Using Technology, Building Democracy

Oxford Studies in Digital Politics

Series Editor: Andrew Chadwick, Royal Holloway, University of London

Using Technology, Building Democracy

DIGITAL CAMPAIGNING AND THE CONSTRUCTION OF CITIZENSHIP

JESSICA BALDWIN-PHILIPPI

OXFORD
UNIVERSITY PRESS

OXFORD

UNIVERSITY PRESS

Oxford University Press is a department of the University of
Oxford. It furthers the University's objective of excellence in research,
scholarship, and education by publishing worldwide.

Oxford   New York
Auckland   Cape Town   Dar es Salaam   Hong Kong   Karachi
Kuala Lumpur   Madrid   Melbourne   Mexico City   Nairobi
New Delhi   Shanghai   Taipei   Toronto

With offices in
Argentina   Austria   Brazil   Chile   Czech Republic   France   Greece
Guatemala   Hungary   Italy   Japan   Poland   Portugal   Singapore
South Korea   Switzerland   Thailand   Turkey   Ukraine   Vietnam

Oxford is a registered trademark of Oxford University Press
in the UK and certain other countries.

Published in the United States of America by
Oxford University Press
198 Madison Avenue, New York, NY 10016

Library of Congress Cataloging-in-Publication Data
Baldwin-Philippi, Jessica, 1985-
Using technology, building democracy : digital campaigning and the construction of citizenship /
Jessica Baldwin-Philippi.
     pages cm
Includes bibliographical references and index.
ISBN 978-0-19-023191-0 (hardcover : acid-free paper)—
ISBN 978-0-19-023192-7 (pbk. : acid-free paper)
1. Political campaigns—Technological innovations—United States.   2. Internet in political
campaigns—United States.   3. Political participation—Technological innovations—United States.
4. Citizenship—United States.   5. United States. Congress—Elections, 2010.   I. Title.
JK2281.B337 2015
324.70285—dc23
2015002142

9 8 7 6 5 4 3 2 1
Printed in the United States of America
on acid-free paper

Contents

Contents

Acknowledgments

So often acknowledgments begin with origin stories, and this project has many. When I was eight, I won an award for citizenship, but had no idea what that meant. Decades later, this book is my attempt to grapple with that question. This book has roots in fourth-grade prizes, undergraduate research opportunities, the doctoral research from which it is most directly born, my scholarship and collaborations since, and the guidance and collaboration I received on this project and others that have shaped my thoughts on the subject in ways that have been invaluable. For those relationships, and their impact on my work and my life, I am most grateful.

Most vital to this project were the campaign staffers and consultants who made it possible. While I cannot thank you by name, know that your help was integral, and that thanks feel like too small an action for my gratitude. Even those I did not interview, but met at conventions or through others, your perspectives and your willingness to invite me into your world were appreciated and thoroughly enjoyed. The campaign that allowed me to work alongside and observe its staffers and consultants deserves specific mention. The experiences I had were not only an essential foundation for my research, but also provided friendships I hope stay with me over the years, and a new understanding of the amount of extra caffeine it is possible to add to your coffee.

As this work came from my doctoral research, my advisers at Northwestern were instrumental in pushing this particular research, and my scholarship more generally, to its height. Bob Hariman, Pablo Boczkowski, and Jim Ettema not only helped me think through this project, but helped me think as a scholar. Their mentoring and that of other faculty in the Media Technology and Society and Rhetoric and Public Culture programs at Northwestern University set an example for rigorous scholarship, asking big questions, and presented a model for the kind of academic I strive to be. A committee on Making Things Happen, Jason DeSanto and Pete Giangreco showed me this project was possible, and then helped make it so. While this project started in coursework at Northwestern and was completed thanks to support from its School of Communication, the roots of scholarly and interdisciplinary inquiry were instilled in me much earlier. I will always be deeply grateful for Christine Bachen and Chad Raphael for bringing me onto research projects as an undergraduate, and providing an entry point into questions of citizenship as an area of study.

My time at Emerson College and specifically at the Engagement Game Lab provided me with an academic community that was more than just academic. My profound gratitude goes to Eric Gordon for bringing me into the Lab and allowing me to become part of what was being built. This work helped me broaden the ways I understood and approached citizenship, and did so in an environment filled with Nerf guns and play, and made me wiser and happier than I had ever considered work a job could do. Working alongside Chris Osgood and Nigel Jacob of the City of Boston's Mayor's Office of New Urban Mechanics also helped expand my vision of citizenship beyond the confines of elections, and has already shaped this and future work. Although I have not been at Fordham long, being surrounded by supportive colleagues and departmental citizens that make up the Communication and Media Studies faculty and the support provided by the School of the Arts and Sciences have both been immensely supportive in the final stages of writing and revisions.

Too many colleagues deserve credit for their input and collaboration along the way. For their valuable insights, criticisms, and advice during presentations, workshops, and happy hours, I am grateful to C. W. Anderson, Eszter Hargittai, Dave Karpf, Dan Kreiss, Ericka Menchen-Trevino, Paul Mihailidis, Rasmus Kleis Nielson, Aaron Shaw, and Steve Walter. For their moments of distraction, hilarity, and genuine support over the years—academic and otherwise, Megan Bernard, Caitlin Bruce, Leigh Meredith, Patrick Wade, and Randall Bush deserve special qualification. It is no exaggeration when I say I could not have done it without you.

My profound thanks go to Andrew Chadwick for his interest in this project, for bringing it to Oxford University Press, and for providing immensely helpful feedback along the way. Angela Chnapko's assistance in moving from proposal to manuscript to book has been exceedingly supportive, and I could not have asked for a smoother experience.

Finally, my mother, Cecelia Baldwin, deserves more credit than I can put into words for raising me not only to value citizenship, but to love this line of work, and for often counseling me through it. My best friend, Sarah Scott, deserves credit for putting up with me during the difficulties it presents.

1

Introduction

Constructing Citizens

How Electoral Campaigns' Uses of Digital Media Articulate Norms for Citizenship

By October, I had spent hundreds of hours in the campaign's communication office, and all I could think was "Where is the bigger picture?" In the frenzy that subsumed July to November and led up to the 2010 midterm elections, no one was having idealistic discussions about people coming together to voice their views and support their vision for their community and their country. There was no talk about the virtues or philosophies behind their approaches to reaching and persuading voters. No one was even saying what they wanted out of potential voters. Dollars, volunteers, and votes are the unarticulated and unparalleled goals of all campaigns, but discussions of desired or impressive forms of participation were notably absent. Beyond any immediate need to fill cash-strapped coffers, what did campaign staffers think about the role of donating and the many channels through which supporters could do so? In addition to getting to the polls, what do campaigns want potential voters to do with the numerous messages the communications departments produce? In short, what forms of action are both strategically valuable, and meaningful representations of what citizens ought to do?

Campaigns are not reflexive, but reactive. Observing and sometimes assisting in a communications department of a federal-level election in the 2010 cycle, I learned this within a week. Senior staff do not explain their goals or reasons for action; they tell people to do things. And those people, in turn, try to carry out those actions as quickly and as well as they can.

Everything is infused with urgency and the sense that your current task will make or break the campaign. Staffers are inundated with and pummeled by the day's work, and their surroundings show it: drafts of flyers for an event at a senior citizen community; an entire wall of a dry-erase board filled with issues and information to be put on the campaign website; a calendar of social media content for the coming week; digital voice recorders with opposition speeches awaiting transcription; a flip cam uploading video footage of the opponent's speech that may or may not be used by the campaign or the national party for television or online ads; an email inbox full of drafts of press releases, information needing to be fact-checked, and a Sisyphean Google Alerts number that refuses to rest at zero; many cups of coffee. Still, despite being literally surrounded by the messages through which the campaign would connect with voters, I found myself confused about where to locate the very processes and articulations of participation and citizenship that I had come to observe. *Where was the citizenship?*

In the midst of frenetically alternating between rapid response, combing the news for events to which the campaign would need to rapidly respond, and searching for valuable information that could be used when rapidly responding, I would observe this lack of reflection on what the ideal forms of political participation were and wonder when people would articulate the goals and purposes of the many messages they were constantly creating and circulating. Sometime during the discussions staffers shared while hunched over computers and takeout, however, I began to unearth where such traces of citizenship existed. I saw that even when campaigns were not talking about the practices of participation that they desired of citizens in traditional terms of deliberation, becoming informed, providing "boots on the ground," interacting directly with candidates, and so on, these imaginings were present in the communications staffers' minds and lived in the texts they communicated to the public. Further, I began to understand that the practices of campaign communication taking place across various digital media platforms were spaces of disagreement, excitement, confusion, and collaboration that produced shifting messaging practices and new visions for what counted as political participation. If states are laboratories of democracy where norms and policies are tested, campaigns are microcosms of it, within which desires for citizenship—both implicit and overt—are suggested, fought over, and decided upon. The texts they create are the result and embodiment of these practices.

Gone are the days of "revolutionary" online campaign communication of the 2004 Dean campaign or the inventive and much-lauded social media strategies of the 2008 Obama campaign. By the 2010 midterm elections, campaigns at the state, district, and even municipal levels realized the necessity of incorporating numerous digital media technologies into their messaging strategies, and the rise of digital campaigning happened across the electoral landscape. As campaigns realized the importance of these tools, "new" digital technologies, such as interactive candidate web pages, grassroots organizing platforms, fundraising sites and widgets, Facebook pages, Twitter feeds, YouTube channels, microsites, campaign and candidate blogs, text messages, and more were used alongside traditional media channels of print, radio, or network and cable television. Rather than replacing "old" practices of creating and purchasing paid-media advertising and pushing for news coverage or earned media, the introduction of digital media channels adds more opportunities for message creation and circulation that must work in tandem with traditional means. Moreover, the boundaries of what constitutes "new" and "old" media meet and blur in digital texts. New technologies often reinforce old norms, while older media channels can be put to use in ways that introduce novel forms of participation or content to citizens. Campaign web pages have been around since the mid-1990s, but they remain innovative because of changing technological capabilities and their use alongside other types of media. Online streaming video has had a much more recent adoption, but is often used in ways that merely reproduce the content of older media—to air the ads audiences already see on broadcast television—resulting in little innovation. As new practices are being adopted and integrated, campaigns believe that the use of cutting-edge digital media tactics for messaging and mobilization can help them win elections, and are simultaneously pulled by the comfort of tried-and-true methods of prior success stories. On the whole, the trends that emerged during the 2010 election cycle and have continued to solidify in the years since illuminate the constant negotiation of digital media practices, incorporating a deep tradition of prior messaging strategies while simultaneously introducing slight, yet meaningful, additions to the process. As tools that were once sporadic and novel are becoming widely undertaken and routinized, they open up spaces in which traditional strategies mesh with opportunities to create and circulate new types of content and encourage different modes of participating in politics. While such a hybrid media system often results in slight changes in content and goals, these changes highlight new ways of thinking about campaign strategy and political engagement.[1]

As campaigns navigate this new media landscape on a widespread scale, the discussions, debates, successes, and shortcomings that occur among staffers in campaign headquarters and within the public texts of candidates' Facebook walls, Twitter feeds, or web pages highlight these shifting practices of campaign messaging. As I observed one campaign's navigation of digital practices in the "post-'08" boom in election technology, larger questions surrounding the possibility of related shifts in norms of political participation and citizenship loomed. What, according to the people who ask us to take political action, does it mean to be political? What is expected and desired of people if they are to be considered active citizens? As this book grapples with these questions, it tells many stories.

Focusing primarily on the midterm elections of 2010, it tells the story of the rise of digital campaigning on a widespread scale, and highlights the strategies and tactics that emerged in a landscape that lacked a manual.[2] By rooting itself in the 2010 midterm cycle before considering the subsequent shifts leading up to 2012 and immediately following, this book is a story of the political consulting class that makes up the vast majority of electoral politics, but is seldom the focus of entire books: those who are more local than the presidential level. These are not campaigns run entirely by the leading names in strategy, nor do they have the money to hire the best developers. They are run by individuals who are navigating the adoption of digital media, not ones who wrote the book on its best practices. Often, they are limited to party-supplied and publicly available tools, and to the skills possessed by a relatively local coalition of the willing. Moreover, as it connects these tactics with those deployed in the years leading up to and including the 2012 cycle, this book highlights how emergent digital campaigning strategies have shifted, evolved, and solidified. Therefore, this is not a manual that investigates what best practices look like or how to achieve electoral victory, but an examination of how both successful and failed campaigns contribute to the development of new strategy standards and tactics at the local level.

This book shifts its focus away from the particulars of what new technologies campaigns are using and instead investigates the ways the adoption of a variety of digital and traditional messaging tools influences the process of message creation, the messages themselves, and ultimately citizens. To that end, it highlights four major strategic shifts campaigns took in 2010. First, it focuses on the rise of the fact-check within a recently popularized form of media, the microsité, and traces its connections to other campaign-produced, blog-content, journalistic campaign coverage. It also highlights two complimentary emerging strategies associated with campaigns' use of social media platforms. On one hand, campaigns are increasingly requesting that supporters circulate campaign material to their own networked publics, with an emphasis on circulating content that is mundane, rather than mobilizing. In doing so, they are changing their approach to audiences in a way that is not about enhanced targeting opportunities, but about networked social connections. Additionally, as it relates to the content of these messages, campaigns are increasingly relying on content that mirrors the offline practice of retail politics and attempts to facilitate interpersonal connections rather than provide policy information. Finally, this book also takes an in-depth look at the practices and organizational culture involved in campaigns' attempts at message control in light of the move toward increased expectations of reciprocal communication and openness in spaces such as social media, blogs, and commenting sections.

The strategies I have described contribute to major changes in what have always been two main areas of interest for communication strategy: the type of information provided to citizens, and the forms of participation in which campaigns ask citizens to engage. Regarding the type of information being created by campaigns, these strategies present two divergent trends. The move toward microsites and fact checking more generally presents citizens with detailed information, proof-bearing, and a level of information that encourages deeper engagement and even skepticism toward political information. On the other hand, the content crafted for social media spaces is increasingly devoid of such details, instead focusing on pictures and graphics that may facilitate emotional attachment. As a result, informational norms within online spaces not only vary, but are likely becoming more divergent. Regarding the methods of participatory action campaigns encourage citizens to take, the requests are relatively low bars; citizens are asked to recirculate campaign content and be able to provide public feedback and engage campaigns and other citizens in public discussion. While both of these involve aspects of control and management by campaigns, they do offer citizens ways to talk back to political institutions and contribute their voice to public discussions.

While these emergent strategies are far from a utopian vision of politics, this book will argue that they do constitute a promising development in the possibilities for citizenship in a digital age. Citizens' voices may not be widely heard, and a local commenter is unlikely to emerge as a new authority in the political sphere, but being encouraged to provide public, visible feedback, even though that feedback may disrupt a campaign's ability to stay on message, is a meaningful development. A large swath of the populace may not engage in participatory political action, but campaigns' efforts to get more and more people on the lowest rung of the ladder of engagement, and their efforts to keep pushing them upward, are a reason to be hopeful. While citizens will be exposed to social media content that is less informative, content that encourages emotional connection could drive future action, and other digital spaces like microsites are seeing improvement in the quality of their information.

Methodologically, this book is most rooted in the tale of one federal-level election taking place in 2010 in Illinois, where I spent over 300 hours observing and working alongside a campaign's communications staff. Thus, it represents the story of their campaign, but it is more than that as well. Combining what happened in one campaign with the perspective of consultants and staffers nationwide, as well as the actual texts created by campaigns in Illinois and beyond, this book uses this constellation of moments, texts, and staffers to tell the story of contemporary campaigns more generally. Moreover, as it combines discussions that reflect on the 2010 cycle with those that looked forward to and occurred during the 2012 campaign season, it focuses on tactics that are common across a variety of diverse campaigns. By putting all these elements in conversation, it simultaneously investigates the practices developed and deployed by campaigns, as well as the purposes, goals, and values behind those tactics. Its work is inductive, rather than experimental, and points to major themes across campaigns that answer the question "How do campaigns engage with digital media, and what does that mean for how we understand ourselves as citizens?" This book is more than just a story of the everyday trials of campaigns as they grapple with tools and navigate emerging norms of campaign communication strategy. It is the story of what it means to be a citizen in a digital era. Rather than merely cataloging the practices of political operatives or the content of candidate's websites, this book investigates the ways that the ins and outs of everyday texts created and communicated by campaigns articulate and reflect norms and definitions of participatory citizenship that are currently functioning within a contemporary democratic public. In doing so, it highlights the messiness of the process of building democracy—a process that takes place in everyday moments and hasty, contested decisions just as often as by the polished hand of presidential speechwriters. This book argues that within these moments, there is much more nuance than is available in claims extolling the rise of radical participation or bemoaning the death of democracy.

Why Campaigns?

If citizenship can be broadly understood as "a shared set of expectations about the citizen's role in politics . . . [that] tell citizens what is expected of them, and what they expect of themselves," then it can be seen in any number of political and civic spaces; from meetings of a local community group to online social movements.[3] So why focus on campaigns? While they are only one of many sites where citizenship is formed and enacted, campaigns are a space where normative understandings of political participation and citizenship are on display and performed on a national—and even international—scale. First and foremost, it has long been argued that campaigns are the way that people "experience" politics in the United States.[4] Dubbed "perhaps the clearest expression of a democracy's continually evolving mythology and perception of its own essential character," campaigns are a cornerstone of how Americans understand civic issues, governance, and democracy in general.[5] As a ritual, Election Day literally creates democracy, and the media ritual that accompanies the months leading up to that day offers the act of campaigning attention, and an interpretive frame about the importance and centrality of elections in democratic culture.[6] Because of these deep connections, the citizenship practices recognized and undertaken within an electoral context—especially those that are new or shifting—are key to those that function within the democratic public. The messages campaign staffers and consultants produce, and their intense amplification through any and all media channels, contain requests and allowances (as well as prohibitions) for action that reflect an understanding of what counts as political action.[7] While campaigns may not occur every day, contemporary politics is colloquially understood as a "permanent campaign," illustrating that electoral contests provide a frame for understanding the political landscape and its surrounding practices of public deliberation and discussion.[8] Moreover, a baseline measure of political participation is often the act of voting itself, and the most bare-bones definitions of democracy often center on the practice of a voting public.

Despite the rise of political participation that is civic, nongovernmental, and nonelectoral, elections remain one of the most salient aspects of politics in the United States.[9] Coverage of electoral campaigns remains an aspect of news that is shared across the nation, and one that citizens are continuously exposed to on a wide scale. Even as campaigns engage in increasingly specific targeting of potential voters, the audience for campaigns remains the potentially voting public—a population much broader than those of issue-based advocacy campaigns or local volunteering efforts. While citizens, especially younger ones, are gravitating toward nonelectoral methods of engagement, elections are still a major player in the development of political messages that are aimed at both persuading and mobilizing.[10] Additionally, cutting-edge advocacy groups often evolve toward or borrow from strategies employed by major campaigns. Even at the local level, millions are spent on individual congressional elections, which are clearly still attempting to reach out to vast swaths of the population and ask them to take political action. Moreover, while the goals of campaigns are rather limited to the ultimate goal of gaining votes, the tactics and strategies that contribute to that purpose often represent the cutting edge of strategic innovation. With more money, more seasoned staffers, and ultimately more at stake for mobilizing voters to take a particular action, campaigns are often the site of innovative practices that other advocacy groups can then use to their advantage. In its focus on the construction of emergent norms of citizenship, this work is not necessarily about how citizens are currently engaging, but how they are *asked* to engage. The practices that campaigns request of citizens not only present a specific model for how citizens ought to take political action during a moment when ideals of citizenship are in flux, but are also likely to shape the actions citizens do take in the future, and provide a useful yardstick by which to measure emerging forms of participation. As political campaigns have been a space where the construction of citizenship has occurred for hundreds of years, they are an ideal space to see citizenship's evolution. While presidential campaigns are often the site of inquiry because of their prominence within the cultural imagination and the public's familiarity with candidates, midterm elections also provide important insight into this process of constructing citizenship. Beyond literally filling in the gaps in technological and strategic development that occur between presidential elections, what happens in midterms shows what practices rise to the top. With limited budgets, less labor from volunteers, and less centralized systems of power than national campaigns, the federal, statewide, and municipal races that are the focus of midterm cycles show what practices are carried over from presidential races, and how they may shift at a different scale. The 2010 cycle in particular provides insight into an important moment of transition: how campaigns dealt with the need to "go digital" in light of the overwhelming success of the Obama campaign's victory in 2008. Additionally, looking at the more recent solidification of what were emergent strategies in 2010 makes it clear that the practices outlined in this book contributed in meaningful ways to more recent developments in 2012 and the years leading up to 2014.

In light of our increasingly mediated everyday lives, these ongoing enactments are themselves digitally mediated. As Rasmus Nielsen argues: "The role of an active citizen is, in short, one people assume by socio-technical means (even if not under conditions of their own choosing)—whether in political campaigns, in social movements, or elsewhere."[11] As new technologies are becoming increasingly common to the creation, circulation, and reception of political messages in general, the relationships between conceptions of citizenship and media technologies are a vital space of inquiry. While innovations in media technologies have impacted all realms of the campaign environment, the communications office is the place where digital strategy meets the public. Not only are digital analytics used to craft messages in the same behind-the-scenes way as they are used to target citizens for the finance department's donation requests or tell field captains whom to speak with, but they are also the media channels through which the public is increasingly accessing information about campaigns.[12] The communications office is the space where digital tools impact both the content and the form of strategic decisions. Despite recent findings that call the efficacy and reach of digital campaign messages into question, citizens report turning to digital and social media for political information in increasing numbers.[13] These messages—just like the television ads and direct mail buys that came before them and still play a major role—are how campaigns speak to the public and ask its members to be political. They are where normative constructions of citizenship are most clearly articulated, and most directly presented to those they ask to be citizens. Moreover, as the goal of these messages is to persuade a public audience, campaign strategy is likely to reflect the type of content and requests for action that are not only necessary to a campaign's success, but likely to tap into citizens' existing proclivities. Campaigns' constructions of citizenship through digital strategy therefore also speak to the active role played by the broader public in contributing to constructions of citizenship. By looking at the processes and discourses of message creation and circulation within the electoral environment, this book gives insight into the ways that campaigns present definitions and norms of active citizenship as they use digital tools to communicate with potential voters.

What Counts? Understanding Citizenship in the Digital Age

Understandings of "citizenship" are often nebulous, multiple, and contradictory, yet the concept is commonly referenced as a key feature of democratic public culture. The ability for ordinary people to actively engage in political and civic life has been the subject of many disciplines, and the myriad ways people may do so have been studied using a wide range of methods that focus on various features or components of citizenship. Studies concerning the object of citizenship have spanned historical time periods involving a variety of definitions of the term itself, and centered around a variety of spaces, from the agora to the bowling alley.[14]

Inquiry into the effects of technology on political participation and citizenship has been taken up within communication studies and political science for some time. Conjectures about the radically democratic interactions and the material capabilities of new technology and counterarguments about the stunting features of these same objects populate the debate. According to some, the fact that the Internet allows people to connect across geographical boundaries or engage with other individuals and perspectives they may not encounter in a face-to-face setting is creative of a new public sphere and a more level, democratic form of engagement.[15] Conversely, others have countered that, despite its capabilities, the Internet has not really changed politics—that elites dominate this media channel as well and that it is littered with many failed attempts and a few well-publicized successes.[16] Deliberative democrats have viewed the wealth of information to which the Internet is home as a way to inform citizens so that they are more capable of informed discussion, debate, and opinion formation,[17] while others argue that an abundance of highly specialized content can fragment people and insulate them alongside fellow-minded citizens and opinions.[18] Or worse, the technology itself, via algorithms, does the job of filtering for citizens.[19]

Yet another area of disagreement among scholars is whether the ability to form online communities both productively returns us to our communitarian roots[20] and isolates us from one another and our civic duties.[21]

While these analyses into various elements of citizenship have provided useful insight and much empirical data, they are most often concerned with judging whether citizenship is being executed "successfully," as measured by a limited number of practices such as voting, donating to a political campaign, or engaging in a very specific type of rational, bounded debate. By these rubrics, citizenship is in disrepair, but that is only part of the picture. In an era teeming with new tools for participation, it is quite possible that declensionists who worry about citizenship have simply measured the wrong things. Some scholars argue that to see the additional spaces of participation and sometimes flourishing examples of engaged citizenship, new measurements that define political action in new and broader ways are needed.[22] Even within more expansive definitions, however, a preoccupation with judging the successful execution of citizenship supersedes questions about what actions and processes reflect active citizenship. While measuring these acts is not detrimental to the study of politics, this research overlooks the fact that acting as a citizen is an ongoing process, rather than a box we can check if the proper actions are taken.

The vocabulary we do possess for speaking about how citizens ought to be, and what counts as citizenship, is limited. In what has become a cornerstone for studies of citizenship, Michael Schudson's *The Good Citizen* argues that norms and ideals of citizenship have changed throughout history and will continue to change according to the social, economic, technological, and political contexts within which we are always situated.[23] Exploring history's models of citizenship, Schudson points to the "monitorial citizen"—someone who monitors information she is interested in and can be mobilized to learn more or act when necessary—as an especially compelling normative model for how people do and should engage with political information. This model, while appropriate for our many modes of media consumption and certainly one form of ideal citizenship, has become a dominant paradigm for how scholars understand the consumption of political information, despite radical changes to the media through which information is consumed. Working to expand the paradigm of citizenship, Theda Skocpol has pointed to the change in citizenship from mass membership in volunteer organizations to managed, professional organizations.[24] Philip

Howard's *New Media and the Managed Citizen* similarly considers citizens' processes of information gathering and other participatory acts, and argues that digital media allow a wealth of ways to control the content and capabilities at their disposal, thereby resulting in "managed" citizens and illusions of political power.[25] Daniel Kreiss echoes this account of allegedly radically democratic changes to electoral politics—as exemplified by the 2004 Dean campaign—showing participation to be heavily embedded in stable, hierarchical, and controlling organizational structures and routines of traditional campaigning.[26] In a more optimistic approach to contemporary citizenship, W. Lance Bennett and colleagues argue that citizens are politically engaged outside of these controlling structures when they act as "actualized citizens" who favor "loosely networked activism to address issues that reflect personal values," rather than "dutiful citizens" who feel a compulsion and obligation to participate.[27] These actualized citizens are less interested in engaging with government than they are in acts that are "personally defined," such as consumerism, community volunteering, or even learning to code and produce their own media and tools.[28] Far from telling tales of civic decline, research that attempts to understand potentially new forms of citizenship and political action contends that online digital media are well suited to such a form of political engagement because they increase the availability of information, as well as the number of tools for mobilizing what Zizi Papacharissi has called our "dormant political consciousness."[29]

These new ways of formulating citizenship and its places of potential enactment are not exclusive or static. Participating in politics can at once be an activity of being managed by hierarchical political organizations and of becoming actualized by using one's own social networks for advocacy. People can monitor information that is produced by a grassroots organization or individual person, or they can keep tabs on traditionally powerful political organizations and news outlets. While these forms of citizenship are some that are currently at play, the complexity and expansion of the contemporary media environment means there are likely to be even more changes to how people interact with campaigns and political information and additional forms of civic and political action. Rather than assessing the quality or amount of participation or citizenship, this research attempts to better understand how this dormant political consciousness is being activated—how citizens are being addressed differently in a digital media environment, what kind of texts campaigns are producing for citizens, what political practices or stances audiences are asked to take as citizens, and what visions for "good" citizenship are encouraged or are present in inchoate form.[30] In this way, this book echoes existing attempts to locate new forms of citizenship that have bubbled up as citizens have veered away from electoral politics, but contends that similarly emergent conceptions of citizenship are appearing within the electoral space as well.[31]

In taking this approach, the norms of citizenship that can be observed often exist outside of campaigns' explicitly desired modes of participation. Campaigns act purposefully toward their goals of dollars, volunteers, and votes, but the ways their persuasive and action-oriented texts might be changing concepts of political interaction and citizenship are not usually on staffers' radar. As a result, the pursuit of everyday goals—especially via the use of digital tools and new practices to achieve them—can result in engaging certain conceptions of citizenship that are different from those that are often the topic of public discussion, whether this is consciously undertaken or not. The shifting norms of citizenship that bubble up within campaign-produced texts are often either vastly different from the abstract goals staffers and consultants articulate outside of the hectic context of the campaign, or in direct conflict with their short-term electoral needs. Staffers' and consultants' democratic ideals of providing a louder voice for or greater information to a wider number of people are genuine and deeply rooted, but the hectic pace and ends-oriented realm of the campaign often reflect more—or less, as the case may be—than democratic ideals. On the other hand, what campaigns see as expedient uses of existing platforms, such as Facebook or Meetup, can lead to unintentionally loosening their stranglehold on control of messages. These mismatches of articulated goals, in-the-moment practices, and lofty ideals are not problematic for the study of citizenship; they make it all the richer. The places of cleavage, disagreement, and definition that take place within discourses surrounding what it means (and should mean) to act politically show the depth of the concept and can begin to unpack the many ways citizenship functions in our contemporary democratic public. Models of political communication and of technology's role in politics that exclude these rhetorical features fail to understand the way that lived practices contribute to how we understand what it is to be political. This book's goal is to remedy such gaps in knowledge and to identify relationships between the ways new media technologies are being used and discussed for political messaging, and the shifting forms of participation and citizenship that these uses reflect and encourage.

Approach to Investigating Citizenship and Outline of the Book

Getting at these emerging definitions and expectations for citizenship requires the use of multiple methodologies. Primarily, this research enlists ethnographic participant observation of a 2010 federal-level campaign in Illinois, focusing on the communications office and the creation of campaign messages and digital campaign texts. This race was chosen for study not because it was positioned at the absolute cutting edge of digital media use, but because it was a well-funded, nationally publicized, yet still local race in which the question of *how* to innovate would be grappled with. The campaign had the resources to hire experienced staffers and consultants who knew the importance of tending to innovative practices, could dedicate money and manpower (although no campaign thinks it has enough of either) to digital tactics if they were deemed necessary, and was in a close race that would ensure the campaign undertook whatever new strategies it could. As a result, this race would provide insight into how digital media contributed to evolutions and shifts in existing strategy within an organization that was truly innovating, rather than following known best practices.[32]

This book goes beyond that single race, however. The ethnographic analysis is bolstered by 40 in-depth interviews with communications and digital media staffers and consultants across the country and makes use of additional conversations that occurred at national professional conferences such as Netroots Nation in 2011 and 2012, extending the analysis to campaigns outside of Illinois. Most directly quoted material in the book is from these interviews, and while the speakers remain anonymous throughout the text, the pertinent details of their positions are provided (see the appendix for a detailed list of the interview participants).

Additionally, the findings of this book employ content and textual analysis of campaign-produced texts from 11 competitive races in Illinois while drawing on culled examples of similar texts across the nation. Largely, the analysis of texts themselves focuses on how the texts do or do not contribute to traditional campaign goals of persuasion, mobilization, and fundraising, and traces themes in the type of content produced (images versus text, tone, aesthetics, etc.), what citizens are asked to do, and discussion of the affordances of the tools used.[33] Though this analysis primarily draws on social media texts, it also includes a variety of website and email outreach produced by these campaigns. Finally, the book examines examples and secondary analyses of strategies taken in the 2012 and lead-up to 2014 to show that the practices that were emerging in 2010 have in fact solidified into widespread tactics. Together, these interlocking methodologies intersect to develop a lens for analyzing citizenship from several perspectives that are seldom combined in the study of political communication. Enlisting multiple perspectives, this research looks beyond the traditional and overly simplistic measures of citizenship such as voting or trust, and challenges research that focuses only on an analysis of texts while ignoring their practices of production or use. In doing so, this book provides a "genuinely sociological account of political engagement" and highlights new ways of thinking through the concept of citizenship.[34]

Beyond the methodologies employed for gathering data concerning emerging campaign strategies and notions of citizenship, theoretical lenses that attend to the nuances of the role of digital tools and citizenship itself are necessary. First and foremost, this book views campaign texts as a fluid combination of the content of the messages themselves, the tools through which they are created and circulated, and the self-reflexive talk about goals, successes, and shortcomings (and those of politics writ large) that occurs in the creation of texts and in reflection on their success. Although the strategies behind the production and distribution of messages come together to produce a single text, they can act either in collaboration or at odds with one another, and contribute to meaning of the text as a whole. To get at such intricate relationships, this research approaches campaign texts as necessarily mediated by technologies' material affordances, their socially situated practices of use, and their contexts of evolution. This construction of such norms is not a unidirectional phenomenon extending from campaigns to citizens, but is a reflexive practice of coproduction between campaigns and a web of actors or "social world" that involves other campaigns, advocacy groups, and the existing political proclivities of citizens.[35] Thus, the digital strategies in this book should be seen as both structuring and structured by patterns of use and existing norms of citizenship. While the content of this book focuses on campaigns' actions—the choices made and reasons given by staffers and consultants—those perspectives are always simultaneously shaped by citizens because of campaigns' needs to create messages that will resonate with and appeal to the public. As a result, prior conceptions of citizenship, of both recent and distant past, are at play in this investigation of the ways that media technologies impact the concept of citizenship—citizens are still managed, and taking a monitorial approach to the news is a productive civic endeavor, but there are changes to these forms of citizenship to uncover as well. This book illuminates the additional, evolving ways campaigns encourage individuals to engage with political information and participatory action. In doing so, it describes sets of emerging campaign practices and investigates how they invoke new understandings of what makes citizens.

Each chapter of this book attempts to provide an account of emergent campaign practices that gives new insight into the role of digital media on shifting norms of participation and citizenship. Following a chapter detailing the slow evolution of digital media in the campaign environment, I provide analyses of four digitally driven phenomena and their impact on how we consider citizenship. Chapter 3 investigates changing persuasive messages across a variety of digital platforms, from official campaign sites, to off-brand microsites, to journalistic coverage, focusing on how these messages construct an ideal approach to political information that is skeptical and based in judgment, rather than mere consumption. This new form of skeptical citizenship goes beyond assertions of how much information people can and should engage or how they should go about selecting that information, instead focusing on how citizens ought to approach political content. Chapter 4 looks at the changing practices of information sharing by charting campaigns' increased drive to get citizens engaged in practices of digital circulation within a social media environment and argues that these changes imply very different views of how citizens are organized in relation to one another and to campaigns, as well as openings for participatory citizenship within "managed" models of citizenship. Chapter 5 investigates the emerging genres of behind-the-scenes and digital retail politics that can be seen in social media content, and how this content reflects a norm that focuses on action over becoming informed about policy or issues. Chapter 6 examines the ways that the tension between needing to maintain control of a message and wanting to foster deliberation and discussion is currently playing out in a digitally mediated environment and how such tensions are navigated by campaigns, ultimately arguing that the concept of control is being redefined in ways that, while still powerful, do provide citizens with options for deliberative practices and opportunities to take campaigns off message. Finally, the conclusion ties together the previous four concepts and shows the ways that these burgeoning forms of citizenship have been reinforced and sometimes slightly modified in the years since the 2010 cycle.

By bringing in examples from the 2012 elections, this chapter focuses on taking a broad view of how emerging phenomena turn into existing practices and highlights important, new trends that appeared on the scene more recently, to contribute to the constantly evolving practice of building our current democratic culture. In each example, we can also see how the dominant orthodoxies of campaign communication are being upended. War rooms are increasingly engaging in constant practice of fact checking that contributes to new forms of negative messaging; even within the study of social media, we find that messaging is about more than microtargeting increasingly specific segments of the population; campaigns are internally very conflicted about their desire to control public discourse and enable citizen participation. The emergent strategies discussed here show that many of our dominant understandings of campaign operations and culture need to evolve too.

2

Incremental Innovation

In 2010, Illinois was home to no fewer than four extremely competitive races. The Senate race between Mark Kirk and Alexi Giannoulias was routinely listed as one of the three most competitive in the country. The Illinois 10th Congressional District was named an important toss-up race for the duration of campaign season, and candidates raised nearly $9 million, putting it in the upper echelon of congressional fundraising, while the 8th Congressional District has been ranked one of the most competitive according to its victory margins from 2000 to 2008.[1] On top of these federal races, the statewide gubernatorial election was tight until Election Day. Although these campaigns were clearly playing at a high level, their adoption of technology was far from overwhelmingly innovative. Of these races, only the Kirk and Giannoulias campaigns employed dedicated, senior staffers to run digital media operations. While staffers led digital or social media efforts in the other campaigns, doing so was one of many other responsibilities. Far from having messaging autonomy, these staffers often replicated the language provided by a press-oriented communications director and placed it in social media channels, leading to similar if not redundant information across channels. Only in 2012 did campaigns in these same districts employ someone whose only job was to tend to digital media.

Despite the general popularity of social media like Facebook and Twitter in 2008, 2010 was the first election cycle in which they were widely used by campaigns, and their capabilities and purposes were not yet clear. One day at the end of August, the campaign manager yelled from across the hall: "Hey, how do I send a message just to some of these people?" Staffers stared at the Administrator interface for the campaign's Facebook page, and despite their deep personal familiarity with the social network, the room was filled with blank faces. The communications director expressed her desire to use many of the same categories available to target the campaign's Facebook advertisements in order to send targeted messages—much as the campaign already divided its email list. "Well, I think you can only do that by place," answered a staffer, as the communication director pointed at the screen, and noted, "It looks like you can do gender too. And age." After a few moments of staring at the screen, she continued, "Well, that's not too helpful." Resigned, she added, "Maybe for GOTV it will be. Whatever."[2]

Campaigns are slow to adopt technology, often waiting until a tool has demonstrated success in consumer markets and is widely used. They are even slower to develop or adopt new tools specifically designed for political campaigns. When they do use newer tools, they often search for ways to reach the same goals. In short, their use of digital media is evolutionary, not revolutionary. As this book attempts to understand new modes of being political within a digitally mediated environment, it also requires an understanding of the history of campaigns' use of digital technology and its contexts of evolution. Before we can attempt to understand the ways these newer tools impact the current practices of campaign communications, we must understand how earlier advances in communication technologies have already influenced campaigns' ability to interact with voters.[3]

Campaigns are notoriously risk-adverse. Despite a common and clearly articulated optimism around what digital media can accomplish, campaigns are reluctant to change or adopt new strategies. One communications director in what was considered a pivotal federal election in 2010 explained, "Politics is not a pioneering business . . . consultants, strategists, and candidates stick with the tried and true."[4] While digital tools are respected for their ability to engage constituents, and consultants recognize the technological successes (and failings) of major races' use of tech, many consultants are also skeptical of digital media's ability to do the most important thing: turn local voters out on Election Day. While winning staffers and consultants often issue clear decrees over best practices after the election has ended, campaign offices in the midst of an election often lack the skills to rigorously test

strategies or new tools to prove their mettle. As a result, proven best practices are few and far between, and innovation becomes riskier. In a campaign
strategy, the devil you know typically wins the day.

Campaigns are a zero-sum game. Though innovative strategies can
impact future campaigns, they are less validating on both a personal and a
collective level if your candidate loses. While the Dean campaign's technical
advancements have been touted in political circles and the direct connection
between that campaign's tactics in 2004 and those of the Obama campaign
in 2008 have been noted,[5] electoral success is what breeds confidence in new
tactics. Aside from being motivated by the satisfaction of electing their candidate for the job, consultants' and staffers' careers are tied to electoral victory, thus raising the risk of adopting new, untested strategies and practices.
As a specialist in digital strategy who joined the Giannoulias for Senate campaign wrote following a close, hard-fought race, "Averageness operates like
a life preserver in campaigns—it keeps you alive, for the most part."[6] Going
on to describe the way that this behavior is "meant to stifle progress, stall
creative solutions, and preserve the status quo," she describes just how disin-
centivized innovative activity is for those who develop strategy. In addition
to potentially confusing staffers, taking advantage of new technology often
means parting ways with strategy that has a demonstrated success rate; a
frightening wager in light of the zero-sum outcome of a campaign. Even the
most cutting edge of campaigns, Obama's 2012 re-election campaign, was
home to deep disagreements over whether adopting new analytics-based
tactics was tantamount to "foregoing the expertise and relationships" that
traditional strategies held.[7]

Even as large-scale changes to campaign tactics such as a move toward
political marketing that focuses on the individual needs and desires of
potential voters occur, campaigns are behind the eight ball. In 2007, Pippa
Norris described campaigns as "running hard to stay in place."[8] Despite
some significant advances, most campaigns have failed to gain much ground
in the years since. Innovation has largely meant using tools that had been in
the hands of consumer marketing and even citizens for years, rather than
driving new developments. Beyond hired help for website development and
email management, nearly every campaign drew entirely from tools that
were either publicly available or party-provided. Databases of voters supplied by the national parties were part of everyday life for all campaigns.
They were used by staffers at virtually every level of the campaign, and aided
in organizing, contacting, and mobilizing potential voters. Campaigns have

long relied on publicly available, nonspecialized tools, from the fax machine in the 1980s, to Meetup in 2004, to social media platforms Facebook and Twitter in 2010. Even after Obama's 2008 success with the original My.BarackObama.com platform, few smaller races had the same resources or technical knowledge to implement similarly original tools. As a result, the landscape of digital political tools in 2010 was filled with publicly available platforms—social media like Facebook and Twitter dominated the scene, alongside party-provided database tools and commercially available email management systems. Waiting for innovative practices to become tried and true before adoption often results in a vicious cycle of playing catch-up. Another result is a trickle-down effect, wherein tactics move from the presidential level to federal and gubernatorial races, followed slowly by state-level races. The practices that have been successful—measured not only by votes gained, but money raised and publicity garnered—not only trickle down from federal to state and municipal levels, but are adopted across campaigns of the same level as they are found to be generally successful.

When campaigns do incrementally take on new tools and adopt new strategies, there is often a tension between meeting traditional goals and attempting new feats. Efficiency, speed, and reach are seen as the boons of using digital media to get out campaign messages, and their benefit is often therefore viewed as one concerned with amplifying that which already exists, rather than revolutionizing that which is possible. Posting events on Facebook (or Meetup, before that) can bring more people to hear a speech or rally for a cause, but the tactic is not designed to change the form of political participation or the role citizens are asked to take therein. Publicizing a message across email lists and social media platforms can amplify and extend its reach, but need not ask citizens to engage with it, the campaign, or their communities any differently than a television ad. With such an approach, the goals of campaigns are not qualitatively altered by the use of digital media; they are merely executed in ways that are more numerous or efficient. Digital media platforms can, of course, facilitate completely new ways of engaging citizens—My.BarackObama.com (MyBO) allowed people to see and connect with other local volunteers and tally and compare the type and amount of volunteering they were doing, making political participation a newly social (and potentially competitive) process. Most of the time, however, the pendulum swings toward the amplifying end of the spectrum. In this way, evolution has occurred, but it has come at a plodding pace, and often been accompanied by reluctant but dedicated staffers who seek to slightly improve known campaign benefits rather than branch out toward new goals. As this book focuses on slight changes that both amplify old forms of engagement and construct completely new ones, it first details the evolutions (and occasional revolutions) in both technology and strategy that have come before.

Digital Media in Politics: Where They've Been and Where They Are

Over the years, campaigns have used technologies in many different forms. They have become an instrument for defining and finding populations, they are used as channels by which to circulate texts in different ways, and they have existed as tools through which the public can engage in interactive participation with the campaign. These uses bleed into one another, and technologies are not bound to a single purpose—Facebook can provide campaigns with information about potential voters, a platform for circulating messages, and a space in which to ask and encourage any variety of participatory actions. Moreover, a variety of technologies are used together and cumulatively, rather than the old giving way to the new. Although database technologies were one of the first uses of information communication technologies (and are no longer very "new") in political campaigns, their use remains an important element within a toolkit that has grown sizably over the years. Despite these overlaps, the uses of digital media to connect with voters can be grouped into three categories: tools to define and catalog populations, vessels to transmit information, and objects conducive to citizen interaction and engagement. Understanding the ways that communication technologies have been and continue to be used for these three purposes provides a foundation from which we can understand the ways that campaigns' contemporary engagement with new media texts is continuing to evolve.

TOOLS TO DEFINE AND CATALOG POPULATIONS

Long before the Internet technologies we now think of as constituting new media were developed, political campaigns made use of cutting-edge computing technology to locate, categorize, and keep track of audiences and populations. In 1973, the AFL-CIO registered nearly 9 million names in its computing system.[9] This new technology enabled political groups and campaigns to keep track of members or supporters and even catalog other information about them (zip codes, demographic information such as age or race, and so on). In addition to databases of members of political organizations, the late 1980s and early 1990s ushered in a new era of computerized voter registration that enabled campaigns to locate past and likely voters and target specific voting groups with their messages.[10] In developing these practices, political parties and campaigns have long looked to and organized seemingly unrelated consumer-marketing databases in order to supplement voting-related and demographic knowledge with "lifestyle" information.[11] In doing so, information that is closely correlated with political leaning or policy opinions (such as subscribing to religious information outlets, to catalogs for guns, or to certain partisan publications such as *Mother Jones*) is combined with other database content to provide in-depth accounts of audiences, neighborhoods, and potential voters. By combining multiple databases, political parties can access information surrounding party affiliation, voting records, policy preferences, level of party dedication, donor history, and demographic features of individuals, and use this information to segment and pinpoint audiences that are most likely to be persuaded by their messages, or to tailor messages to specific audiences.

Even as political organizations have enlisted database technologies since the 1970s, their use in political campaigns has been highly varied and surprisingly unsystematic. Because of the incredible value put on data, it was, until the past decade, seldom shared—even among similarly interested groups. Private firms would sell information to political campaigns, which would often horde these lists. Only in 2002 did the Republican Party begin to consolidate the information from a variety of such databases, resulting in an information cache of over 175 million names in the party's "Voter Vault" by the 2004 election. On the other side of the aisle that same year, the Democratic Party was still without a centralized system and was on the losing side of data management. Instead of an organized and shared catalog of information, campaigns at all levels still relied on unorganized and ad hoc compilation by state offices. Far from the image of efficiently run political machinery, state party offices and individual campaigns had to purchase information from political information firms and data-mining corporations, often reverted to stacks of handwritten three-by-five index cards that were difficult to use and went uncataloged for future use, and failed to share information across state lines.[12] It was only after losing the 2004 presidential race that the The Democratic National Party (DNC) followed suit, developing the VoteBuilder database and the Voter Activation Network (VAN). While some data are still owned by private data firms or proprietary information of political groups, they are often shared with or available for purchase by the parties with whom the owners share political values or goals.[13]

These practices continue to evolve as new media platforms develop, often allowing campaigns and political organizations to access greater amounts of, more specific, and newer types of information than ever before. Although the purpose and design of databases has largely remained to pool and categorize information, the systems of both parties have been added to and made compatible with other platforms in order to put the data to use toward campaign goals of transmitting information to an array of audiences and engaging citizens in activism. On the Democratic side, the database technology used across Democratic campaigns, VAN (used alongside Democrats' VoteBuilder technology), recently partnered with NGP Software, a company devoted specifically to fundraising and new media software. This new hybrid database/organizing tool called NGP-VAN allows campaigns to mobilize citizens to take action in addition to locating, organizing, and categorizing people. Aside from using technologies created specifically for political use, political campaigns and organizations also enlist existing information from simple methods of tracking and categorizing populations as consumer marketing, such as cookies (small data files that are stored on a computer's hardware and gather data about Internet habits), search engine optimization (SEO), off-the-shelf email management systems, and accessing information willingly divulged to social media platforms. As social media has become a place where people disclose a large amount of information, campaigns are often able to gain access to this information, and use it to categorize people based on geography, interests, issue-salience, or demographic information.[14] These technologies allow campaigns to better know their audience, locate specific audiences, define and create their own audiences, and then target them with specifically tailored messages. Targeting has become one of the most valued capabilities that political communication experts have at their disposal, and the information in databases can be used throughout a wide variety of media technologies, from email to online ads.[15]

Although certainly productive for campaigns, the conceptions of citizenship that emerge from such practices are varied. While some commentators are optimistic about their effects, others fear problems for democratic participation. A primary disagreement concerns the appropriate scope and level of information required to attain informed citizenship. On one hand is the argument that targeting populations provides people with the information they are most likely to care about and is therefore more likely to actually engage audiences and lead to further participation, especially those already somewhat engaged.[16] On the other hand, many have argued that the ability to carefully and specifically divide populations (and the resulting differences in information received by various audiences) leads to fragmentation, polarization, and a lack of the common knowledge that's necessary for a functional public sphere.[17] These arguments between the importance of breadth versus depth of knowledge are met with a third alternative that does not measure preexisting norms of citizenship, but contemplates the possibility for a new type of citizenship altogether: that of the managed citizen.[18] This normative account posits that although people think they are engaging in information interpretation or participatory techniques, the infrastructure and architecture of database technologies are always at work, affecting the information and calls to action people receive, and constantly evolving as more information is recorded. These information-gathering technologies provided the structural foundations for further advancement in the ways campaigns could communicate with potential voters, and would also influence the ways in which they could engage and harness new digital media for in future campaigns.[19]

VESSELS FOR TRANSMITTING INFORMATION

Campaigns have long used a variety of media tools—"new" media as well as public addresses and advertisements via mail, broadcast television, and radio media—to circulate their messages within the public. These texts, in addition to their persuasive goals, are how the public attains information about officials, candidates for office, and policy decisions and debates. As media act as a vessel to circulate content, their technological affordances allow for differences in the content and form of the messages as well. While the media may not actually be the message, they do allow for potential shifts in the types and amounts of information that have been argued to have various effects on participation and citizenship.

Ever since television coverage of political news and events resulted in fundamental changes in the ability to present visual information to the public in ways that are often argued to have transformed politics writ large, new technologies have long held the promise of revolutionizing campaign communication.[20] While radio and TV technology allowed campaigns to reach mass audiences, subsequent advances in technology also contributed to campaigns' ability to reach a variety of audiences through various channels. One of the first "new" methods of bringing unmediated information to voters took place in the late 1980s with "blastfaxing," allowing campaigns to distribute messages directly to politically active groups or news agencies without having to physically share the same space.[21] Since Dianne Feinstein became the first candidate for elected office to develop a web page in 1994, yet another medium has existed through which campaigns could reach a mass audience.[22] The use of campaign web pages would grow rapidly, as over two-thirds of congressional candidates in the 1998 cycle had websites; now they are expected and nearly universal, even for small, local races.[23] While campaign websites might now be considered mundane and relatively static, they remain fundamental spaces in which campaigns can construct their own image, and have become tools by which campaigns can establish emotional or parasocial connections with citizens and enable limited actions on the part of citizens.[24]

Direct email communication, first used to great success by Jesse Ventura in 1998, was applied similarly, but also allowed messages to be sent to groups as well as individuals who were activists. Not only were these media used to aid communication between campaigns and elites such as journalists and known activists, but they allowed for direct communication with potential voters and everyday supporters as well. These advances in technology provided more avenues of communication by which to circumnavigate news outlets and communicate directly with a greater audience.

The recent import of social media platforms into campaign communication has led to even more channels for message dissemination and circulation. Candidates have developed their own YouTube channels (in the 2008 cycle, 72% of major party Senate candidates and 28% of House candidates had their own channel; in 2010, this jumped to 78% combined rate of Senate and House candidates) and use them as a place to publicize television ads, web-specific ads, and informational videos or footage from public events.[25] In September 2009, there were 166 representatives and 39 senators using Twitter; by March 2012 these numbers had risen to 367 representatives and 87 senators.[26] Consulting firms specializing in digital messaging have grown exponentially in number, and increased in specificity, with entire firms devoted to mobile phone and SMS (Short Message Service) text message technology or website design. Moreover, campaigns are increasingly turning to social media channels of Facebook and Twitter to spread their messages and interact with citizens. These numbers, as they have rapidly increased, are likely to continue to grow through the trickle-down effect under which campaign strategy operates, wherein technology use tends to be adopted at a greater rate by smaller, more local elections as time goes on.[27]

Through their use of the slightly different affordances and social uses of digital media channels, campaigns have made a variety of different types of content available, and various media have come to be characterized by different norms of content. These norms are influenced by both the material affordances of media technologies and their socially constructed instances of use. While blogs, websites, and microsites all allow for a wide variety of material capabilities, including video embedding, long-form descriptions of policy or messages to potential voters, and links and buttons to other action or web pages, the material constraints of social media exert a more limiting effect on the type of content that can be circulated. While Facebook allows campaigns to post many kinds of content (video, news stories, links to the campaign site, etc.), the posting format strongly encourages shorter messages. It enables campaigns to share their own website content or that of other media outlets with the click of a button, and provides campaigns the option to frame the story themselves by providing an opportunity to caption and share content. Twitter and SMS have even more obvious material constraints, as they only allow for 140 and 160 characters, respectively. Even when the material capabilities of technology are similar or identical, various media channels can develop different norms of content. Campaign websites are a space for detailed, candidate-focused information on a wealth of topics, from candidate biographies to issue and policy positions to information about contacting the campaign.[28] Campaign blogs give more personal accounts of the day-to-day happenings with campaigns.[29] As a medium that often both circulates campaign messages and renders judgment on their persuasive capabilities, feasibility, and political leanings, news blogs provide campaigns with yet another specific type of earned media coverage that is geared toward reaching niche audiences, geographically specific content, or content that gives in-depth explanation of already-existing political and news texts.[30] Part of the project of this book is uncovering the emerging practices across a variety of media tools—for instance, social media have become home to "behind the scenes" content and digital "retail politics," as is discussed in chapter 5—in an effort to better understand both the practical use of their tools and their implications for political participation.

Opportunities to transmit messages via paid media coverage have expanded through new media as well. Just as the new form of cable television brought a change to the capabilities of political advertising in the 1990s, web technologies have done so again.[31] There is a wealth of ways to advertise online, from paying to advertise on certain search terms to producing banner ads that are carried on various blogs and other websites. Web advertisements can tap into slices of demographics, just as cable television or direct email can, but can do so for less money and with greater ability to control and target messages. Additionally, campaigns can optimize their online ads or campaign texts like microsite and official websites so that search engines return them more frequently and alongside requests for related information. Even as these are paid-media channels and therefore are not free of cost to a campaign, they significantly lower the cost of broadcasting messages online, and thus the barrier to entry for online communication is very low.

Equally consequential to the patterns of campaign production of these texts across multiple media are the findings that citizens encounter and interpret these messages on an increasingly common scale. While television is still the most prominent mode of accessing political information, use of digital media is on the rise. In the 2010 midterm election, 54% of adults, which amounts to 73% of Internet users, went online to get news or information surrounding the elections, a number that far surpasses the previous midterm election's number of 31%.[32] The same study found that 24% of all adults (32% of online adults) used the Internet as their main source of political information. Going beyond conceptions of the Internet as one monolithic technology, the project finds that a whopping 31% of online adults viewed campaign-related videos, such as online ads or coverage of campaign events. Additionally, 22% of online adults used Twitter or social networking sites for political purposes. More specifically 18% used the platform to see how people they knew voted, and 14% used it to get candidate or campaign information.[33] Twelve percent of all adults used their cell phones to keep up with political news.[34] The use of digital media as a vessel by which to circulate campaign messages not only results in the ability to target populations with specific single messages, but also creates a web of interconnected information that keeps audiences on the messages campaigns want them to see. As one communications director from a congressional race explains it, "Capturing people and getting them stuck in something like flypaper—they go to your website . . . then they're looking at your education plan, and go to the Facebook page, and the Facebook takes them to the Twitter feed, Twitter feed takes them to the YouTube page . . . they're continuing to browse and they're staying on your message."[35]

Just as there is a mixed bag of citizenship claims concerning digital media's use as tools to categorize populations, so, too, are the claims about their use as vessels for messages contradictory, and the goals of campaigns often stand at odds with ideal forms of participation and citizenship. Through these different uses of digital media, campaigns are also able to get their messages directly to potential voters without relying on the rapidly dwindling news media and often without subjecting their messages to reframing. The production of these more narrowly purposed and easily targeted texts holds promise for electoral success, but also contains the conflicting rewards and pitfalls for citizenship examined in the previous section. At one level, the much-desired flypaper effect of campaign messaging is equivalent to an echo chamber, and is thus seen as problematically insulating audiences from the contradictory information that leads them to question messages or gain a diverse perspective. Despite this apprehension, others see the ability to get audiences an influx of messages they find important as most likely to change supporters into volunteers, directly aiding campaigns' primary goal of electoral success, and potentially leading to a higher level of participation.[36] Although the ramifications of the content citizens access can be debated, use of digital media for circulating political messages has definitively opened up an increased space of owned and earned media and lessened the barrier to entry for many candidates. While candidates once had to hound the press and hope for coverage or shell out massive sums for radio, television, or print ads, digital media taking the form of candidate web pages, microsites, direct email communication, and social media tools such as Facebook, YouTube, and Twitter have provided more channels that are of low or no cost for candidates. For many consultants, this is a primary benefit of digital campaigning. While traditional, more expensive forms of print, radio, network, or cable advertising are still necessary to a successful campaign, these new media technologies allow more information about a candidate or campaign to enter the public and potentially break through. While the political arena is still dominated by party politics and political elites, grassroots candidates are now better equipped to get their message out, gain the necessary levels of name recognition, and enter and influence the local and national political conversations and elections. Consultants often reference new media's ability to level the playing field for smaller races or candidates. "You're not trying to get some board member from the *New York Times* to pay attention to you.

You can take the message straight to the audience, right? You can get them to pay attention."[37]

TOOLS FOR CITIZEN INTERACTION AND ENGAGEMENT

While the aforementioned developments have led to what have by and large been amplifications of previous needs for organization and message transmission, shifts in media technologies have also enabled a more radical shift in attempting to more deeply engage citizens. Rather than approach citizens as receptors of messages or types to be categorized and subsequently marketed toward, campaigns have embraced technical changes that have increased the amount and types of ways citizens can participate in the political process. Most importantly, digital media have changed the dynamics of the communication process by increasing the opportunity for feedback and two-way interaction between campaigns and voters. Additionally, they have contributed new capacities for citizens to engage with one another and be mobilized, providing easy opportunities to participate in politics on a variety of levels and a wealth of options for action that match a variety of needs or preferences.

While we currently think of "interactive" technologies as being cutting edge and of the moment, digital media have fostered various forms of interaction between campaigns and the general public for decades. Just as the earliest forms of online technology such as message boards and chat rooms fostered interaction and community among members, technologies of direct email and comment pages have afforded these same feedback loops between campaigns and citizens. As early as the 1970s, campaigns began to use computerized systems to produce form letters from constituents, thus vastly increasing the amount of citizen input received by campaigns and officials.[38] While citizens could always contact campaign offices as a response to the messages or platforms they heard on the radio, television, or in person, they are able to do so much more easily with the help of digital technologies. Citizens can directly respond to campaign-produced emails or easily find contact information on campaign websites, and the asynchronous aspect of email makes matching schedules with a busy and often sidetracked campaign staffer unnecessary. In most cases, these opportunities for conversations are not even limited to a candidate's constituents, but can be undertaken by any interested member of the public, although traditional markers such as a provided zip code enable campaigns to organize citizens according to their relevance to the local district. Moreover, as technologies have advanced, mobile phone communication, social media, and commenting capabilities on blog posts or campaign websites all allow for and encourage dialogue between a campaign/candidate and citizens. Contemporary campaigns even try to encourage this two-way dialogue, as one 2010 communications director described the office's goal of "providing a forum" through social media.[39] Another described the importance of dialogues on the campaign Facebook page, saying staffers ask questions and encourage supporters to answer, because "you get people roused up when you create that conversation."[40] Some digital consultants explained how social media tools like Twitter can be used to engage in one-on-one conversations with constituents or potential voters by retweeting people's comments on the race, the candidate, or a policy in order to bring them into a conversation, and how closer to Election Day, you could use the platform to digitally "canvas" by talking to individual people who were still undecided.[41] As elected officials began to use the platform in earnest in 2010, they also saw it as a space through which to engage their constituents in reciprocal communication. In what is now a fabled example and one of the first massively publicized political uses of Twitter, Newark mayor Cory Booker used the medium to connect with constituents during a blizzard in order to help shovel out those who tweeted at him for help, and ultimately bring one constituent much-needed diapers for her infant.[42] After Cory Booker's use of the platform to truly interact with constituents, rather than merely campaign at them, consultants began to see the platform as more than a way to amplify their existing messages; it could instead transform the kinds of interactions citizens expected of campaigns and candidates. Incidents of valiant acts enabled by digital media clearly get more publicity than posts about policy, but the use of these media to communicate directly with the public can be seen across a variety of topics.

In addition to an increased ability to communicate with campaigns, digital media provide additional avenues for public discussion and the articulation of viewpoints among citizens, interactions that need not be led or directed by political institutions such as campaigns or those in power. Blogs and online news sources can often be commented on and can be spaces of legitimate, productive debate and discussion (often thanks to the work of moderators). These spaces have become the site of multiple types of participation, with Daily Kos standing as the prototypical example of a space where people can go to get information (via blog content created by editors), create and share their own information (via "Diaries"), discuss and debate topics (via comments), and also plan offline action. Blogs are not the only space for such interaction, though. Microsites and websites stand as spaces for public commenting and debate, and discussion is often present on websites and microsites produced by campaigns as well, though to a lesser degree.[43] Social media furthers this feedback, allowing citizens to comment on and respond directly to campaign texts via media platforms that are seen by their peers, and groups who are interested in the campaigns at hand. In doing so, these platforms allow citizens easy mechanisms by which to engage one another in political matters and conversations. While not exactly widespread, these texts are used by substantive portions of the public, and especially by communities of activists. Message boards have been places of discussion and deliberation since the early days of the Internet, and were engaged by 6% of online adults during the 2010 election. As early as 1992, Ross Perot promised an electronic town hall, and during his time in office, President Obama has been the first to make use of such technology. YouTube has been used to solicit questions for debates and town hall meetings from a public that expands beyond the usual gatekeepers since 2007, and in 2011 candidates and politicians began using Twitter and Facebook as spaces for these dialogues and to solicit input and reactions.[44] Beyond simply discussing political information, citizens share texts and pass along political information in new ways—through email, social media platforms, text messages, and blogs—as well. In 2010, a full 16% of online adults sent email related to campaigns to their family, friends, and others, and 12% of voters went online to reveal their candidate of choice on Election Day. Moreover, 8% of all Internet users (13% of social media users) posted their own political content to these sites.[45]

Aside from simply opening up lines of communication to campaigns and among groups of citizens, digital media have also provided avenues for other forms of citizen participation as well. Emails, websites, and online ads that request acts of participation such as donating money, signing petitions, or public discussion and debate encourage new modes of participation and provide a new avenues for old forms of participating. Even though direct-email communication was primarily used by campaigns to send messages to political organizations and individuals in the 1990s, it is still argued to be of utmost importance to mobilizing, despite being a rather "mundane" technology.[46] Similarly, online petitions have become a common mode of participation that occurs across multiple websites, social media platforms, and email campaigns, and through candidates, political parties, and political organizations. While donations have long been solicited (and still are) through phone calls, mailers, and face-to-face meetings, Internet technologies have become extremely important to this form of participation. In 2000, Republicans began to seriously harness Internet technologies for fundraising, using direct emails and websites of campaigns as well as supporting political organizations to do so, and the Left responded in 2004 with ActBlue, its wildly successful networked donation system for candidates and progressive causes. Currently, campaign websites, microsites, and social media channels routinely (and sometimes constantly) contain links to donation sites, and 4% of Internet users donated to campaigns during the 2010 cycle, and 1% used their cell phones to contribute via text message.[47]

Websites such as Meetup.com were extremely productive as places to set up offline meetings in the 2000 election, and were the predecessor of later campaign-produced technologies such as MyBarackObama.com—a campaign website that allowed users to network and acted as a central location for many opportunities for activism—which also attempted to connect online and offline participation. This continues to be a productive method of participation, as 7% of Internet users went online to get information or organize offline events, and 5% went online to participate in volunteer efforts for the campaign cycle, 10% of social network users joined a political group or cause, and 2% even started their own group.[48] Even mobile phones have become a medium through which to engage in political participation beyond disseminating information. In the 2008 election, volunteers were asked to sign up for instant text message alerts, the then-nominee Obama first announced his pick for vice president via SMS, and although the campaign did use this point of contact to send them one-way messages, subscribers were also asked to mobilize. In the 2010 cycle, 6% of adults used their cell phones to let others know about conditions at local voting stations, 4% to monitor these conditions as they occurred, and 3% to shoot or share video about campaigns.[49] While this same type of participation had previously been done without the assistance of digital media, newer technologies enable faster, easier engagement.

Despite their increased use, the merits of these forms of engagement are debated. Because they are "easier" to undertake (one need not even leave the house, devote much time, or have much more than a cell phone), these acts of political participation have been criticized as less meaningful than prior forms of political engagement such as physically signing a petition or writing and mailing a letter to the editor. Such critiques not only negate the efficacy of new methods of participating by dubbing such actions "clicktivism" or "slacktivism," they also argue that online participation can actually discourage long-term activism and voter mobilization efforts.[50] As campaigns and consultants began to realize the value of mobilizing online advocacy in a major way in 2010, they were especially concerned with getting people engaged in easily enacted forms of engagement, which they hoped would lead to greater amounts or more involved forms of activism later on. "Once we know you'll sign a petition, we can try to get you to forward them to friends, or donate money. . . . So you want to turn people who are on your email list into donors and/or volunteers; you want to turn donors and/or volunteers into supervolunteers. It's a constant ask."[51] Echoing this, a national-tier new media consultant explains, "We know who's a supporter, who actually signs petitions, and we can try to turn them into level 2 volunteers. Then supervolunteers—we try to get people up the ladder of engagement."[52] These campaigns are so invested in the concept of gradually increasing levels of participation that they inform the ways they organize their requests. The consultant continues: "We go in steps. First we'll ask you to give us contact info, then sign or support something, then donate.[53] Viewing these actions in a vacuum, it is easy to judge them as mere clicktivism, but within the overall campaign context, they become vital stepping stones of overall messaging and mobilization goals.

Not only do these forms of participation occur, they seem to be the future of the role of technology and politics. Whereas new media firms were once largely focused on web design and maintenance, online advertising, and general message dissemination, practitioners are now concerned with the participatory elements that new media can bring to the table. Entire organizations are being built upon the promise of digital media for political engagement, and training occurs across the country in an attempt to bridge what used to be separate departments of communication and field organizations.[54] Opinions on the importance of using the unique capabilities of digital media are strong: "If you're not using social media to *engage*, you're failing," says one social media consultant, adding, "What's the point of these if you only use them to broadcast? That's not what people want."[55] While using all avenues of digital media to "blast" a message is tempting, most argue against such practices, however appealing they may be. Says one consultant: "Clients [campaigns] only want to get the message out. And enough consultants now try to say no. We've got to engage these people on their level. Talk to them about what they're talking about, not about what you want them to talk about."[56]

Evolutionary Strategy

Within these three categories, campaigns largely use new tools for old reasons. Moreover, even outside of the realm of communications offices, this rule holds true. One of the most productive uses of what was then new technology came in 2000 when the GOP began fundraising online. A so-called revolutionary development occurred in 2004 with the launch of ActBlue, a platform that enabled anyone to raise money online for any candidate on the Democratic ticket. Today, "new" tactics include using social media to raise money by posting pictures of a campaign office with price tags attached to equipment like photocopies, direct mail, yard signs, chairs, and so on.[57] In these and many other cases of adoption, campaigns' goals remain traditional, even as their tactics for reaching those goals shift. As with any case of evolution, what is moving too fast for some moves too slowly for others. Expressing her distaste for those who call old, traditional goals innovative, one consultant described how similar digital tactics were to those involving mass media of television and radio: "All they're really doing is targeting messages to segments. They're not personalizing. There's no actual nonlinear content assembly. People aren't grabbing different versions of messages that emphasize different points based on the individual, they're just microbroadcasting."[58]

When these early adopters and reluctant incrementalists come together in the contemporary campaign environment, what emerges is a hybrid environment for campaign strategy, in which new strategies are devised to deal with old problems, and occasionally, new goals are added to the "big three" of votes, volunteers, and dollars. These confusing, and often confounding, environments are spaces where strategies and responsibilities are ambiguous, undecided, and thus constantly being negotiated. Although innovative tactics such as using text messages for GOTV have been empirically proven to be easy ways to improve turnout and many cutting-edge consultants preach a "culture of analytics" in which only empirically tested strategy makes it to voters, local campaigns still find themselves without a clear strategy when it comes to crafting individual digital messages.[59] The following chapters investigate these emerging practices, the contexts from which they spring forth and which they may in turn affect, the goals with which they are pursued, and the forms of action or engagement they encourage in citizens. With each advancement in media technology, campaigns have gained additional channels for the content they put into public circulation, and the possibility for new tactics and new goals grows exponentially. Navigating these new areas is no easy task. While grasping at straws and moments of confusion happen, new practices also solidify. Consultants and staffers gain their bearings, and strategies solidify. Some of these maintain the status quo, and others signal new directions, new affordances, and new expectations for how potential voters act and what they want. The question then becomes how campaign messages and strategies might be changing in a digital environment, and what new additions to traditional genres of message might imply for the state of political information. The following four chapters detail some of the changing goals and strategies of contemporary digital strategy and their implications for what it means to be an active citizen within such a context.

3

Constructing Skeptical Citizens

Much of the content campaigns produce ends up on the cutting room floor, or, in trendier campaigns, the whiteboard walls. Erased only when in dire need of more room, the walls of one such campaign's communication office told the future through messaging calendars, documented the past in faded marker, and held alternate versions of reality in its jettisoned yet unerased content. Forty-three days out from Election Day, a lead communications staffer erased a square of whiteboard that had already been long forgotten by the campaign. "We're building a microsite!" came the communication director's voice. This site—a smaller website or single page produced by and connected to the campaign, but containing a different web address—would, according to the communications director, "show who [the opponent] really is." It was to be a top priority. In 2010, races in Illinois and across the country were turning to this medium as a place to go negative on opponents. In them, an image of Speaker of the House, Nancy Pelosi, emanated fire, Majority Leader Harry Reid's head was 10 times a normal size, and Senate candidate Christine O'Donnell was cackling in front of a cauldron.[1] The campaign was, as of that moment, on the bandwagon. Information was compiled through email chains and in shared Google Docs, punchy headlines were yelled across the hallway between the two offices of the communication director and the rest of the staff, and the site grew in front of everyone's eyes as the staff sketched the outline of a microsite on a wall of whiteboard. The content on the wall expanded, containing best attempts at titles (largely bad wordplay and tired clichés), columns that could potentially be sections or whole pages devoted to choice quotes, media coverage of the opponent's wrongdoing, the ever-condemned flip-flopping on issues, and rows of the opponent's allegedly extreme views, ready for attack. Debate and discussion over what to include on this site that was supposed to reveal the opponent's faults occurred often. "We have to make sure people really *get* that he's just not who he says he is" was a common sentiment during brainstorming sessions.[2] Although staffers would often add events to the board and compile them in a shared document, a month later the "microsite" still only existed on that wall. Even though the site never launched, it was the campaign's firsthand encounter with a form of campaign text that seemed to be sweeping the nation, from nationally publicized Senate races to those that were only countywide. When the site lay abandoned, what was left were reams of fact-checks, some of which were cannibalized for the campaign website, blog posts, or press releases as the weeks went on.

Even before the microsite, fact-checks were a part of everyday life in the communications office. Staffers spent their days creating and editing fact-checks, sending them in email chains for others to proof before posting. They shared Google Docs, with lists of facts and corresponding citations, so they could easily be pulled down at a moment's notice. Fact-checks were in press releases, had their own section of the campaign website, and were emailed to reporters regularly. The campaign focused on producing, circulating, and requesting them in almost every media channel: the press releases sent to reporters were also used in the news section of the website and shared in bits and pieces and as a whole through social media platforms. Staffers also focused on circulating the fact-checks completed by other reporters or news agencies. Proving their version of the truth—be it in a microsite or a fact-check—was a major part of the campaign's goal.

In addition to being trendy, these messages stand as a prime example of the ways digitally mediated campaign tools are imagining and encouraging new forms of citizenship within their messages. Microsites and campaign-produced fact-checks, along with political blogs and journalists' recent emphasis on the process of fact checking, act as a space for political content that is substantively different from that of traditional campaign communication. While the overarching narrative these tools tell is often remarkably similar to other media channels (after, all, staying on message is important), the affordances and socially constructed uses of these digital technologies are forming new practices of content creation that reflect and encourage new versions of citizenship. Despite the fact that the use of websites is nothing new, microsites contribute to new types of negative content, and their content questions candidates' statements and, more generally, what counts as valid or factual political information. As campaigns have, in some ways, moved beyond the enthusiasm surrounding microsites that dominated 2010, their excitement at creating and circulating texts that encourage citizens to develop skeptical and critical competencies has been funneled into other digital media texts. This content allows for and fosters a form of "skeptical citizenship" that recommends citizens question and ultimately judge the validity of political information.

This concept of the skeptical citizen marks an expansion on traditional associations of citizenship with practices of news or information consumption, by encouraging consideration of the ways that citizens are expected to engage this information. Additionally, it differs from assertions of the cynical and consequentially malaise-ridden or apathetic state of citizenship, as it focuses on how citizens are encouraged to approach political messages and information, not government itself, skeptically.[3] By encouraging this skepticism, microsites advocate a realistic account of the attitudes toward information that are necessary to navigate the rough-and-tumble world of contemporary democratic politics. Beginning with the microsite and its role as a new and seemingly successful tool in 2010, this chapter investigates how the 2010 and 2012 cycles saw a rise in content that constructs and reflects a vision of citizenship that not only necessitates consuming information, but consuming information in a specific way. From microsites to political blogs to websites devoted to election/candidate fact-checks, much of communications offices' time is devoted to content that develops a critical approach to political information. Through these texts, citizens are constructed not only as those who devote their attention to political news and information, or what Zizi Papacharissi has called "civic monitors," but as those who critically examine the information before them and render judgment on its credibility—as skeptical consumers of the political information they are monitoring.[4]

Beyond Citizenship as Information Consumption

Political communication research has long approached the study of political participation and citizenship through the lens of information consumption.

Awareness of news and public events and the capability to make informed decisions concerning politics has long been a central component of politics and informed notions of what democracy is. Theories of deliberative democracy hold that people must be informed in order to debate civil issues and reach consensus.[5] Although social scientists since Lippmann have found citizens unable to maintain fully informed perspectives and contemporary polls routinely showcase citizens' uninformed state, information is still at the heart of empirical measures and normative understandings of what constitutes political action and citizenship.[6] Even models of citizenship that are considerate of the unattainable nature of omnicompetence emphasize the central role of information. In these, rather than being called on to consume massive quantities of information in an effort to become universally informed, citizens are called on to monitor information that is of their particular interest or concern, or focus on specific issues of interest that warrant activism.[7] Acknowledging the productive possibilities of allegedly passive forms of engagement, such models of citizenship still focus on gaining access to and encountering certain types of information as the foundation for engaged citizenship. From this core association of democratic citizenship and information, the fields of political science and political communication routinely link the study of citizenship with levels of knowledge about the political system, measuring access to appropriate information and the effects of information on participation.[8]

As the Internet brought forth new capabilities in making information available, utopian visions imagined a public that could be deeply educated in a wealth of topics and for whom "a new source of political power lies in [information's] wide-spread dissemination through telecommunications."[9] This optimistic view is tempered by the paradoxical possibilities of information overload, wherein individuals can now choose to ignore information of a shared public in exchange for personalized information, and concerns over the veracity and legitimacy of information found in online texts abound.[10] With 54% of people getting their political information from online sources during the 2010 campaign, studies not only investigate the content of information, but look into people's practices involving information as well. They keep tabs on how people access it, investigate information seeking and avoiding behaviors,[11] study its retention or salience, and enter into debates over the state of research concerning relationships between participation and information, directly linking information with engaged citizenship.

Currently, even in the face of discussions about what types of participation a "new citizenship" should measure, theories of how citizens approach political information or may question its validity have been largely underdeveloped. Schudson's foundational vision of the monitorial citizen who superficially surveys a vast swath of news for interesting content, rather than consuming all that comes her way, is still pervasive, as are the developments of similar notions of "watchdog" or "standby" citizenship, which emphasize the need to publicize troubling or controversial events.[12] While these approaches are appropriate to many methods of political participation, they focus only on whether citizens receive information (and what that information is), rather than how a text can or should be interpreted. In doing so, they treat the process of encountering information as naive consumption—citizens either attend to content or they do not, and those who attend are either persuaded by its content or they are not. Even in analyses that account for why logical and persuasive appeals may fail, these theories of information consumption either assume a universal approach to political information or are unconcerned with how citizens approach this content. While cultural studies has long asserted that people are active interpreters of texts, political communication has largely assumed that texts exert their influence over readers, and that failure to influence is merely a result of faulty persuasive tactics.[13]

Far from simply being a fault of disciplinary blinders, politics itself—the world of campaigns and elections particularly—treats citizens this way. Campaigns regularly tell audiences to go to a candidate's website for information without any hint of incredulity at the expectation of truthfulness. Despite the cultural image of lying politicians, the news media exhibit constant surprise and shock over politicians "misstatements." This gap in thought is precisely where the concept of the skeptical citizen picks up. It stands not as a model for saying what type of information or fact is better or more important, but that all information must be approached with a shrewd and questioning mindset that views political information as necessarily complex and layered, and is skeptical about what counts as a legitimate fact. Through analysis of microsites, political blogs, and fact-check sites and pages, this chapter argues that the contents of specific digital media are beginning to reflect and encourage this questioning and active encounter with political information. In doing so, it puts forth another expansion of the monitorial citizen—that of the skeptical citizen.

Illuminating the Digital Texts

By 2010, political blogs and fact-check sites were largely a known quantity—political blogs are typically understood as sites for aggregating, interpreting, discussing, and rendering judgment on political information; fact-check websites or pages are places where the backtracks, flip-flops, and inaccurate statements of campaigns and candidates are cataloged and publicized. Microsites, however—and their evolution as political tools, their material capabilities, and their uses within campaigns—are newer to the electoral scene. As a rule of thumb, microsites are attention-grabbers. Although their roots go back to ideas floated as early as the 1996 Dole-Kemp campaign, as of 2010 microsites were described as "the hot new thing" by national-tier new media consultants, who are saying, "I *love* microsites" and "Every campaign wants one."[14] As a result, microsites have generated buzz as fruitful new tools that draw the interest of potential voters as well as earned media. These sites attempt to make up for what they lack in size with flashy graphics, strong (often inflammatory) claims, amusing interactive games, and attacks that are pithy, witty, and often harsh. More importantly, by multiple measures, they seem to work. In 2010, FireNancyPelosi.com raised over $1.5 million; WitchesForChristine.com received over 25,000 hits on its first day.[15] As a result, campaigns want them. As one digital media and web design specialist describes campaigns' overzealous reaction, "Omigod, Nancy Pelosi is on fire and it's on Fox News and it's making money and I need one now!"[16]

Despite the recent explosion in their use, the material technology of microsites is actually quite simple. Microsites are websites connected to and funded by a person, organization, or company not identified in the domain name. Although they are typically smaller in size than websites—often in the range of just one to five pages—microsites have the same material capabilities. Although the web design skills needed to create numerous microsites were less readily available in the past, and the cost of creation was therefore greater, the medium itself has existed for numerous election cycles now, although it was used sparingly for many cycles. Microsites were used by the Gore campaign in 2000 and considered a productive medium for Howard Dean's 2004 presidential run, but despite their early existence, their adoption remained slow. This reluctance to take up new forms of communication is common no matter what the media channel, and in a campaign environment in which the use of new tools must prove impressively productive before widespread use will develop, microsites have only recently been adopted on a larger scale. Far from being a one-time tool in 2010, campaigns have used microsites widely in the years since, and they have become especially prevalent in advocacy work. This type of site became more meme-like and less substantive in the electoral campaigns of 2012. For instance, EtchASketchMittRomney.com and RomneyGekko.com were two more notable sites of the election, and neither provided much more than a slick set of images. The first featured an Etch-a-Sketch displaying two contradictory Romney statements or policy positions whenever the user clicked to "shake" it, and the second made use of Romney's ties to Wall Street and featured a picture of a young Romney alongside other Bain executives posing with cash. This type of site also did much of the same work for both national parties, individual campaigns, and advocacy work.[17]

Microsites are small and therefore tightly focused. One national-tier new media consultant explains their true purpose as negative sites: "They give you an opportunity to hit one message, and to hit it big, hit it loud, and hit it hard, without messing up your brand."[18] While self-focused microsites certainly have and currently do still exist—Hillary Clinton's 2008 campaign led the way, launching two popular ones: TheHillaryIKnow.com and HillaryHub.com, and in Illinois in 2010, the Giannoulias campaign for Illinois' Senate seat launched TruthAboutAlexi.com, a site about the candidate himself—even though consultants nearly universally speak first about attacking one's opponent through microsites. Even after acknowledging sites that are positive, consultants raise questions: "Why have a microsite that echoes who you are? Why isn't that on your site?"[19] Some strategists have simply dubbed them "hit sites," even when examples to the contrary are explicitly noted. Moreover, these sites are largely informative in their negativity, rather than mobilizing. Despite the large amount of press attention surrounding sites such as the RNC's FireNancyPelosi.com for its impressive mobilization of donors, engaging audiences in participatory action is not the most common purpose of campaign microsites.

In Illinois in 2010, six campaigns produced nine microsites, and two campaigns drafted one site each but never took the pages live. In these sites and others developed in 2010, a pattern of content emerges that is, as this chapter will show, consistent with content created and disseminated by campaigns elsewhere, as well as that of statewide political blogs, and nationally known fact-checking endeavors such as FactCheck.org. Drawing on textual analysis of existing microsites, fact-checks, and local Illinois politics blog coverage as well as discussion about both developed and planned sites' creation, this chapter illustrates that they all demonstrate the need for a skeptical approach to information.[20]

While this chapter focuses largely on the media of blogs, fact-check sites, and microsites, there is good reason to believe that the emerging practices found within these sites are more stable than their current distribution channels. These emerging practices are recurring within specific media channels other than microsites and are mirrored in digital tools throughout the campaign environment. Political blogs are not only for citizen journalists, but are increasingly created by campaigns and interested volunteers that have always been the campaigns' boots on the ground. Fact-checks are an increasingly common feature on both local and national scales, and often show up not only within microsites, but in official campaign sites and journalistic enterprises as well. These digital texts exhibit similar emerging patterns of content and processes of creation that impact day-to-day operations of communications staffers and encourage and invite audiences to approach information as skeptical citizens.

Effects on Traditional Campaign Communication

While the content of microsites, fact-checks, and journalistic blogs may vary across districts and offices, these media channels are important across the board and impact the everyday activities and organization of campaigns in significant ways. Although this chapter focuses on the content of these sites, the processes of producing the content also impact the organizational culture of campaigns and their interactions and reveal important insights into how both journalists and academics approach digital campaigning.

As the campaign I observed set out to produce content for a microsite that largely became content for a fact-check portion of the campaign website, the process of culling and organizing information in fact-check form became an important organizational tool for the communications office. Almost anachronistically, the campaign had boxes full of paper versions of content. From press questionnaires to print ads, there was content generated in both the primary and the general election stages of the campaign, and information about the campaign as well as its opponents, most of which was ignored in no small part because it was unsearchable except manually. The digital information that was unpublished was most often saved in email chains for quick mobile access, and while it was locatable if someone could remember appropriate search terms, standard organization systems were something of a luxury in the chaotic world of a tight race. Because much of the work was a collaborative effort between three or four communication staffers, work on content that required many citations often occurred over the span of many link-filled emails, often sent repeatedly on an as-needed basis. In the development of the fact-check/microsite content, however, things began to change. Because of the anticipated size of the microsite, staffers needed a common space to see the content together in order to ensure its categories were coherent and exhaustive, and Google Docs was the logical choice to fill this role. When staffers contributed to the shared Google Docs, evidence was at hand for all staffers and easily available to use within a different message or to quickly reply to a reporter's question. While use of the tool began as a way to make the work of finding citations for fact-checks and the microsite more efficient, it became a meaningful aspect of how the communications office kept track of information. Fact-check pages created in September were occasionally added to, only to be used weeks later. For example, while details from Federal Election Commission (FEC) reports were not always deemed important enough to make it into sound bites or warrant press releases, they were organized into one giant FEC document to be used as needed, and occasionally placed in other issue-oriented communications.

An overwhelming amount of both journalistic and academic coverage of the 2008 Obama victory centered upon the campaign's revolutionary use of relatively new media tools like social networks and the data gathering and analyzing associated with microtargeting. As a result, coverage of digital campaigning is rife with proclamations of forever-changed landscapes and a widespread focus on how campaigns use social networks. Although these platforms are certainly important to campaigns, continued reliance on microsites, fact-checks, and journalistic blog coverage highlights the fact that digital campaigning is about more than social media. In fact, although many have criticized campaigns' uses of social media for controlling citizens, microsites, fact-checks, and the like are forms of digital campaigning that do even less to enable interaction on the part of citizens. Instead, they provide yet another broadcast platform. Although this sort of campaign communication is published on websites that could have interactive features, fact-checks only make use of broadcast features. Yes, blogs offer space to comment and campaigns and fact-checks offer boilerplate options to share pages via Facebook or Twitter, but interactivity is not a primary feature of these sites. While this reflects a limitation of digital campaigns' ability to allow citizens to take meaningful action, it ought to remind those investigating digital political communication that important changes can and are occurring in digital spaces that are less interactive. The particular approach to information taken by these texts does, in fact, point to new ways that citizens are encouraged to approach political content.

While campaigns have long divulged information about opponents, these texts are not merely recreations of negative ads or repositories for campaign-produced press releases, despite the traces of each genre. Importantly, they also contain specific types of content that invite audiences to act as skeptical citizens more than other campaign texts. First, their content is directed at publicizing political shortcomings and is often the place of negative assessments of people, policy, scandal, untruths, or other information. Importantly, these texts not only provide information, but do so within a frame of revealing that which is hidden or covered up. Additionally, because of their material capabilities and their practices of use, they provide a much more detailed and nuanced depiction of political information. The sheer amount, variety of content, number of sources, depth of information, and dedication to presenting information in a contextualized manner sets them apart from most other messages, traditional or digital. Finally, as a result of revelatory framing and nuanced depictions of information, these texts directly ask audiences to question and judge information they are given, whether it be from another candidate or a news source. As these sites exhibit such characteristics, they not only provide people with more information by which to make political judgments, but also encourage an attitude of skepticism toward political information, encouraging the practice of analyzing and judging what counts as valid political information and as "fact." In doing so, these sites expose an important distinction between citizens' relationships to information, which can extend beyond the role of the consuming, monitorial citizen, to that of critic and "skeptical citizen."

NEW VERSIONS OF NEGATIVE

For as long as there have been political campaigns, there has been negative campaigning. Andrew Jackson and John Quincy Adams may have used pamphlets before Lyndon B. Johnson or the Swift Boat Veterans for Truth took to the television airwaves and before 21st-century campaigns moved toward quirky online attacks, but the mudslinging is not new. Traditional negative advertisements and opponent hits are still common—one need only turn on the local news during an election year to be bombarded—but within a new crop of digital texts such as blogs, microsites, and fact-check sites, negative content is being used and presented in new ways.

In Illinois alone, eight out of ten microsites were attacks on the candidate's main opponent, while one was used as an attack on President Obama. The very names of each site (see table 3.1) reflect this one-track focus, wherein each site's name identifies the opposing candidate (e.g., the microsite produced by the Mark Kirk campaign was called RealTruthAboutAlexi, and the site produced by the Alexi Giannoulias campaign was called WhoIsMarkKirk). Additionally, many campaigns bought extra sites with their opponent's name and some variations of "facts," "truth," or "real" in the URL. As precautionary measures, campaigns even purchased domain names with their own candidate's name. After all, if you own it, your opponent cannot. Consultants' reasons for focusing on an opponent invoke the pseudo-anonymity that the material technology of a microsite offers, but the FEC's regulations requiring "paid for by" language on campaign-produced documents prevent. Despite the presence of this disclaimer, consultants and staffers rely on the ability to disassociate microsites from official campaigns, saying: "You can brand these sites completely differently"; the "different branding, different look and feel—it could confuse the voter to the extent that they don't know which [sites] are associated with whom . . . and the campaigns will play on that." Consultants even assert that such sites are a place for "stuff you don't want your name on," immediately after acknowledging the required presence of the FEC's "paid for by" text.[21] Not only do microsites highlight opponents, they ignore the campaigns' own candidates as well.

Microsites tend to be hit sites not only because negative ads dominate our airwaves, but because they rely heavily on earned media coverage to gain publicity. Because the story of a politician giving factual information is not a newsworthy event, fact-checks, as a genre, are only meaningful insofar as they disprove the validity of a statement. While truthful statements do sometimes make nationally oriented sites like FactCheck.org, the very idea of needing such a site implies the reason is to bring factually incorrect statements to light. As fact-checks overwhelmingly focus on untruthful

Table 3.1 **List of Campaign-Produced Microsites and Purposes**

Candidate producing	Office and Party	Site name	Site purpose
Pat Quinn	Governor (D)	WhoIsBillBrady.com	Attack on opponent
Alexi Giannoulias	Senate (D)	WhoIsMarkKirk.com	Attack on opponent
Alexi Giannoulias	Senate (D)	TruthAboutAlexi.com	Defense of self
Mark Kirk	Senate (R)	RealTruthAbout Alexi.com	Attack on opponent
Joel Pollak	Congress (R)	ExtremeJan.com	Attack on opponent
Joel Pollak	Congress (R)	StopPlayingGolf.com	Fundraising (via attack on president)
Potential site	Federal (anonymized) (R)	n/a	GOTV effort plus attack
Potential site	Federal (anonymized) (D)	n/a	Attack on opponent
Joe Berrios	Cook County assessor (D)	ForrestClaypoolFor Assesor.com	Attack on opponent
Joe Berrios	Cook County assessor (D)	ForrestClaypool.org	Attack on opponent
Forrest Claypool	Cook County assessor (I)	JoeBerrios.com	Attack on opponent

Note: A handful of campaigns that said they "thought about making a microsite" but showed no significant content creation or development toward that goal are not included in this examination. Because the two sites about Claypool are so similar, I used ForrestClaypool.org (the more widely publicized site) to gather data.

statements, they often act as a negative ad, even when produced by bipartisan entities.

Moreover, although contemporary microsites have the potential to be much more interactive than those published by Gore in 2000, these affordances are seldom taken advantage of. Microsites serve to organize and house much information, but even the most cutting edge only allow visitors to donate money to a campaign or party or find an interesting format through which to transmit information to visitors. The *Jeopardy!*-themed WhoIsMarkKirk.com from 2010 provided its information in a game format, wherein the visitor would click to reveal answers, but did not feature any actual game mechanics such as points. EtchASketchMittRomney.com, from 2012, revealed and erased information by imitating the drawing and shaking process of an actual Etch A Sketch, but users could not submit their own ideas for content or draw on the screen. Although these features were not beyond the technical capabilities of microsites, they are outside the text's genre, which is focused on the one-way broadcasting of highly detailed negative information.

Political blogs—both partisan and nonpartisan—are of a similar nature in their tendency to highlight the negative elements of candidates, news coverage, and campaigns in general. Partisan blogs do this most overtly—while their purpose is to aggregate, interpret, and discuss the news they deem important, interesting or relevant, they also serve as clearinghouses for campaign attacks, taking down a slew of candidates from of the opposing party while upholding their own. In addition to simply republishing campaign-produced materials from Republicans in the week leading up to the election, the greater-Chicago area blog *ChicagoGOP* ran stories about eight specific Illinois Democrats up for election, highlighting relevant controversies in which they were embroiled and problems with depictions of the races in the "liberal media."[22] A more locally focused blog from an always-contested district, *Ellen of the Tenth*, took on the Right, using the same approach of publicizing the wrongdoings in local and statewide races, focusing attention on congressional candidate Robert Dold, Mark Kirk's Senate bid (Kirk was previously congressman for the 10th District), and occasionally gubernatorial contestant Bill Brady.[23] Beyond simply searching out this information, partisan blogs enjoy especially close relationships with campaigns of their own party, often receiving tips and ideas for content from communications directors and campaign managers.

Frustrated with the state of the campaign on a day late in September, the communications director of the campaign I observed walked into the staff's office one day. "No one at the *Sun-Times* or the *Trib* will pick up this story," she announced with a huff. "I don't want us to put out a press release . . . it'll look like we're just whining." The story in question—the content of which failed to interest a larger, nonpartisan blog—ended up on a local partisan blog. The next morning, looking at the day's news clips, the communications director gestured toward the story, still frustrated with its lack of publicity. "Well, it's still better than us saying it."[24]

Stories like these are common, as partisan blogs often serve as a site where campaigns can dump negative information about an opponent and avoid the damaging effects of going negative while still getting the information out. Nearly all communication directors, whether working for congressional districts in a midterm election or the regional offices of presidential campaigns, emphasize the importance of maintaining connections to local bloggers in order to drum up media coverage with a smaller-scale story. "This [hit on an opponent] is going out to all the local blogs," emailed a local partisan blogger after receiving a tip from the communications director. Within a day the story had been picked up by nonpartisan news blog *The Capitol Fax*, and within a few days, local newspapers began to report on the story as well.[25] These characteristics do not seem to be an artifact of local context, but part of a larger trend. While local campaigns leverage the journalistic ties they have, so too do national-level campaigns, with the Right routinely leaking to publications like *Drudge Report*, and the Left leaking both to progressive media and to grassroots activist sites such as *Daily Kos*.[26] While nonpartisan blogs don't focus on hitting any particular side, they often hit both, and take some swings at the news media covering the election as well, and fact-check sites function similarly. In displaying the misinformation at play in public discourse and condemning the politicians and campaigns spreading such "facts," fact-checks largely amount to spaces in which campaigns and politicians (as well as the occasional news organizations) are taken to task. These new forums for attacks on individuals, campaigns, and information itself do, however, contain content that is very different from the 30-second attack ads the public usually receives.

REVEALING, NUANCING, AND PROVING THE FACTS

The most notable difference between these digital texts and traditional ads, however, is not in the amount of negativity, but the revelatory framework within which this content is provided. According to major fact-checking sites PolitiFact and FactCheck.org, their primary purpose is to "help you find the truth in American politics" and "reduce the level of deception and confusion in U.S. politics."[27] Focusing largely on ranking the veracity of politicians' claims, assessing whether or not they've kept promises, and pointing out other instances of online fact-checking, these sites highlight the amount of misinformation that exists in the public. Sure, these sites also highlight truths (PolitiFact gives a "Pants on Fire" rating to pure falsehoods; Dennis Kucinich has zero such ratings), but the very premise of needing a fact-checking site is that misinformation exists and must be revealed. These websites have gotten much publicity and positive feedback. PolitiFact won a Pulitzer in 2009 and has received two Knight-Batten Awards for Innovations in Journalism, and FactCheck.org won the Sigma Delta Chi award from the Society of Professional Journalists in 2010 and has been named by *Time* magazine as one of "25 Sites We Can't Live Without" and one of World E-Gov Forum's 10 sites that "are changing the world." Their form has been adopted by campaigns in the digital environment as well. While fact-checks have long been a standby of press releases, specific pages on official campaign websites exist as a space for such content now. Microsites, political blogs, and fact-checks not only provide information; they contain a fundamental emphasis on revealing or uncovering information that is portrayed as hidden. Audiences are not simply told that a candidate's policies or viewpoints are bad, but the process of proving this is the case is spelled out, and the flaws of prior information are put on display in detail. Moreover, readers are explicitly told that the information they know about candidates (and possibly politics on a larger level) is likely limited, insufficient, and potentially wrong.

Fact-check websites are perhaps most clearly positioned as revelatory, as their goals of publicizing nonfactual information necessitates revealing its status as untrue (or partially true, as is often the case). PolitiFact does this by providing a quote from a person or organization, and then an icon of a "Truth-o-Meter," which ranks the information as true, mostly true, mostly false, false, or "Pants on Fire." Making the site a source for a variety of types of information, audiences can click on individual politician's "files," which contain a summary of all of their PolitiFact ratings and the totality of states' discussions, and track specific promises people have made. The FactCheck.org headlines that preface their fact-checks add to this sense of revealing, often including questions about the veracity of multiple sides of a specific topic or issue, such as: "Does Washington have a spending problem or an income problem? We offer some key facts."[28] Headlines like "Sorting out the truth..." and "Fact-Checking Boehner and Obama" similarly imply that there is almost always a mix of truth and fiction that the site will parse.[29]

These sites not only reveal information about candidates when they provide the correct information; they reveal acts of lying, backtracking, flip-flopping, or breaking one's word to the public. Additionally, this practice of revelation is not limited to politicians or campaigns, but involves other political orga- nizations such as super PACs or grassroots groups as well as the news media, and PolitiFact even contains special sections devoted to pundits, many of whom are journalists.

Campaign-produced microsites also contain this same emphasis. While campaigns' main websites serve as information central—where everything that is said is taken at face value as the policy or value of the candidate—these microsites frame information as difficult to know, secret, or debated. The names of many of the sites invoke this revelatory frame, with titles such as RealTruthAboutAlexi, TruthAboutAlexi, WhoIsBillBrady, and WhoIsMarkKirk. Beyond explicitly asking who a candidate is (or *really* is), or what the truth about a politician may be, these sites walk audiences through a process of discovering this information. Using a combination of visual choices that emphasize revealing secrets and content that purports to do so, these sites employ many tactics to reinforce their revelatory frame. RealTruthAboutAlexi led with an all-capital letter headline, "we won't get fooled again" (see figure 3.1). This is supplemented by an image of Giannoulias made to look like a suspect—a candid image of him with push pins and string connecting his photo to those of other people's Polaroid and mugshot-like photographs, mimicking the boards of crime-drama television shows that pinpoint guilty parties. Debbie Halvorson's campaign website contained a section devoted entirely to fact-checks, illustrated using an image of the definitive file for the 11th District (see figure 3.2). WhoIsMarkKirk makes similarly productive use of imagery, as its whole format is a play on the *Jeopardy!* game (figure 3.3). With answers such as "This politician claimed to be 'the only member of Congress to serve in Operation Iraqi Freedom,' even though that claim is not true," answering the *Jeopardy!*-style "Who is X?" questions links Kirk to these damaging facts and events, while simul- taneously driving home the message that voters still may not know exactly where Kirk stands (and encouraging people to keep asking, "Who is Mark Kirk?" in real life). While the WhoIsBillBrady page does not overwhelm- ingly emphasize its revelatory nature, the single image of Bill Brady looking downward in an ashamed way, next to the direct "Who is Bill Brady?" head- line lends itself to this depiction, as it implies that Brady has something to hide, or at least to be ashamed of.

Figure 3.1 Screenshot of a microsite, produced by the Kirk for Senate campaign, depicting the "real" Alexi Giannoulias as a suspect. (TheTruthAboutAlexi.com.)

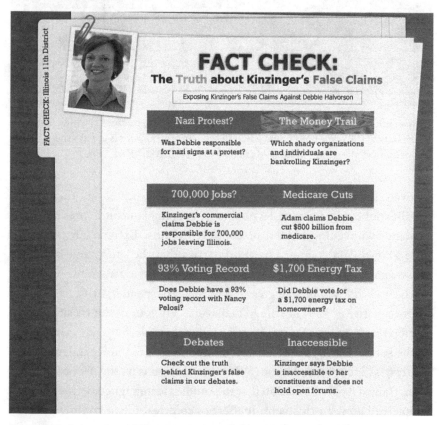

Figure 3.2 Screenshot of Congresswoman Debbie Halvorson's campaign website, which featured a FactCheck section depicting a file for the 10th District. (DebbieHalvorson.com.)

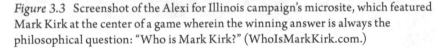

Figure 3.3 Screenshot of the Alexi for Illinois campaign's microsite, which featured Mark Kirk at the center of a game wherein the winning answer is always the philosophical question: "Who is Mark Kirk?" (WhoIsMarkKirk.com.)

Even sites whose revealing nature is not indicated in their name (JoeBerrios.com, ForrestClaypool.org, ExtremeJan.com) present their content as unveiling hidden or contested truths. ExtremeJan publicizes little-known data compiled by third parties that the site's namesake, congresswoman Jan Schakowsky, is "the most left-wing member of either of the two houses of Congress," the "biggest spender in the House of Representatives," and "hostile to taxpayers." On four of the six sites, information that is open to the public and easily accessible, but seldom looked up or the subject of news articles, such as donor lists and independent expenditures, is highlighted. Although this information is public, fact-check sites often framed it as information that the candidate impugned or doesn't want people to know. In this vein, JoeBerrios.com features a common official document—a Freedom of Information Act request—but frames it not only as proof of a claim, but as revealing information that was purposefully hidden and subsequently unearthed by Claypool's campaign.[30]

As the site of commentary and expansion of news coverage and political events, blogs also make revealing and contextualizing information a top priority. While the news media often investigate that which is hidden, partisan blogs take it is as their purpose and goal to provide some sort of expansion on this coverage. Despite critical views of blogging as little more than a release valve for blowing off steam and a medium filled with complainers, blogs expand upon traditional information such as news coverage or press releases in many ways. By discussing the significance or insignificance of a news item, debating the validity of an article and its facts, pointing out shortcomings of the original news content, or conducting additional reporting, "bloggers help us asses the news if news organizations can't or won't."[31] Blog content, rather than merely providing information, contextualizes and complements information. Fundamentally, as blogs flesh out and comment on information, they contribute additional content and guide readers through the information environment.[32] *ChicagoGOP*'s post titled "What the Chicago Tribune Wouldn't (Couldn't) Print" and long accounts of election coverage and analysis directly reveal the problems (and successes) of recent mainstream news coverage.[33] Similarly, many will use news articles as jumping-off points to showcase responses to the stories as well as opinions on the elections, as illustrated by local blog Ellen of the Tenth's routine use of stories from the national-level liberal political blog, Talking Points Memo.[34] As noted earlier, because of the many close ties between bloggers and campaign staffers, blogs are also known to break smaller-scale or more local stories and cover races that are given less attention by major media outlets.[35] Journalist Rich Miller's nonpartisan news blog, *The Capitol Fax*, often aggregates election coverage, devoting whole posts to rundowns of the latest ads or a wide array of coverage of one story from many news outlets. In grouping this content and also providing his take on it, Miller uses his blog to supplement news coverage and make it more holistic, engaging in what Axel Bruns has described as a "guide dog" function that productively brings together varied perspectives of events or policies on a variety of sources, including both news coverage and original documents, and can provide insight into the multiple ways to frame an issue.[36] Additionally, with numerous posts that clarify or explain the half-truths of news information and information from campaigns, these blogs further support findings that blogs' main purposes are to direct people to political information, and engage in greater description or judgment of that information that highlights errors, biases, shortcomings, or important aspects.[37]

A significant portion of the production of skeptical citizenship is not only pointing out that there is unknown or misinformation around, but pointing out that all information is nuanced and contextual, and therefore must be engaged with a degree of skepticism and analysis. Even while some traditional television and radio ads invoke revealing narratives that are conceptually similar to those on microsites or fact-checks—for instance, the Pat Quinn campaign had a series of well-received television spots that also questioned his opponent's, Bill Brady's, fitness for governing and asked. "Who is this guy?"—their ability to illuminate the complex nature of political information falls short in relative to that of microsites, political blogs, and fact-checks. These digital texts call attention to the nuances of political information in a variety of ways. First, their material capabilities and socially situated patterns of use result in a level of information that is highly detailed. Second, they routinely turn to discussions of context, showing how information and what counts as truth is relational, complex, and contingent. Finally, they explicitly show how arguments progress, breaking down logical moves in a process that is multistep and unfolds and shows the details that are necessary to engage political information.

A reason that these digital texts are able to showcase detailed, contextualized, and long-unfolding arguments is their material capacity to hold a large amount of information at virtually zero cost to the campaign. Considering how much every second of a television ad costs to air, spending time on intricate details or complex arguments is an unthinkable use of funds, even in cases where the campaign coffers seem quite full. Even other traditional advertising platforms such as direct mail and radio are costly, and holding viewers' attention is difficult. With the online spaces of microsites or official campaign web pages, a campaign need only pay for the cost of producing such content. Blogs and fact-checking journalistic sites are equally equipped to devote space to detailed explanations, and can take the necessary time and space to reveal information in a way that situates political information and "facts" as nuanced, contextual, and needing to be critically interpreted in a way that advertisements cannot. The affordances of fact-check sites and political blogs, while not campaign-produced, are just as amenable to large amounts of information. Moreover, readers are more likely to be interested in the content they are reading than audiences subjected to radio or television ads. While major campaigns' large purchases of Internet ads have recently made headlines, the vast majority of traffic to microsites, blogs, and campaign fact check pages is from people who seek them out through search engines or click on links recommended by campaigns or friends.[38] As a result of seeking out these materials or trusting the source who supplied them, readers are likely to spend more time on the sites. Because of these material and social affordances, campaigns can use the microsite as a place for more (and more detailed) content, and blogs and fact-check style journalism have become a space for in-depth discussion and contextualization of facts and events. In stark contrast to contemporary print and television news content that is often labeled (and condemned) as part of a "sound bite culture," the content of these texts provides an approach to political and candidate information that is broad, well rounded, and conscious of context, and goes through specific steps to prove or debunk information.[39]

Fact-check websites or pages of campaign websites exist as spaces devoted entirely to inquiring about the validity of what campaigns or candidates have said or done, myths, or discourses that are circulating within the public. By attending to the specific details of information and pulling news accounts and candidate quotes apart in order to analyze whether they should be believed, these fact-check sites show that information is complex and in need of dissection and critical insight. PolitiFact begins with direct quotations from politicians and parses the specific details and meaning, attempting to understand what sources and facts the statements could have come from, and other information or evidence that may contradict such claims. As a result, a politician's short sentence can lead to a nearly 1,000-word assessment of the quotation that delves into its many possible meanings and its intent. Fact-check sites use these techniques to gauge the validity of a claim with recourse to a politician's past actions, and PolitiFact even has a specific tool to gauge whether or not people have changed their policies, stances, or speeches. This shows readers that information should not be seen as static, but as always tied to past and present contexts. FactCheck.org often provides overviews of all sides of a debate in articles such as "Debt Limit Debate Roundup" and gauges the validity of arguments within the confusing discussions that go on about a particular topic or event.[40] The fact-checks that have begun to appear on campaigns' official websites are not as concerned with showing the possible readings of statements or alleged flip-flops, as they are with proving one version of the event, much like microsites. In doing so, fact-checks highlight the variety of political information occurring within a larger field of discourse and often consist of responses and reactions to other information, showing how facts exist within in a larger context that should be taken into account in order to understand the information at hand.

Far from being single-issue sites, these microsites cover a wide range of what is often damaging information about an opponent. WhoIsBillBrady, WhoIsMarkKirk, and JoeBerrios.com are veritable grab bags of information on a wide range of topics. JoeBerrios.com features video of Berrios agreeing with a tax hike (and a politician) that was widely despised, and lists a "Greatest Hits" page that includes quotes from organizations such as the Better Government Association calling him "pay-to-play, personified." It highlights the fact that he was then under investigation by the board of review for corruption, had pushed property tax increases, and had been condemned for nepotism. WhoIsBillBrady contained information "revealing" Brady's stances on six major issues (economy, women, families, guns and crime, ethics, and civil rights). Additionally, these specific issues are bolstered by broader categories of news (coverage of Brady's misdeeds and missteps) and quotes (a compendium of things Brady said). The interactive game that makes up the WhoIsMarkKirk site similarly features six "categories" (Iraq and Afghanistan, Military Miscellany, Teaching, Health Insurance Reform, and National Security and Foreign Policy) for *Jeopardy!*-style trivia that always resulted in the question "Who is Mark Kirk?"). ExtremeJan was not focused on one issue or example of her allegedly extreme views, but on 17 different topics—from votes on legislation involving product safety, abortion, healthcare, and card check, to third-party assessments of her shortcomings in areas of national security, "free market policies," spending, and tax policy, to linking her to corruption. ForrestClaypool.org covered a wide range of issues that go beyond the site's headlining message: "He doesn't care about tax payers." In addition to information related to property taxes, budget cuts, and corruption within his campaign and the Better Government Association, the microsite includes an expansive breadth of allegations. It gives equal room on the page to criticisms involving Claypool's Republican donors, raises given to staffers, and a slam of the *Chicago Tribune* for favorable coverage of Claypool. In the most conceptually bounded microsite, even as the front page of RealTruthAboutAlexi remained largely focused on Giannoulias's role in giving loans to criminals during his tenure at his family's Broadway Bank, the rest of the site covers a vast swath. The "Fact-check" portion of the microsite took aim at Giannoulias's views on TARP and the fact that he received a tax rebate, took money from special interests, and was a "rubber stamp" for Democratic policy—all in addition to numerous claims related to the bank. On the "Media Coverage" page of the site, information critical of Bright Start (a failed higher education endeavor of Giannoulias's during his time as state treasurer), of his general inexperience, and of his lack of debate participation rounded out the wide array of information.

Not only are a variety of news stories referenced, but the candidates themselves are often cited as well. In every single site, candidates are quoted or paraphrased, and video footage featuring candidate gaffes and unpopular statements are used on JoeBerrios.com and RealTruthAboutAlexi. This information is substantive too; entire news articles or multiple paragraphs make up the entries, rather than just choice quotes excised from their context. Just as a variety of issues are covered by these microsites, so, too, is an assortment of sources used to make claims. Culling information from multiple news organizations is common practice within each of these microsites. RealTruthAboutAlexi and WhoIsBillBrady had entire sections devoted to a cache of damaging news stories, while the other microsites wove multiple news stories throughout.

Microsites have not only become a space to prove information that is true, but one for debunking information as well. This takes the form of illustrating how opposing candidates may lie, flip-flop on issues, hold unfavorable positions, or behave in ways that do not match a positive narrative about them. RealTruthAboutAlexi had a fact-check page that shows where, when, and exactly how Giannoulias made seemingly suspect claims. Interestingly, Giannoulias's own similarly named site, TheTruthAboutAlexi (about the candidate himself) also employs this fact-check technique to dispel what it calls "myths." The two ideas for microsites in this study that were not carried out were also described as employing a fact-check. In one case, it was to show that an opponent "isn't who he said he was," and in the other it was to show that "the policies [our opponent] previously backed aren't what voters support." ForrestClaypool.org described Claypool's position on an issue as "inconsistent at best," citing conflicting votes over the years. The WhoIsMarkKirk game largely featured content that showcased embellishments that Kirk made of his own record, revealing that the "facts" Kirk had previously asserted were not factual statements. ExtremeJan argued that Schakowsky was associated with people whose views on Israel (an important issue in Chicago suburbs) go against her voting record. In one case, this debunking even extended to implying that the news coverage of their race has been biased. ForrestClaypool.org quoted a *Sun-Times* article detailing Claypool's raises to staff, and added: "The *Tribune* ran a similar story but omitted this same information about Mr. Claypool." In doing so, this micro-site not only debunks the information produced by an opponent, but also implies that even news sources should be approached skeptically. Within the vast expanses offered by microsites, blogs, and fact-check sites, sources are compiled, contexts are investigated, and the credibility of information is questioned. Readers are then also asked to judge the "real truth," and the result is that "facts" are repeatedly checked, corrected, and reassessed. One microsite even specifically requested that citizens make judgments about what constitutes valid political information when it asked readers to con-tribute anything they deemed to be a "myth" about their own candidate (TruthAboutAlexi.com). Now, certainly any campaign would no doubt be pleased if voters believed all negative content about their own candidate to be myth and all negative content about their opponent to be true, and cer-tainly fostering a critical mindset in citizens is not at the top of their list of goals for these texts. Still, in their attempts to inform, persuade, and con-vert opinions, the vast amounts of contextualized, analyzed, and proven (or disproven) information these texts provide situates them as encouraging a skeptical and shrewd approach to assessing information.

Campaigns are beginning to encourage this behavior within other digital messages as well. In August 2011, long before the presidential Republican nominee was even decided, the Obama campaign began to pursue similar tactics via email requests. On the evening of one of the many Republican primary debates, the campaign instructed its supporters to watch and to keep score of candidates' statements and misstatements, and to share the results on social media. Complete with a scorecard and point values for Republican talking points like "socialism," "Obamacare," and "9-9-9," the campaign combined an amusing version of Bingo with a live fact-check event, and brought this fact-checking behavior to social media as well.

Political blogs offer up a slightly different attention to detail. Still focused on providing specific details for which news or ads have no room, they pro-vide more detailed information and context alongside additional interpreta-tion and opinions. Offering extensive detail, an October 27, 2010, post on ChicagoGOP provided information on key state-level house races, includ-ing the phone numbers of campaign offices for 12 races. As these texts pro-vide a greater quantity of content, they also provide layers and nuance to the political information the public receives. In a ChicagoGOP post labeled "analysis and opinion," specific vote totals of years past were presented in detail, going back as far as 1998, along with predictions about how many votes would be won in specific counties in a variety of state and federal elections.[41] In a *Capitol Fax* post concerning the Illinois Democratic Party's failure to send out absentee ballots, journalist and blog author Rich Miller not only relayed the story from the major news outlets, but updated it twice through his own reporting, provided additional comments and opinion on the event, and highlighted and then answered questions being raised about the topic around the Internet.[42] By the same token, these blogs have space to parse and judge the specific word choices of candidates. One blog took the time to parse a recent 14-word quotation from Governor Quinn, while another honed in on the specific language of local municipal politicians' press releases or analyzed television ads, sometimes frame by frame.[43] In such analyses, blogs exhibit a skeptical view of a variety of campaign texts.

Additionally, a large amount of content is devoted to elaborating the information provided by quotations or news accounts. Because a common feature of blogs is to provide information in addition to that produced by the news media, stories about the validity of news accounts, in-depth explanations of scandals, candidate missteps, or allegations of impropriety, and judgments about these topics are often the topic of political blogs. *The Capitol Fax* has extensive content of this type—rather than simply providing the top lines of polls, as most news agencies do, the blog often delves into a variety of polls at once, discussing top lines, the possible problems with sampling or reasons to believe pollsters' assessments, and quotations from other sources about the polls. Additionally, Miller looks at controversies and conflicting information with this approach, systematically including quotes from candidates over the course of years, and input from both sides concerning news stories. Similarly, in partisan blogs, attention to the complexities of political information often takes the shape of analyzing things candidates or campaigns on the opposite side have done or written, and critiquing positive coverage or reception of their ideas, events, or actions. As blogs engage in these critiques, they mirror microsites' propensity to illustrate the nuance and complex contexts of political information. Through their process of nuancing and contextualizing, these digital tools encourage skeptical approaches to information, and a view of all information as "news-as-process: a continuing and necessarily unfinished coverage of topics and events inviting user participation, aiming to achieve what can be described as 'deliberative journalism.'"[44]

In all of these cases, the messages at hand go beyond previous campaign conventions of simply telling audiences to "look deeper" or providing very brief quotes from newspapers or other authorities. While those tactics may have endeavored to incite skepticism, they did not do the work of contextualizing information or walking audiences through the steps of proving or disproving information. Surely, these newer messages are descendants of those traditional tactics, but the changes they have undergone across a wide variety of digital channels have qualitatively changed the practices that citizens are asked to engage in—namely what to look for when determining a message's validity.

The emphasis on systematically questioning, proving, or disproving information exemplified in these sites differentiates them from traditional mass media and digital texts alike. It's obvious that a campaign's official website will contain a positive portrayal of its candidate, and an opponent-based microsite will contain negative content, but there is also a substantive difference in the way information itself (whether positive or negative) is contextualized, legitimated, and questioned (or, in the case of official campaign sites, often unquestioned). While microsites portray information in a way that calls the validity of information into question, official websites by and large provide information that, while substantive, is "documented" by simple assertions rather than practices of proof bearing.[45] Issue pages consist of candidates' reported positions and values, only sometimes giving specific examples of legislation they have or would support, and even then often without cited sources. Even in cases of sites that have endorsement pages, which can give legitimacy to a candidate (i.e., a candidate's claim to be pro-choice is legitimized by support from the National Organization of Women). Similarly, in cases where there are fact-checks on official campaign websites, they are the only space in which information is checked, debunked, or systematically proved, whereas that framework runs through the entirety of most microsites. The information on official websites is not framed to assuage audiences' doubts, but to give supporters more reasons to agree. Indeed, as research shows that official websites are unlikely to act as persuasive tools,[46] trying to convince audiences of the validity of a site's information is perhaps a poor use of time and resources. These processes of debunking and proving fundamentally situate information as contested, as in need of being checked. This process of proof-bearing signals that we are operating in a world in which the veracity of facts must constantly be skeptically questioned and implies an audience who engages shrewdly with political information, who will not take it at face value. The implied mode of consuming and interpreting political information—of engaging in civic matters and acting as a citizen—is to skeptically approach, parse, and judge, and citizens are expected to engage with political information as skeptical citizens rather than naive consumers or even uncritical monitors.

Multiple Truths and Critical Citizens

More detailed, informational, and covering more topics than traditional negative advertising, these sites function as clearinghouses for information, revealing the "true" facts of the election. Just like their advertising brethren, campaign-produced messages are attempting to get voters to believe their side of the story, and often spinning news and events in order to do so. Still, the wealth of information they offer—the long lists of misdoings, numerous examples of outside coverage of such misdoings, explicit "fact-check" sections, and the emphases on proving or debunking information—not only lend credibility to the arguments made, but provide complicated, nuanced, and layered accounts of political information and "facts" that readers must parse. Moreover, throughout all of these microsites, the process of distinguishing "valid" information from "invalid" information is a priority. In doing so, these sites imply that people should take a skeptical view of the political information they encounter. These texts argue that some political information counts (which is revealed by the sites) and some doesn't, and in some cases even explicitly assert that there are facts that are "real" (and therefore ones that are "fake"). In making these designations, these tools put forth a form of citizenship that asks people to judge political information and "facts." While critics like Keen have argued that these tools fail to provide more truth to more people, this alleged shortcoming is precisely where their benefit lies.[47] Rather than proclaiming truth, these digital tools complicate the assumption that information should always or uncritically be considered fact, and invites citizens to skeptically approach and analyze the multiple contexts and validity of information.

Clearly rooted in traditional campaign communications of negative ads, campaign websites, direct mail, and so on, these messages expand on those forms to position political information as in need of serious analysis. They focus on the act of revealing content rather than simply reporting it, and strategically complicate notions of what should count as "fact." In doing so, they perform a questioning and skeptical encounter with political information, and construct a normative model of citizens who ought to use similar measures to discern between what should and should not count as valid information. As these messages span the information landscape—from campaign-produced to journalistic in nature, from low-traffic Blogspot blogs to news sites that have won national awards, from interactive to information dumps—their qualities speak to a wider phenomenon within political communication as well as outside of it. Skepticism, in its similarities to irony, is a disposition that is likely alive and well if not bubbling under the surface of an era in which irony has been proclaimed "the ethos of our age." While it may be too soon to tell whether, as has been proclaimed, "Facts has finally died,"[48] these practices certainly frame information as in need of a skeptical assessment.

These practices also impact dominant understandings of campaign culture and work. While the war room is understood as the center of strategy—full of communications operatives taking on big questions about the narrative of the campaign—energy peaking when news breaks or staffers try to break news—the constancy of fact checking disrupts that idea. While communications offices, like all campaign work, have always been more of a grind than is recalled in our cultural memory, the rise of fact-checks has shown this work to be constantly occurring in the background, and in many cases to be more granular. Moreover, the processes of message construction that do happen there often pull from the same general well of information, which has become increasingly well organized, and can be used across a variety of purposes.

The digital tools and texts that encourage these practices are not only widespread, they appear to be growing in number and reach. In its coverage of the 2012 State of the Union address, the *New York Times* unveiled an interactive fact-check feature that allowed readers to scroll over text and view pop-up windows that explained and contextualized the speech and rendered judgment on its veracity. In the following week, a similar feature emerged within the paper's online election live coverage "dashboard."[49] Providing live blogging coverage of the January 26 Republican primary debate, the *Times* not only brought together highlights, commentary, and Twitter discussions concerning pivotal moments in its blog, but continuously fact-checked debate content. Moreover, inviting readers to "Ask The Times," the Election2012 dashboard provided a forum (or encouraged people to use Twitter) that asked people: "What should we fact check? As you watch the debate, ask us questions about candidate's statements you think deserve a second look." While campaign tools may change—from blogging platforms to microsites to interactive dashboards—practices of questioning, contextualizing, and proving what constitutes facts and valid information remain an important and central concern of political information, whether it be campaign-produced or journalistic in nature.

It is not that campaigns producing these sites specifically set out to create skeptical citizens. In fact, the campaign goal is often, to the contrary, allegiance above all else. These sites are produced by campaigns in order to persuade, and campaigns are not concerned with what citizenship or politics means, so long as they are winning votes. In many cases, campaigns are not very reflexive about their reasoning behind putting up a microsite; upon asking a national new-media consultant why so many campaigns wanted them, she answered: "It's because Obama and also Hillary did that. Then everybody needed one."[50] Use by major campaigns that garnered intense enthusiasm showed that microsites were not only safe, but likely worth the time and effort. With little to lose, campaigns' increasingly widespread use of microsites is much more a case of using everything but the kitchen sink than upholding democratic ideals. In fact, according to traditional measures of levels of citizenship, such as voting, these tactics and texts can be argued to diminish citizenship because of their potential to lower turnout. As one national new-media consultant admits: "With negative messages . . . the political goal there is keep them from voting, keep them from helping out the other guy."[51] Even with a goal that is often condemned as harmful to democracy, the consequences for citizenship that these texts foster must also be given attention and approached as potentially changing citizenship, rather than just depleting it. In the midst of a political environment often described as bitterly partisan, entrenched, and full of politicians and voters who are unwilling to listen to the opposition's arguments, concerns about the relevance and impact of information-heavy, contextualizing, and nuanced texts are apt. The persuasive capabilities of blog posts, microsites, and fact-checks remain largely unclear, and the intractable nature of strongly held political beliefs has been found to significantly impede people from taking up or believing information.[52] Still, despite the fact that these digital texts might not change the mind of an entrenched supporter or detractor (or even of a persuadable voter), the way they present information is still of importance. Even those who refuse to be swayed or need no swaying are presented with a model for what ought to be necessary to prove information as fact. Ultimately, that these digital tools invite any and all audiences from across the political spectrum to investigate information and present "facts" as necessarily detailed, contextualized, and therefore contingent is an important change in how political information is depicted, and results in political information being framed as something that should be approached critically and skeptically.

Many say that we live in a time where citizens are already skeptical of the information we encounter, that we're deadened to the advertisements we receive in the mail or in a newspaper, the logos and coupons on the backs of our grocery receipts, and to the banner ads we see on web pages. Illustrating that point, the difficulties involved with reaching saturation or breaking through are well-trod territory within campaigns. While a certain level of cynicism or immunity to messaging clearly plays a role within campaigns, these texts model a skeptical attitude toward information that encourages engagement with the information at hand, rather than avoidance or dismissal. In this way, the behavior of skeptical citizenship invited by these digital texts is the opposite of a cynicism that means lacking trust in government or politics and has been shown to lead to lowered rates of civic engagement and political participation.[53] Indeed, such a disposition is a truer recognition and representation of what it takes to navigate the current state of democratic politics that exists within the terrain of strategic accounts of events and information that is constantly being spun to fit into competing narratives. The breadth, depth, and complexity of the information provided by these microsites promote and idealize an approach to information that attends to its complexities and asks audiences to be skeptical of the informing mechanisms and institutions of our political system.

This new potential form of citizenship—that of skeptical citizenship—differentiates itself from other preexisting concepts and adds to the aspects of civic engagement they cover. While some have argued that negative advertisements produce better citizens because they expose potential voters to important, controversial issues, the skeptical citizenship that microsites encourage not only exposes people to the same type of negative information, but asks them to be leery of the veracity of most political information they encounter.[54] This version of citizenship is thus more interactive, as it expects citizens to judge, rather than just consume, information. While the concept of the monitorial citizen provides a model by which to understand how much information people can and should engage, and how they should go about selecting that information, it does not consider how people encounter this political information. Similarly, while descriptions of managed citizens are productive for understanding the very real structures and influences under which citizens are operating, they also assume that to be managed is to be unaware of these structuring forces, and to necessarily approach content uncritically. Although political actors' engagement with the digital media environment surely does involve structuring hierarchies and organizational dynamics, new possibilities for political participation and civic engagement—new possibilities for what being a citizen means—exist as well. As these digital tools represent emerging practices of political content that emphasize variations on traditional negative advertising, focus on the act of revealing information rather than simply reporting it, and strategically complicate and question notions of what counts as "fact," they perform a questioning and active encounter with political information, and encourage citizens to engage claims with an equally shrewd mindset and approach political information as a skeptical citizen.

4

Digital Circulation
in Networked Publics

"And you *better* do it yourselves!" came the communication director's voice, barreling through the hallway between her office and the rest of the communications staff. What was so important that the room full of chattering computers had to put off fact checking an opponent's recent ad, editing press releases, and drafting hits on the competition with one week to go until Election Day? They had to change their Facebook picture. More specifically, the staff was instructed to make one of the many newly digitized campaign logos their profile picture, which would be accompanied by a notification to their friends' Facebook feeds, hopefully encouraging friends to do the same. Almost two months prior, on September 1, the start of the election season home stretch, the entire staff had similarly been instructed to "like" the candidate on Facebook, "follow" him on Twitter, repost interesting stories, and tell any volunteers they came in contact with to do the same. The digital circulation of texts—described to the staff as "taking the campaign viral"—was something the campaign had decided was integral to its overarching strategy. They weren't the only ones. Out of the 16 gubernatorial, senatorial, and congressional campaigns in the Chicago area, all but four—one third-party gubernatorial and three congressional candidates—made these requests via social media, often repeatedly asking such action of citizens.

Simultaneously, and seemingly unrelated, campaigns across the state and country were looking for a different silver bullet—a video, image, website, or any other text they could imagine that would go viral. In the governor's race, the Quinn for Governor campaign produced an online-only ad that referenced the hit TV show *Glee*. Bob Dold's congressional campaign produced one featuring a talking seal. Mark Kirk's campaign for Senate put shark costume-clad staffers in front of their opponent's headquarters, shot footage of the stunt, and distributed it to their email lists in hopes that it would be forwarded.

Beyond produced content, capturing revealing or secret content was seen as one way to get a message to go viral. In any campaign worth its salt, volunteers and staffers were sent out with voice recorders and video cameras to "track" opposing candidates. While campaigns in Illinois failed to uncover much of serious interest, the hope for all campaigns was to reproduce the magnificent impact of the recording and subsequent circulation of former Senator George Allen's 2006 "macaca moment." Filmed by a tracker, Allen's use of the racial slur "macaca" was seen by over 400,000 people online and millions via television news, and is widely regarded as the reason Allen lost his reelection bid. While no campaigns in Illinois that year broke such major news, the tactic was part of individual campaigns' toolkit, and was even specifically recommended by the national parties. While campaign-produced ads differ from explicit requests to circulate information or caught-on-tape moments via social media, they are all designed with a common goal in mind: going viral. No matter their form or argument, videos and texts that would go viral were seen as a holy grail for campaigns.

By 2010, the assertion that we reside in a network society, in which people are more connected to a wider array of people across vast geographical terrain, was commonly accepted wisdom.[1] Electoral examples have fanned this flame and provided examples of the strength and impact of these networks: Howard Dean's meteoric rise in 2004 was on the backs of supporters connected through the online-offline forum Meetup.com; Senator Allen's shockingly steep plummet due to a YouTube video was reincarnated in 2012 in the form of Romney's candidacy-ruining comments denigrating 47% of the electorate; Barack Obama's 2008 campaign has been idolized for its capacity to get supporters to activate their social networks to support and turn out for Obama via the My.BarackObama.com platform; the right-leaning FreedomWorks invested in their own social media platform, launching FreedomConnector in the first months of 2011. While the messaging tactics of producing potentially viral videos and encouraging supporters to "like" candidates are different in scope, they are both part of a strategy that aimed to harness the power of social relationships and networked patterns of organization that the contemporary digital landscape enables and highlights. This chapter details the drive to produce "viral" content, the tactics deployed to do so, and the goals of such content.

Going Viral

As these novel uses and exceptional successes have become more frequent, the particular practice of encouraging voters to digitally recirculate campaigns' own texts has become an increasingly widely used campaign tactic, rather than a one-off practice. What began as a phenomenon mostly related to the quick dissemination of video content, "going viral" has come to encompass media texts of all kinds, and concerns the broader, emerging phenomenon of encouraging citizens to spread campaigns' digital texts.[2] Despite the contagion metaphor's inherent gesture toward the uncontrollable, campaigns see virality as a controllable strategic device that can be both created and harnessed. In the current campaign environment, campaigns across the board both desire such action and are actively encouraging its uptake and undertaking.

Campaigns have long attempted to get supporters to circulate or pass along information by asking people to talk up a candidate, spread literature, or post yard signs about a campaign, and these practices are being complicated, bolstered, and changed by the evolving digital environment. In 2010, consultants and campaign staffers began to emphasize the potential power of specifically digital pass-along—requesting that people "share" or circulate campaign-related content across digital media using their own social networks. As they do so, campaigns recognize and highlight the importance of citizens' connections to each other and voice a desire to engage this networked public, rather than simply reach a mass audience.[3] In attempting to encourage and harness what Daniel Kreiss has called a "digital two step flow" campaigns are focusing on creating viral messages through a variety of content-related choices, and developing content that runs the gamut from amusing to news-breaking to mundane, all of which can include direct appeals to circulate information.[4]

Even before the 2010 cycle, the acts and outcomes of information sharing within social networks has been an important component of political communication research. Traditional models of messaging within campaigns rely on reaching correct audiences, whether they are encountered via widespread dissemination of a single message, a two-step flow model of communication that understands mediators of a message as either opinion leaders or gatekeepers, or even targeted messaging practices that split a population into demographic or lifestyle groups and send them messages that specifically apply to their perceived interests and opinions. In each of these models, campaigns disseminate a message to generalized, large-scale populations (whether that population is a general public or one that is more targeted). Networked media, on the other hand, are able to create mediated relationships that are different from those we've seen before, from "many to many," in which peer-to-peer sharing, discussion, and engagement occur, to "many to one," wherein technologies such as polls or responses to emails have allowed many citizens to provide feedback to previously unavailable individuals or groups such as campaigns or officials.[5] Social media platforms' very existence enables the in-network circulation of messages via material affordances of sharing. In these networked publics, information flows "bottom-up, top-down, as well as side-to-side" and holds the potential to reach what danah boyd has called "invisible audiences" that might encounter content through the network's potential for recirculation and reproduction.[6] Such peer-to-peer circulation is important not only insofar as it may reframe the understanding of the public or audience of political information, but because it marks a shift away from taking part in traditional modes of political participation, toward a model of interactive "actualized citizenship" in which looser personal engagement with peer networks maximizes individual expression.[7]

Countering the optimism of such claims, others have argued that social networks have not resulted in peer-to-peer and reciprocal communication, but reproduced traditional top-down communication practices.[8] At their core, social media, mobile media, and even targeted digital media channels such as direct email and mobile/text messaging are vessels whose content is disseminated on a public level, in much the same way as what we know as "mass" media. In terms of content, campaigns' social media messages are remarkably similar to those of mass media and its multiple models of dissemination—they serve to push out public messages and break through on a large scale. In their form, the process of dissemination is identical. Social media messages are public in nature, and are in fact less targeted than either traditional mailers or email messages. Fundamentally, campaigns rely upon this system of mass messaging in order to educate and persuade the general public. The question at hand, then, is how the digital messaging strategies currently enlisted by campaigns are different from traditional messaging approaches, in terms of what they look like and what their impact is. To draw out the intricacies of this debate, this chapter investigates campaigns' uses of networked publics to actively recirculate content.

The Drive for Digital Circulation

As the new inventions of campaign tactics settle into norms of campaign communication, encouraging voters to digitally recirculate campaigns' own texts stands as one such rapidly normalizing practice, with campaigns singing its praises for a variety of reasons. On one hand, consultants linked the practice of sharing content within social media networks to the broader goal of creating viral content. One campaign manager described a primary digital tactic as looking for "anything that we could use online with the goal of making it viral . . . every campaign out there is trying to look for that little video, that little sound bite, that little blog post."[9] Perhaps too optimistically, recirculation was seen as not only reaching audiences, but doing so in a more efficient way. "Creating a viral buzz around something via YouTube or Facebook or Twitter is certainly an economical way to go if you can get traction with a message," adds another communications director.[10] But social media are not the only ways to drive people to circulate information. One online grassroots specialist explains the relevance of older digital tools over their more novel counterparts, saying, "People will share a lot more on Facebook, but the email tool, it actually brings in more people [who end up taking action]."[11] To some consultants, the prospect of not trying to solicit citizen recirculation seemed almost ludicrous; one answered, "Yes! Yes! A thousand times yes!" when asked if she encouraged such behavior. While most campaigns mention Facebook and Twitter as the main venues for soliciting and observing behaviors of digital recirculation, consultants also referred to the ease and importance of encouraging messages to be passed along via mobile technology.[12] "It's so easy. I'm shocked that more campaigns didn't go this route in 2010," notes a consultant who specializes in mobile.[13] "It's only six [sic] phone characters," says another. "'PLS, space, FWD' is please forward. If there is space, include it in every single text message you send out."[14] Telling the story of a campaign where even she was surprised at the amount of participation generated from people's use of mobile circulation, she adds: "Simple things like that are actually really powerful." This practice of getting people to circulate content is not only important for getting specific messages out on a larger scale, but for adding to the public that might be interested in a campaign's content in general. "So, I don't think that the 'Like' button is the end-all, be-all," explains one digital media consultant, "but I think that having Like buttons and share functions—making your content sharable—that is vital to being able to spread your community."[15] Certainly, some visions of the success of digitally circulated content are ripe for embellishment. Consider communications directors' inflated hopes for messaging channels and their effects: "Your circulation in the end is something like a million, right?" "Even if no press picked it up, maybe five or our most engaged volunteers sent it to ten friends each, and they sent it on, and it had a viral effect."[16] Although it is certainly overly optimistic, consultants' excitement over digital circulation is indicative of its role as an important tactic within contemporary campaigns.

As campaigns attempted to develop content that would have the viral effect they so desired, three genres of viral content emerged: revealing, live footage that was newsworthy; comedic or gag-oriented content that was produced, rather than candid; and mundane content that was often accompanied by a direct request to circulate. While many other possibilities for viral content exist—emotional content, for instance, has been shown to have much better recirculation from citizens—the combination of the cash-pressed nature of any midterm cycle and lack of knowledge of best practices made these three categories the most compelling.[17] The first two were tantalizing for campaigns simply because they could be relied upon to gain traction within the news media as well as through individual citizens.

The idea that a candidate might say something inappropriate on a live camera, as Senator Allen had in 2006 and Romney would in 2012, is tantalizing. As a result, by 2010, trackers were deployed by nearly every campaign, with both national parties producing how-to manuals, and communication and digital media staffers spent many hours sifting through recordings and splicing together videos to publicize what they'd found. More often than not, these efforts were in vain. Most frequently, content that showed a candidate backtracking on a minor issue would be held up as a smoking gun, but the response from the public was limited—and reasonably so; the claims were often overreaching and underwhelming. In one such instance, following weeks of tracking with no payoff regarding top issues, the campaign I was observing obtained a copy of what it considered controversial remarks made by the opponent at a recent debate. A digital staffer spent hours combing through debate footage, eventually finding half of the recording unusable. Following more time devoted to splicing in text that detailed the inaudible parts of the recording, the video was put up on YouTube and linked by the campaign, but only viewed by roughly 100 people.

In lieu of any smoking guns, many campaigns turned to amusing, gimmicky, and fun content that would be well-received and circulated by their base. In the Chicago area alone, this trend prevailed. The Dold for Congress campaign produced a video in which Dold won the endorsement of a seal that had previously seemed likely to vote for his opponent, Dan Seals. The Kirk for Senate campaign made videos of staffers attending events of their opponent, Alexi Giannoulias, dressed as sharks to signify his ties with a convicted felon with the nickname "Jaws." In August, the Giannoulias for Senate campaign made its own offering of gimmicky content in the form of a *Jeopardy!*-themed game that mocked Kirk. A supporter-created video for the Quinn for Governor campaign followed the aesthetic and pacing of ads for the popular show *Glee*, highlighting all of the missteps and problematic statements of Quinn's opponent, Bill Brady, but using a tone and quick cadence that added some levity to the criticisms. Each of these garnered coverage from statewide and local political blogs as well as mainstream Chicago-based and national press coverage. Moreover, the "Seals for Dold" video and the *Glee*-inspired web ad were among the most well received during an otherwise overwhelmingly negative campaign cycle, and were also the most widely shared.

Requesting Recirculation: Mundane Content and Digital Yard Signs

Because these types of content required resources or a significant dose of luck or both, campaigns were left with another, much more simple, tactic for upping circulation: just ask citizens to do the distributing. Not only do campaign staffers and consultants talk about the potential of digital circulation of texts, but the importance of this strategy is also apparent within the actual texts of campaign communication. Just as nearly every consultant and staffer interviewed said they engaged in this tactic, nearly every campaign's public communications displayed this trend, through a simple directive at the end of a campaign email, Facebook post, text message, or another medium. Campaigns did not think this type of message would go viral on its own, and direct encouragement would be necessary to push people to circulate the content. As a result, this tactic became laminated to rather mundane messages to aid in their circulation. Focusing more specifically on social media, as they were most often invoked as campaigns' media of choice for this tactic, analysis of all of the campaigns' Facebook pages shows that, out of four gubernatorial, two senatorial, and ten House races in the greater Chicago area, only one third-party candidate for governor and three smaller congressional races did not once use this tactic (see table 4.1). Although campaigns' use of this tactic was by no means regular or heavy-handed, it did recur throughout campaigns in the final two months of the election.

With 75% of all candidates employing this tactics, they differed not only in terms of total number of posts, but in when these posts came. While some

Table 4.1 **Number of Facebook Posts Dedicated to Requesting Supporters Recirculate Messages**

Candidate	Total recirc. posts	Total posts	% total posts
Brady (R, governor)	9	170	5.3%
Quinn (D, governor)	3	125	2.4%
Whitney (I, governor)	9	120	7.5%
Giannoulias (D, senator)	16	157	10.2%
Kirk (R, senator)	4	223	1.8%
Dold (R, congressperson)	3	110	2.7%
Halvorson (D, congressperson)	3	82	3.7%
Kinzinger (R, congressperson)	4	71	5.6%
Pollak (R, congressperson)	4	270	1.5%
Schilling (R, congressperson)	2	79	2.5%
Seals (D, congressperson)	5	73	6.8%
Walsh (D, congressperson)	1	89	1.1%

Note: Candidates not requesting this action are Cohen (R, governor), and Democrats for Congress Bean, Schakowsky, and Hare.

campaigns made such requests only a handful of times, those who made fewer requests were often those who began the practice toward the end of the campaign. The Giannoulias campaign most actively encouraged some form of digital circulation, doing so roughly twice a week, followed by the two gubernatorial candidates, who were active in the social media space.[18] Candidates within especially contested congressional districts also made use of this tactic, including the 10th District's Dan Seals (D) and Robert Dold (R) and the 11th District's Adam Kinzinger (R), requesting people recirculate messages roughly once a week. Senatorial candidate Mark Kirk's campaign only made use of this tactic four times in the eight-week span, but also made use of mobile technology via QR codes (Quick Response bar-codes) and incentivizing people to share campaign information on Twitter with promises of retweets. While engaging direct requests for recirculation dropped off after these cases, a handful of congressional candidates and the incumbent governor requested readers do so. This rate of use makes sense within the context of campaigns where technological and tactical innovations are adopted through a trickle-down model, and where larger, better-financed, publicity-generating campaigns are first to adopt tactics and new media.[19] While presidential races were encouraging these practices on a meaningful scale in 2008, this tactic was adopted slowly across down-ballot races. Thus, not only are citizens provided with the tools by which they can recirculate content, but the practice is explicitly asked of them as well.

Moreover, as the productive value of such behavior is recognized across both the political and consumer-marketing arenas, the tools that enable and encourage such behavior will likely become more prevalent and easy to use. During the 2010 election cycle, Facebook's "Share" button, which has since become a staple of the platform and enables the recirculation of content with the click of a button, did not exist. The system's only affordances in terms of interacting with posts were "Like" and "Comment" buttons on a page or a post. Of course, users could, and were encouraged to, share content by cutting and pasting links, but it wasn't until early 2011 that the Share button was added, further motivating the act of recirculating messages (regardless of content) by making it an easier interaction and highlighting the option on every post.

As these practices were still solidifying in 2010, campaigns often encouraged this behavior without fully conceptualizing their connection to a specific strategy beyond "it helps us win"—such as a call to action or raising particular issues. Despite being unsure of the exact effects of digital circulation, campaigns are hopeful of its success for a variety of reasons. Often staffers will acknowledge that new media feels like throwing everything at citizens and seeing what sticks: "We don't know the impact [of digital circulation], but we certainly don't dissuade campaigns from doing it," says one consultant, emphasizing the importance of using best practices that have been experimentally tested.[20] Another communication director admits, "[Its effect] remains to be seen. Even talking to specific new media consultants, they are trying to figure out how they even begin to measure its effect," but simultaneously asserts its importance, saying, "Any way to advocate is helpful to the campaign."[21] The cash-strapped and penny-pinching nature of campaigns provides a logical reason to encourage and cultivate practices of digital circulation among supporters, as it holds little cost and is seen as potentially beneficial, even if that benefit is relatively unknown. "Liking and friending and all that stuff," notes one communications consultant, "it's an easy thing to do because it doesn't cost anyone any money."[22] In the Illinois-based campaigns' Facebook posts, a large percentage of all requests to share content with one's own social network were attached to content that lacked any external goal, such as "Show people this to raise money," "Tell your friends to like this page and GOTV." Instead, these requests merely ask people to "tell your friends," "pass this along," and encourage them to get others to read materials and distribute content.

This purpose outpaced all others for nine of the 12 campaigns using this tactic, with just a few instances of using digital circulation to aid other mobilizing efforts such as GOTV, event attendance, and so on (see table 4.2). This request to foster the campaign's growth often came in the form of inviting people to share with friends in an attempt to reach a certain number of supporters, or announcing their proximity to a landmark number of followers such as 5,000 or 10,000. "We have 9,640 fans—we're so close to 10,000! Like this page and help us get to 10,000 fans!" reads one such post by the Quinn campaign. Increasing numbers was seen as especially beneficial for many campaigns because when a user "liked" the campaign, the platform would announce the act of liking to the user's own social network.[23] Alongside requests for sheer numbers came repeated requests for people to adopt the campaign logo or a picture of the candidate as their own profile picture in order to show their support. "Steal this avatar!" reads the Facebook page of one congressional campaign, continuing, "Show your friends that you're supporting Dan Seals for Congress!" Alexi Giannoulias's campaign page contains a post saying, "Show your support for our campaign by changing your Facebook or Twitter picture

Table 4.2 **Purposes of Campaigns' Requests to Recirculate Facebook Messages**

Candidate	Total recirculation posts	Mobilization, GOTV	Mobilization, donate/attend event	No additional motive
Brady (R, governor)	9	2	0	7
Quinn (D, governor)	3	0	0	3
Whitney (I, governor)	9	0	3	6
Giannoulias (D, senator)	16	6	7	3
Kirk (R, senator)	4	2	0	2
Dold (R, congressperson)	3	0	0	3
Halvorson (D, congressperson)	3	1	0	2
Kinzinger (R, congressperson)	4	1	0	3
Pollak (R, congressperson)	4	1	0	3
Schilling (R, congressperson)	2	0	2	0
Seals (D, congressperson)	5	3	0	2
Walsh (D, congressperson)	1	0	0	1

Note: Candidates Cohen, Bean, Schakowsky, and Hare, who did not request such action, are not included.

before Election Day!" (see figure 4.1), and Brady's gubernatorial campaign wrote, "I'm ready to go, but could really use a sign of support from my FB Friends and Fans. How about it . . . if you haven't already, update your profile picture with a Bill Brady / Jason Plummer sign" (see figure 4.2).

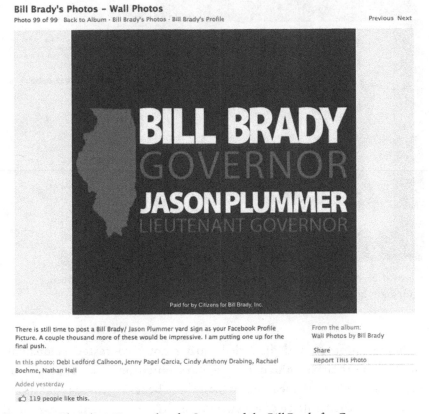

Figure 4.1 The Alexi Giannoulias for Senate and the Bill Brady for Governor campaigns both asked supporters to share virtual signs of support.

By refraining from engaging with the three major campaign objectives of dollars, votes, or volunteers, these requests served largely as a digital equivalent to campaign yard signs: visual markers to show support, but whose persuasive or mobilizing value is largely unknown. These digital yard signs often literally replicated the images found in lawns across Illinois, merely importing the image into a new platform that was more easily distributable. Even in cases where the size of the typeface was changed and information was added—Joe Walsh for Congress added the campaign website to its image, Giannoulias for Senate made one image in which "VOTE" was the dominant text and gave the date of Election Day, Kirk for Senate's read, "I support Kirk"—the implicit message remained the same: "I support this candidate, and you should too."

Digital yard signs enable and encourage replication, just as their physical manifestations do, while also providing freedom from the dangers

Figure 4.2 The Alexi Giannoulias for Senate and the Bill Brady for Governor campaigns both asked supporters to share virtual signs of support.

of being uprooted and discarded during hotly contested campaigns, and despite their seemingly rudimentary imitation of an analog strategy, their use is more meaningful than these benefits. These requests are part of the broader drive to get citizens to circulate content across social networks, and by investigating the reasons campaigns give for turning to these practices, we can begin to see whether the capabilities offered to both campaigns and citizens through social media are adding to or changing campaign goals. Even though some of these changes amount to slight shifts rather than the radical uprooting of norms, there are nonetheless important changes within the relationships between campaigns and citizens that point to spaces of opportunity for democratic participation. As campaigns invoke all of these tactics, the strategic goals of the messages extend beyond reaching masses of people, and involve the recognition of new actors as vital opinion leaders for their public messages and new ways of seeing the audience of citizens to whom they are constantly sending messages. Additionally, as campaigns ask citizens to pass along messages, they simultaneously encourage citizens to take additional action and construct a type of opinion leader that is more than a vessel for campaign-sanctioned information. These emergent modes of participatory action show promise for understanding how to begin to take autonomous action, while working within the constraining forces of institutional power like campaigns or professional politics.

Moving toward Networked Publics

Even cutting-edge campaigns operate within a world where traditional, baseline needs of increasing the publicity and reaching greater audiences are a concern. Name recognition, issue awareness, and increased exposure to both a mass audience and particularly productive segments of the public—women, businesspeople, blue-collar workers, and so on—are still necessary elements of all campaigns, and a significant reason that digital circulation is seen as politically productive. Within these goals comes a vision of the public of campaign messages as either a mass audience, or a mass audience segmented or divided according to demographic categories or interests. In each case, the public of campaign messages is understood as a massive group; however targeted, the goal is to bring more citizens into the fold and provide them with the (appropriate) message. Campaigns' drive for digital circulation, however, troubles this simple view of what a the public of campaign messages looks like and adds depth to traditional understandings of how opinion leaders work, and who they are. Ultimately, these tactics speak to a differently organized public in the process, even while they echo some aspects of traditional visions.

As campaigns explain their reasons for emphasizing social media, the language of reaching more people dominates, and consultants often default to the perspective that reaching more people is the general purpose of each message. "It's mostly about the eyeballs," says one campaign communications staffer, referring to the goal of distributing the campaign's message more widely.[24] "We had messages that we really wanted to get out," asserts another new media consultant, "rebuttals, endorsements, and stretching out paid media . . . making sure we had more eyeballs on those."[25] Reductive measurements of whether a message broke through, such as "eyeballs" on a page or bare numbers, were common measures of social media success. "It was a big thing when we passed our opponent's number of Facebook fans," remembers one former communications director, even as she immediately acknowledged, "That means nothing. Of course, ultimately, that's not votes," she adds: "but it does help, and you definitely want to. . . . It shows a lot of support."[26] Not only might it reach citizens, but it will do so cheaply and easily. "It's certainly more of an efficient way to do it in terms of money. It's free, whereas a pamphlet you might pay six cents a copy. So in that sense, there's a measurable benefit."[27] One campaign was so desperate to even appear as if it was reaching a vast number of people that it paid a third-party company to accumulate Facebook friends for it. Far from a benefit that improved the campaign's reach, the resulting faux supporters were not only not particularly interested in politics, but were nearly universally from outside of the voting area, and often outside of the country. The campaign saw the futility in sending these individuals messages or even trying to target them for ad buys, and eventually had to devote staffers' hours to deleting them from the account so the campaign's analytics would begin to make sense again.

These goals of pushing messages to more potential voters are not new. They add to the continued presence of mass media blitzes on television and radio and mirror their goals of "breaking through" and increasing a candidate's name recognition; they echo timeless encouragement to "tell your friend's candidate X is running for congress," and the consideration of how many people, in how many homes (and which specific homes), an ad will be heard by has been such a central question that quick and easy algorithms for assessing breakthrough based on ad buys are readily available. Moreover, even the language, though slightly different from that of "breakthrough" or "saturation" usually devoted to advertising, implies the same goal of simply reaching people exclusive of concerns of persuasive appeal or ability to mobilize. Repeatedly referencing the need to "get more eyeballs" on the ads, press releases, and media they produce, campaigns use the synecdoche of "eyeballs" as a stand-in for viewers or citizens, revealing the primacy of the act of encountering, without a large amount of concern for subsequent judgment. Interestingly, this preference for quantity—more eyeballs, more people, more encounters—over the particulars of who is encountered marks a much more traditional approach to campaign goals than the often-publicized (and frankly, often-pursued) goals of microtargeting that are enabled by both the data provided within digital environments and digital tools' capabilities to take advantage of these data.

Despite the use of such traditional, passive language regarding what supporters and citizens can and should (or should not) do, campaigns' actual practices show a new vision of the public, emphasizing and highlighting the connected nature of media texts as well as individuals. The goal of circulating campaign texts or images across social networks is more than just getting more individuals to see particular messages; it provides an understanding of digital messages as belonging to a network of other campaign-produced texts, and reorients the relationships among citizens as well as those between campaigns and their constituents.

In a digital campaign, traditional goals of getting more people to encounter a campaign message are also interlaced with the goal of getting people to see other campaign content that supplements or is related to that which is digitally circulated. Described as "flypaper" by some consultants and a sticky "web of messages" by others, the digital messages campaigns create lead to one another and reinforce the messages that campaigns push. The practice of citizens digitally circulating campaign content can further campaign goals of "getting people stuck in that flypaper," "because it gets the word out, and people start going to your website, and then they click on your Facebook page, and they want to see what's going on with the campaign."[28] Another communications director gives an example of someone who connected with the campaign through a Facebook post: "We struck a chord with someone and they ended up coming back and signing up for newsletters in their own right."[29] Another echoes this approach of saturating multiple channels, saying: "We used everything from Twitter, to YouTube, to Flickr, and blogging and that sort of thing [in addition to Facebook] to get the message out online."[30] As they exist within such a web, campaign messages themselves are networked, exemplifying a different relationship to the audience of citizens than the mass media texts that came before.

Despite their structural similarities to mass-mediated texts—social media messages are, after all, publicly broadcast messages—content that campaigns request to be circulated digitally is seen differently. Although the spaces of social and mobile media, much like the TV airwaves, are filled with messages, their content and the way campaigns speak of them reflects a much more interpersonal, engaging form of communication. In these cases, the immediacy of a "user-centered disruption" in how campaigns communicate with the public—and the fact that they will have to communicate with individuals rather than large-scale publics—is often invoked.[31] Acknowledgments that these messages are "public" insofar as they are released to the general public and lack specific recipients are paired with talk of deeper interaction. "If you're not engaging with people, and interacting

with people, you're doing it wrong," describes one communications consultant with a mix of frustration and pleading in his voice.[32] Not only are
these texts allegedly personal, they are described as one-to-one moments of
communication. "All these new tools that are coming out are really looking
at individual voters and their processes," notes one consultant who specializes in developing new tools inform citizens. The move to a user-centered
disruption in political communication is not only about giving attention to
the micro level, but engaging with individuals in a personal way. "You have
conversations with them," illustrates a digital media consultant who handles numerous campaigns each cycle. "You can ask them to do things and
share things in their own circle, and those are conversations with people."[33]
Emphasizing the importance of considering whom you message and when,
one digital consultant constantly reminds clients that "behind each tweet
is a person, okay? Behind each tweet and behind each Facebook status,
behind each email message or text message, there is a person."[34] Going on
to explain that thinking of people as "allies . . . not sheep, not slaves, not
digits or numbers," he emphasizes the importance of seeing citizens as more
than megaphones and motivating and communicating with important supporters, even when reciprocal communication is too large an undertaking.
Despite the fact that the campaigns do not respond to the vast majority of
citizen comments (not to mention that many campaigns have definite policies in place that involve never commenting in social media messages from
citizens), consultants consider such interaction to be responsive, interactive,
and, as one consultant describes it, very personal:

> You're reaching them in a very personal way, in ways you wouldn't
> normally be able to reach them. For Facebook, you don't have to
> know someone and you're able to see their personal photos. Once
> you become friends with them all this other stuff starts to happen
> on a personal level. You start sharing friends and recommending
> other friends that you guys have in common, and you're connected
> to them.[35]

This practice—especially as it is discussed by campaigns—is rooted in
traditional campaign attempts to get citizens to tell their friends and family about a candidate. People get texts from campaigns and provide them
to others, resulting in multiple instances of sharing texts and information
across one-to-one relationships. And for good reason: research supports

campaigns' beliefs that people are more likely to be persuaded by people they know and trust than advertisements or campaign-produced communication.[36] In addition to expanding one's geographical reach, the digital circulation of social media texts also expands beyond the strong ties that were leveraged in traditional pass-along of information. At one level, the relationships that exist in venues such as Facebook, Twitter, partisan platforms such as MyBarackObama.com, and within people's mobile phone contacts encompass looser ties than relationships involved (and empirically tested) in traditional practices of pass-along. Additionally, there are design elements built into the Facebook platform that make sharing posts more productive in terms of increased visibility. As more people share a post, the Facebook algorithm gives it greater priority on people's newsfeeds (thus incentivizing campaigns' requests to share these texts), and also alerts new users if multiple social connections share the same content, regardless of how strong any of the social ties at hand are. All told, the technological affordances, in tandem with campaigns' and consultants' discussions of the potential of digital circulation, result in a partially mass media, partially direct communication model of messaging strategy. This model of communication combines both networked and mass models of communication and, in doing so, highlights how the "public" of campaign messages is changing. Rather than pointing to campaigns' descriptions of their actions as individual in nature yet publicly available as contradictory, these divergent terms point to a space where old descriptions of practices cannot describe the communicative patterns and relationships that occur within the new digital landscape. Such hybrid digital media landscapes ultimately necessitate the recognition of relationships between campaign and citizens and among citizens themselves, and involve slight changes to who is being addressed by campaign texts, and therefore the publics of these messages.

Using Michael Warner's definition of a public as constituted not only by being addressed within a text or discourse, but by mere attention, or coming into contact with a text, we can observe how the circulation of digital campaign texts enlarges the public of campaign messages beyond an originally assumed audience.[37] Mass media, while broad in their reach, are both rhetorically and materially addressed to specific populations. Television ads are purchased according to geographically based media markets, newspapers are often regional in scope, direct mail is tailored and targeted based on demographic and lifestyle information, and online ads are targeting to citizens according to those same qualities, as well as online search terms. By actively encouraging citizens to pass along the campaign texts they receive, campaigns show they have recognized the potential for a secondary public (and potentially many more levels of publics after that), and anticipate networked relationships to be brought into the fold of a campaign's public. While campaign messages may be drafted in a universal voice that appeals to an audience that is like the mass public—as Warner has described, a case "in which one might say 'The text addresses me' and 'It addresses no one in particular"—campaigns and citizens alike are now being asked to consider exactly which people within a social network a message addresses.[38] Now, rather than mass publics that are made up of individuals who are indifferent to other members of the public, a request for digital circulation specifically refers to the extended network of individuals who will receive recirculated content. While campaigns have long wanted messages to reach additional degrees of audiences, this case marks a difference insofar as these messages directly address the second-degree citizens as part of messages' public. As they are addressed as the hopeful audience of these messages, they are brought into the public, which is not invisible so much as it is anticipated, but unknown.

The change to conceptions of publics is not only to the organization of the public at hand, but to the ways of understanding its members and the relationships between them. The circulation that occurs within these networked publics—the digital two-step flow—configures citizens themselves as media, and positions social relationships as media channels.[39] While this is true (and can be said of the traditional model of the two-step flow as well), it ignores the fact that campaigns not only turn social relationships into channels, but also ask us to reflect on the presence of these channels in our lives. The request to "share this with your friends" or even the more vague "Share this!" calls on the reader to consider and recognize the audience that is their social network—not a mass or demographic slice, but a set of networked individual relationships she has with those in her social circle. When citizens recirculate campaign messages, they may not be speaking into a megaphone, but neither are they speaking into the air. In these moments of recirculation, citizens are asked to consider their own networks as members of a shared public and be aware of their tangible digital connections with others. While Benedict Anderson's oft-cited concept of an imagined community connects individuals to a larger perceived public, the members of that public are nebulous—they are not bound by interest or social relationships, but exist as a faceless mass.[40] The publics that circulation activates, however, are populated by individuals who are both identifiable and knowable to some degree. As campaigns tend to rely on networks that are based on "real" identities such as Facebook and Twitter, this is especially true.[41] When individuals circulate, post, text, or tweet political content, they are not only entering into a conversation about politics, they are politicizing relationships that are not already defined as political. In this way, social ties become important potential spaces for politics. Although the move to encourage this practice can be seen as purely practical and in line with long-standing goals of all campaigns for political action—for instance, to get more eyeballs to view a message—it should not be written off as lacking implications for larger notions of political participation and citizenship norms. By implying that good readers pass information along through their online social networks, campaigns approach social media platforms not just as vessels that can potentially hold political content, but recast them as potentially political channels themselves. Face-to-face pass-along has always relied on a system of strong ties—trusted neighbors, friends, family, and opinion leaders were the ones to provide political information (if not providing outright directions on how to vote and think). The encouragement to activate social media networks as modes of political action expands the practice of political persuasion beyond close relationships such as family and close friends to the "weak ties" that dominate social media networks. These practices do not create new bonds between and among citizens, but do activate those that already exist as political, rather than purely social.[42] Because these relationships are reciprocal, one need not share information in order to activate these bonds as political; one only needs to encounter the political content of another person within their network. In activating these relationships as political, citizens are doing precisely what scholars have recommended as a method of increasing participation: "strengthening participatory associations" through the use of social contacts that blend the distinctions between public and private.[43] That these relationships among citizens have been explicitly politicized through the practice of digital circulation (whether executed by oneself of friends) opens our eyes to the fact that any and all of our "social" media relationships can immediately and without warning become "political" media relationships.[44]

In recent years, much journalistic and academic attention has been given to the immense increase in the use of analytics and advanced targeting techniques in campaign communication practices. While it is certainly the case that improvements in database technologies, the use of increasingly refined algorithms, and the development of a culture of testing campaign messages across a variety of populations have increased the amount of targeted content and the populations campaigns target, the development of networked publics shows there is more to the story. Instead, the organization of social media publics reveals that campaigns do not merely see populations only as increasingly tiny slivers to be differentiated and appropriately targeted, but as interconnected and communal. Analytics and targeting do play an important role in contemporary campaign communication, but this work highlights the fact that this must not be the only way to approach or understand audiences for this content.

Impact of Networked Publics: Opinion Leaders and Active Citizens

As the ways campaigns understand the public of their messages change, so, too, do the tactics and goals of disseminating messages. Moving beyond simply wanting more potential voters, these campaign strategies focusing on digital circulation also imply they want more active citizens and are excited to work with new opinion leaders within the digital space. This active view of citizenship focuses on participation—whether it be online or offline—as a necessary element of being an engaged citizen, and as connected to future action, rather than isolated. In addition to emphasizing and encouraging active modes of citizenship, these changes in strategy also expand the population of valued opinion leaders.

Occasionally, communications offices are called on to collaborate with field offices in order to drive people to events or encourage specific acts volunteering—coming to a rally, knocking on doors, and donating money are commonly the subject of digital messages. Requests to circulate campaign content, whether they contain additional content of advertisements, press releases, or news of an event, fundamentally involve taking the initial action recirculate or "share" content. In 2010, when campaigns would make such requests, the act of sharing on Facebook required copying and pasting information into one's own social media page and manually reposting content (although Twitter automated this process earlier, in late 2009). As a result, the opportunity to comment on, frame, or add to the campaign's existing message was at the forefront of the act of recirculation. Even when Facebook streamlined this process in 2011 by allowing users to share any post, image, or linked content with a single button, the ability to comment on, frame, or add to the original content was still a prominent feature of the automated version. When citizens share or circulate campaign texts via Facebook, they therefore can laminate their own comments to this political information, providing a substantive frame to the text, giving it new and different meaning—it can be condemned, mocked, enthusiastically supported, or even debated in the process of circulation. An unmodified recirculation of a campaign press release, update, or event may voice the same positive response as a statement of support framing the text, but there is also room to radically change a text's meaning, resulting in a "new" overall text that combines the citizens' view (even if it echoes that of the campaign) with the original content. Without making any changes to the content of what the campaign created, citizens can reframe the text with their opposing views. For example, while hundreds recirculated a reminder from President Obama to watch the 2012 State of the Union address, some of the texts circulated were recast to advocate forgoing the event: "No. Why would I want to spoils [*sic*] my dinner by listening to a bunch of lies?" asks one, while another professes, "I can give you the State of the Union in two words: It sucks. Democrats, Republicans, third party, etc. It's all madness." In addition to circulating a political message with the intent to undermine it, citizens can contribute any variety on lenses to issues, and can even attempt to *de*politicize content. In such a case, one woman frames a post about White House First Pets with "Because I love animals, I decided to share these photos. It's not meant to be political." In each of these instances, readers actively frame and reconfigure the messages they are circulating without changing its original content, and hold the potential for wresting control of a text's meaning.[45] As individuals pass along content and navigate the opportunity to contribute to existing messages, they are more than simple receivers of messages, and are instead taking direct political action. Although the assertion of rising levels of citizens producing political content is not novel, campaigns' discussions of such practices as common, easy, and oft-requested, framing the actions as a norm or participatory practice, rather than an exceptional case, are an emerging trend.

Additionally, these requests to be creators of content are connected to ongoing and future action, as social media use is seen as a prior step to traditionally valued offline activities such as contacting the campaign or coming into the headquarters to make phone calls or lick envelopes. On one hand, fostering discussion in and of itself is engaging in a deeper level

of participation and a long tradition of encouraging an ideal of deliberative democracy. A consultant describes the routine social interaction that
occurred on Facebook with a level of awe, saying, "They are talking to a page,
to the candidate," and pointing out that despite this action's simplicity, most
people never contact an official or candidate for office.[46] A communications
director relays his attempts to engage people in reciprocal communication
with the campaign: "It's a matter of engaging them by asking them a question and by having them respond and talk about it. . . . I know our candidate,
I know he was following and he was commenting himself. . . . you can easily
engage with them from your home."[47]

The desire to encourage active participation was relevant for both the
online and offline world. A consultant who discussed their goal of getting
people "stuck" in the campaign's messaging web also described how circulating messages could productively lead to more action, relaying her excitement when citizens who circulated messages then started "saying they
wanted to come in and do something—that was great." Another shared
this view of the act of digitally circulating campaign texts as a means to an
end, saying, "I mean, the whole notion of getting your supporters to share
information and interact with the campaign is to get them more engaged.
It's important for building the small-dollar [donations] for the campaign."[48]
While consultants often refer to the fact that "you can't take your eye off the
big picture" of winning votes by focusing on minutiae, some see a direct correlation between their use of digital media and big-picture goals like increasing the number of volunteers in headquarters and voter turnout.[49]

> Our campaign got more votes than the gubernatorial campaigns
> and the federal senatorial campaign. It was insane, and I think a lot
> of it has to do with the fact that we were able to mobilize college
> students and the Facebook crowd and the Twitter crowd that these
> other campaigns just didn't have the drive for.[50]

While online action was a benchmark, offline action was often the ultimate
arbiter of success for a campaign, even in their social media messages: "I'm
less interested in getting them to do things online and more interested in
getting them in the door," asserts one such consultant. "There is this online
to offline goal trajectory we have."[51] In doing so, they use social media to
highlight and call attention to offline events such as rallies or meetings, and
ask people to volunteer for the campaign as well. "When you say, 'Hey the

next three Saturdays, we're phone-banking, and we're going to hit canvasses from these locations. Come and tell your friends,' that's giving someone something to do."[52] Like the goal of increasing a message or campaign's publicity, encouraging the digital circulation of campaign texts in order to increase participation is nothing new. Since volunteers are a main tenet of all campaigns—one of the three goals of votes, volunteers, and dollars—it's no surprise that campaigns would use new media channels to ask people to do so, positioning requests for circulation as a means to the end of future or potential additional action.

In doing so, campaigns are displaying a view of participatory acts as connected to future participation and campaign involvement. Citizens are not expected to simply engage in a single form of participatory action and be done, but are assumed to be ripe for future action as well. As they label these concepts "daisy chains" of participation, where actions are linked (e.g., instances where signing a petition will result in being asked to donate to a cause shortly thereafter), or the "ladder of engagement," where a citizens' participation in one event is cataloged and campaigns will ask them to repeat or engage in a stronger level of action in the future (for instance, if you donate enough times, you are likely to be asked to volunteer at headquarters or attend a particular event in the future), campaigns articulate a nuanced approach to encouraging and measuring participation. These forms of linking participatory actions illustrate that campaigns do not think of political participation as occurring in single, individual actions occurring in a vacuum—as often measured by those studying such activities. Requests for action now, despite the urgency and temporal specificity of requests for participation, are never simply that. Rather, they imply continued action in the future, action that crosses online/offline spaces. Additionally, as campaigns are almost always looking to future, potential actions, this view of participation necessitates the constant surveillance of citizens—what messages they respond to, when, and so on—in order to assess their availability or willingness to contribute and to target citizens' most likely and productive actions in the future.

Finally, campaigns and consultants see encouraging the practice of digital pass-along as potentially putting them in contact with and harnessing new opinion leaders. On a widespread scale, claims that new digital media would provide a platform for new voices to gain traction have largely failed to meet the mark. The hierarchies of online elites whose voices are amplified within digital publics are remarkably similar to those of the traditional news media and are extremely difficult to enter.[53] Despite these shortcomings, however, developments in how campaigns consider the networked individuals that make up the publics of their messages give reason for optimism. Rather than providing citizens with an opportunity to amplify their voices to such a degree that they become widely read or encountered, campaigns are seeking out new and different people as opinion leaders who could be influential in particular, more limited networks. Despite campaigns' inability to truly extend these voices far and wide, by approaching new and different individuals, campaigns are actively seeking to elevate new voices, even if it is in a more limited context.

Fundamentally, campaigns and consultants see social and mobile media as capable of reaching and engaging individuals and target audiences that were previously untapped. "Like a business leaders list, we now have a 'viral leaders' list," says one seasoned communications director.[54] Another consultant, extolling the virtues of a similar model, discusses the importance of getting one such "viral leader" to push out a message: "If you can get [progressive consultant and activist, John] Hlinko to post it, he has this huge club he can wield himself . . . if somebody notable pushes it—if it's a *Daily Kos* editor that tweets it out or posts it, we see a big hit."[55] Similar approaches abound across the spectrum, and even more communications directors focused on earned media and press relations have adopted these tactics. "Our primary goal with new media is—we call them talkers—we get the talkers talking. And they really help drive the message through," notes one such communication director.[56] Within this approach to circulating a message, campaigns emphasize the difference between just pushing information out, and pushing it to the right people, saying, "You really want to get three or four retweets from people who are known to have a giant audience on Twitter."[57] Elaborating on this concept, another consultant counters a long-standing belief within campaigns: "Sharing information isn't necessarily the challenge. In many places, the biggest challenge is you have a piece of information, and the biggest challenge is trying to figure out to whom that piece of information is relevant."[58] While these lines of communication produce texts designed to reach opinion leaders of old such as activists connected to political organizations or heading up local groups, they also offer the possibility for more people to become opinion leaders by circulating texts—different people than those voicepieces from local and national organizations. "There are still influentials," says one consultant, considering the level of democratization of the media landscape, adding, "They're just not—they don't have as big an audience, and it's not like one guy, or like three white dudes on TV anchoring a news channel. It's amazing that any-one can become an influence. Anyone can start a blog and become like the most authoritative blogger on this topic. Anyone can start a Twitter account and develop hundreds, thousands of followers."[59] Another consultant agrees with the fact that social media texts and their potential for digital pass-along are all about seeing who the *new* influentials are, saying: "It's all about find-ing champions in unlikely places."[60] Perhaps even more intriguing are the cases in which citizens are not only asked to amplify or spread message, but to give feedback and help political elites. One grassroots consultant explains how they use digital tools to contact people at local or state levels who seem active in those media channels: "We get feedback and ask, 'Hey, what do you guys think of this senate race?' And kind of asked them what they think and get feedback that way and that kind of shape our endorsement, that shape how much time and energy we spend there."[61]

As staffers monitor media for mentions of their candidate or race, they routinely take note of who is talking, and begin to notice those who repeat-edly demonstrate interest, whether it's positive or negative coverage.[62] Most often this does result in a "long tail" of citizens who are given a minimal level of attention without actual response, but insofar as it is a direct attempt to attend to the possibility of rising opinion leaders, campaigns are extend-ing the population of individuals they recognize as potentially important. Describing the ability to talk to specific people who might not be part of the traditionally targeted messages, one digital consultant remarks that social media help organizations like hers "reach out to those people in kind of unconventional places or unconventional groups that haven't necessarily always agreed with us and get support where we can."[63] Emphasizing the fact that digital media enable campaigns to turn to a new population of opin-ion leaders despite the fact that traditional voices often still garner the most attention, one campaign manager explains that it's best not to use social media to reach traditional opinion leaders.

> In terms of sort of the traditional opinion leaders, going after a chamber of commerce president or a business CEO, or somebody that would be a traditional third-party validator of a particular pol-icy, that needs to be done through true conventional methods, call-ing them up on the phone and talking with them and getting them to write an op-ed in the newspaper that we would then publish on our Facebook page.[64]

As campaigns make concerted efforts at reaching new opinion leaders, it is not the case that the Internet or social media necessarily or even accidentally lead to the dismantling of power laws wherein major media voices command a disproportional majority of attention while smaller actors command very little, but that campaigns see strategic benefit in doing so.

Still, even campaigns' desire to speak to new opinion leaders is tempered by their reliance on traditional practices and local-level technical capabilities. Campaigns are, technologically speaking, capable of measuring who their potential influencers are within some social media. However, Because of a lack of savvy staffers, a constant dearth of resources, and an overflowing workload, this was seldom the state of messaging in 2010. At Netroots Nation 2011, a national meeting of progressive, digitally inclined consultants and activists that followed that election cycle, a new media consultant asked her audience of roughly 40, "Who tries to get people to share their messages on social media?" Properly socialized to value the benefits of harnessing networked technology, nearly everyone in the room raised a hand. When the next question asked was, "Who's measuring who they should talk to? Who's aware of how influential their Twitter followers are? How many of you even know who your top 20 people following you are?" nearly all hands went down. Even within a highly specialized group of people who are active in politics, only about 10% of the consultant-heavy audience seemed to have the knowledge and skills necessary to properly evaluate and hone their tactics. Other consultants have experienced this same divide between the possibilities offered by social media tools and staffers' ability to implement them (whether because of skill level or a lack of time). One digital strategy consultant explains the disjunction:

> I don't think a lot of campaigns are really being able to detect it as well as they could be. If you really look at the kinds of things that they are doing—in terms of tracking all of that and keeping track of, "Every time we tweet, this guy sends us something back," and really keeping track of who's responding and how often they are responding, the kinds of things that they are saying back to you—that would give you the ability to reach out to those people and bring them into the fold as your field organizers or your ground team.[65]

Within local elections such as congressional and state-level races this problem is painfully apparent. Although Illinois' 10th District contained one of the most hotly contested and nationally publicized congressional races between two of the largest-spending congressional campaigns in the country, neither had a senior (or even full-time) staffer dedicated to or specifically trained in new media. Instead, interns handled much of this work, or communications directors delegated the creation of websites or answering of campaign emails to outside consultants while maintaining a high level of control over the production of texts across media platforms. Even while campaigns discuss their desires to reach what they understand to be "new" opinion leaders, their tactics for doing so are often confined to tried-and-true forms of interaction that predate social media.

Despite the common reversion to applying traditionally successful practices to the realm of social media, some have begun to see the need for new practices that actually make use of digital media's potential for reciprocal contact and communication between campaigns and citizens, and recognize a greater number of individuals as potential opinion leaders. While campaigns long shied away from direct engagement online, they are now not only actively producing social media messages, but engaging in one-on-one contact with citizens.[66] A consultant discussing a candidate's proclivity for dialogue online relayed the frustration these new practices can bring: "His communication director literally had to pull him away from the computer. He'd be up at all hours responding to comments on a blog post or something, and the campaign was like, 'We need you in call time [to solicit donations].'"[67] A consultant describes his preference for using Twitter to get out the vote (GOTV) and directly contact people who have discussed their undecided status online.[68] Here it is precisely the interpersonal elements of the medium—individuals, rather than organizations or campaigns, can reach out to citizens—that is compelling to those with institutional power. For example, the Obama administration's continued use of Twitter by multiple individual White House staffers (designated by the "44" after their name) allows for more personal interaction. Individuals and their messages are not tied to monolithic entities like an entire campaign or administration, but are still connected to an official status, lessening the divide between individuals who are considered private and impersonal organizations that are considered public.

It is important to differentiate this practice from the tactic of microtargeting, which is often touted as the dominant mode of digital-era campaign strategy. While microtargeting uses big data and user analytics in order to segment populations into increasingly precise slices based on any number of variables (demographics, interests, Internet browsing history, engagement with campaign emails or other materials, and so on), this is a decidedly different process with entirely different goals and different views of citizenship. Engaging with networked publics is, first and foremost, about recognizing the audience as connected, rather than segmented, and relying on those connections for the spread of information, rather than direct communication from campaigns. Because microtargeting ultimately aims to provide each individual with the information most relevant to him or her, publics do not end up with a shared text, and widespread circulation of a text is not part of the goal of messaging. In many ways, the rising strategies of microtargeting and encouraging viral content pose fundamentally opposed visions of what audiences and publics ought to look like, though both strategies are often employed to some degree.

Circulation and Citizenship

When campaigns ask citizens to take action by circulating content, these campaign messages become more meaningful than the digital equivalent of yard signs. These messages encourage citizens to create their own political information through the act of circulation, and request that citizens recognize their own social networks as part of the ecosystem of political information. Of course political campaign's attempts at encouraging digital circulation are self-serving—this form of action represents a cheap, easy method that holds the possibility of getting campaigns everything they need. It is a way to get a message out, and holds the possibility for capturing many levels of the always-desired trifecta of votes, dollars, and volunteers. Still, simply because this action is not undertaken with idealism and a noble cause in mind does not mean its effect cannot contribute to such productive democratic tenets. The cynic will posit that citizens who engage in digital pass-along are merely acting as pawns of a campaign—as amplifiers of a constructed message, and their actions are not autonomous or empowering but are merely further proof that the dominant mode of engagement is that of the "managed citizen," a puppet taking actions that are prescribed and limited by traditional power structures of campaigns, parties, and professional politics.[69] What this chapter shows is that even within such an environment, these are also spaces for productive political engagement.

While not an explicitly articulated goal of campaigns, the act of encouraging digital circulation fundamentally displays a more participatory ideal of citizenship. The very process of circulating campaign messages represents a normative account of citizenship that is more active than those emphasizing the consumption of information. By encouraging and expressing the desire for citizens to engage in practices of digital circulation, campaigns encourage the foundations of actualized citizenship—sharing and producing civic or political content among peer networks—despite their connection to institutional politics. While individuals' uses of these media channels still exist within such a "management model" of political action (many members of the newly constructed campaign public are, after all, supportive members), the texts' encouragement to activate one's own social networks as political points to additional spaces for creative and unrestrained action. Moreover, not only are these actions possible, but they are being encouraged by campaigns themselves and point to the fact that a completely managed system of action may no longer even be tenable in the current digital campaign environment. As a result, we should not consider the actualized and managed realms as separate spaces, but observe there is room within campaigns for autonomous and creative action. Thus, while designations between "managed" and "autonomous" experiences are useful in many arenas, these sharp divisions are becoming blurred within the arena of political campaigns, and the managed and the autonomous should not be considered separate spheres in which participation of one type excludes the possibility of the other.

By observing campaigns' attention to these networked social ties as potential sites for political action and engagement, these findings build upon Theda Skocpol and Zizi Papacharissi's arguments that the potential spaces of participation have changed and must be located and fostered. Illustrating the historical change in the structural organization of political participation from community-based to professionalized organizations of citizens (which can be seen as a decline or thinning of democracy), Skocpol argues that while a decrease in democratic norms and behaviors can be seen, the demise of participation is not the only possibility for professionalized participation, and that "we Americans can and should look for ways to recreate the best of our civic past in new forms suited to a renewed democratic future." Papacharissi's explanation of the blending of public and private political spheres is an example of one such space.[70] This does not mean replicating the practices of old, but finding opportunities within our current conditions.

The practice of digital circulation by citizens stands as one such opportunity for meaningful participation within the professional realm.

While the material capabilities of social and mobile media and citizens' uses of these technologies for political engagement have transformed the political landscape, campaigns' specific attempts to harness the powers of these technologies by encouraging practices of digital circulation have led to greater changes than previously identified. By recognizing and fostering, through their practices, messaging that encourages actualized citizenship, consultants and campaign staffers have engendered slight changes to their own messaging tactics by actively searching out and contacting "new" opinion leaders in addition to those of traditional organizations or interest groups. They have engaged in a hybrid form of messaging that uses the material capacities of mass media alongside the socially situated practices of personalization and one-to-one contact that culminates in an enlarged version of their campaign's public. They have politicized the social relationships that were previously thought to be largely separate from the realm of the political, thereby producing options for autonomous, creative political participation within spaces that were too easily designated as managed and therefore not politically viable.

Though the practice of digital circulation may look remarkably like passing along campaign pamphlets, the practice, as it is executed and discussed by campaigns and consultants, points to additional ways of thinking through understandings of a public for these messages, and understandings of the opportunities for citizenship that exist within these messages. These goals for the practice of digital circulation point to additional ways of thinking through what have been campaign goals for a long time. Both gaining "eyeballs" and reaching new opinion leaders are related to the general goal of getting a message out—breakthrough and reaching the correct populations are still, generally speaking, of utmost importance for campaigns. Similarly, getting citizens to participate, whether it be through GOTV efforts or campaign events, has always been a need. However, in all of these cases, consultants' and campaigns' discussion of these goals points to new understandings of how they work. The emphasis on participation gestures toward a good citizen as not only one who participates (and especially one who participates by maintaining interaction and communication with the campaign), but one who participates continuously. Participation, as understood through practices of circulation and elites' discussion of them, is not a specific and single action, and it does not occur in a vacuum. Instead, it is always tied to future (and past) acts of participation, and is idealized as ongoing and continuous. The combination of an emphasis on "eyeballs" and discussions of audiences as individuals marks a move toward conceiving of these messages' public as a hybrid of mass and one-to-one, wherein new levels of members are directly addressed, and all members as asked to reflect on their relationships to other identifiable individuals, as well as the political nature of these relationships. Finally, the process of activating these relationships as political not only marks a mode of citizenship as an active embodiment of versions of actualized citizenship already theorized, but shows the ways that allegedly oppositional norms of actualized and managed citizenship can function simultaneously, without surrendering autonomous action, and while still working within the constraining structures of political campaigns.

5

Digital Retail Politics

Interpersonal Messaging via Social Media

For tools that staffers were intensely familiar with and used on a daily basis outside of the campaign, social media were a surprisingly consistent sore spot for the communications office. Not only did other priorities constantly overtake the time that was supposed to be devoted to creating social media content, but there were also very few ground rules for what constituted "good" messages. Despite a nearly constant underlying drive to take advantage of these social media platforms—moments not laced with the frenetic air of deadlines and rapid response were often used to consider the social media messaging calendar—the campaign was seldom impressed by its own social media content, and often defaulted to content that it had deemed "good enough."

Occupying the top left corner of the communications office's central whiteboard wall was the social media calendar, mapping out two weeks' worth of content across Facebook and Twitter, yet never seeming full enough. Major campaign events, anticipated endorsements, and planned press releases that matched the overall messaging strategy held definite places on the board, marked with blue ink, but much of the other content was constantly at risk of literal erasure. Staffers would add their own ideas or those mentioned in email chains in red, and brainstorming sessions with the communications director would bestow the blue ink of permanence on a lucky few. Largely, such sessions would result in a string of "noes" or silent disapproval: "Local legislative meeting? [silence]"; "Mexican Independence Day parade?

[silence]"; "Tax cut extension?" "No." This process often sent staffers back to scanning hundreds of thumbnail images from small events to find a picture worth showing off, or trying to reframe national policy discussions in ways that were specific to their electorate. Instructions for what made good posts were in some ways redundant to what made good campaign messaging in general—it had to be timely, it should grab interest, it should speak to targeted populations, and so on—but these rubrics still often proved inadequate for determining acceptable messages. As this process was repeated over the weeks and months, one of the only constants in deciding what would become a campaign message was that anything became more likely to pass muster if it came with a photo. It didn't have to be visually arresting—a not-blurry shot of the candidate or supporters would suffice nearly every time. Beyond the "no picture, no post" litmus test, the rules were fuzzy. The staffers were in relatively uncharted territory. Best practices were largely defined in much the same way as obscenity: you'll know it when you see it.

In 2010, social media messaging was a still-emerging space. While most candidates were using social media tools, campaigns were largely uncertain about what type of messages worked best. Tactics were haphazardly put together, and best practices were far from codified, but during this period certain norms began to become dominant. Though social media platforms are still about informing audiences, as were earlier channels used by communications professionals, the information created for and distributed through them differs. What began as sites for traditional campaign content like press releases and endorsement announcements have increasingly become a space to highlight the pleasant interpersonal elements of campaigns. Retail politics, the baby-kissing, hand-shaking, bread and butter of campaigns have found a home online, as have descriptions of the everyday ins and outs of life on the campaign trail and behind-the-scenes views of campaign headquarters. Often amplified by a heavy reliance on images and subsequent development of aesthetic sensibilities, this "fun," interpersonal content cropped up in a variety of spaces in 2010 and marked the beginning of a continued trend of realizing and appreciating content that once seemed frivolous. The emergence of this new genre of interpersonal content not only marks an addition to the landscape of information, but an addition that emphasizes very different goals than messages traditionally produced by communication departments. Campaigns social media messaging has moved away from providing information and attempting to persuade, in favor of strengthening the social connections that are necessary to mobilize citizens. While there are potentially negative consequences for this move away from policy, seeming inefficiencies can be productive for campaigns and civil society alike.

Political Information and Campaign Goals

Throughout the pursuit of major campaign goals of dollars, volunteers, and votes, it is the act of informing—whether in service of persuading or mobilizing—that is the primary job of communications and digital media staffers. Messages as materially divergent as printed pamphlets and campaign websites share this goal, as do television, radio, and Internet ads. Providing strategic and persuasive accounts of information such as issue stances and policy positions is a goal that spans campaigns' efforts at paid and earned media alike. Simply put, campaigns constantly create the content we come to know as political information and rely on audiences to make informed judgments concerning a candidate's fitness to lead and whether her values and stances match their own. Their power to create and circulate this content in a way that it reaches new populations of potential voters is increasing not only because of the technical and strategic changes discussed in the previous chapter, but also because of the changing environment of local journalism. As a result of all of these factors, 2010 marked a change in the type of content that campaigns are producing, and that shift has only continued in the years since.

In order to fulfill their goal of informing citizens in order to garner campaign support or participation, campaigns have long worked in tandem with news media to get campaigns' messages to the public. As campaigns vie for earned media coverage and push content that emphasizes their message or issues, the news media stand as an important mediator of campaign messages to the public. Changing this relationship, however, are the severe budget cuts to print media, both local and national newspapers and magazines. Reductions in resources have led to restricted coverage that, while certainly a theoretical problem concerning the ability of the news media to inform citizens, has also been a practical problem for campaigns. Expressing frustration with the state of political coverage in general, one communications director declares, "Frankly, the media really isn't covering anything any-more. So in the old days when you would have an event or speaker, or announcements or something, you'd have a couple of TV cameras and daily reporters. Now you don't have any of that. They don't show up."[1] This prob-lem is perhaps felt by all campaigns except the most-covered races that attain regular national publicity. In 2010, even in major cities with large news oper-ations, communications directors found it hard to drum up coverage. "It was a difficult time," describes one such communications director, "because the [area] was adjacent to a major media market, but given the incredible shrink-ing newsroom, it was difficult to get mainstream media out that way, unless there was major breaking news."[2] Even in a major city like Chicago, the majority of campaigns were drowned out by coverage of the mayoral elec-tion that was slated for January, and even high-profile races for the Senate and governor felt the crunch, with those at the congressional and more local levels bearing the brunt of the coverage drought.[3] Even more affected are suburban and rural areas with meager journalistic resources. One commu-nications consultant explains what he calls "a real dearth of local coverage," saying: "Last time I picked up my local paper in Wisconsin, half the content was written—it was like from a syndication service. It was from the AP or it was from McClatchy. There were very general articles about suburban life, but there wasn't much specific to my community."[4]

A complete lack of coverage isn't the only problem campaigns run into when trying to get their message out in the traditional avenues of earned media. As newsrooms and resources shrink, the coverage not only dimin-ishes, but changes as well. Over time, less coverage has been devoted to topics requiring large amounts of resources such as investigative journal-ism and detailed accounts of policy stances and platforms, in favor of horse race coverage and attention to the process of campaigns rather than the issues.[5] Major news organizations such as the *Chicago Sun-Times* have even announced an end to endorsements, a process through which campaigns can make their stances on issues public and which ultimately holds the promise of a persuasive message courtesy of the publication.[6] As a result of these changes, fewer opportunities for campaigns to reach audiences with persuasive content exist, and communications offices are feeling the crunch.

As this alleged failure of the press has become a hot topic of conversa-tion in the new millennium, social media are seen as the answer for both campaigns and citizens to break and circulate the information they deem relevant. The communications director who announced that "the press no longer show up" relayed this need matter-of-factly: "So, how do you get that information out? Now, you have the responsibility to communicate your message, which, in the old days, the mainstream media would have helped you do."[7] Although earning major press coverage remains a primary goal of communications departments, supporting these earned media efforts with campaign-produced social media content is seen as a way to circulate information when the press is otherwise occupied. One digital director within an advocacy organization expresses her understanding of why social media have become a popular space for political information, saying, "I think people feel that their media has failed them. And they're creating their own narratives because they feel that the press institutions that are out there are failing them."[8] Campaigns, as well as citizens, can use these new tools of publication and circulation to their advantage. Seeing their news coverage drop dramatically and sensing an opportunity to wrest control of the messages that circulate in the public sphere, campaigns have made the capacity to circulate campaign-produced messages via social media an integral part of the information equation.

Despite their clear and sustained goals of persuading citizens or mobilizing them to take specific actions, informative messages have certainly changed over time. Scholars have traced the rise and possible effects of phenomena such as infotainment, sound bite culture, an allegedly "post-network" era, and parody as tools of the news and of providing information.[9] While much of this research concerns news coverage (which is indeed swayed by political campaigns' earned media efforts), changes in the content of campaign-produced messages have occurred as well, including similar moves toward emotion-based appeals in place of "hard" facts.[10] Examinations of these shifts in content have led to conflicting assertions of their impact on the state of democracy and political participation—such as the perpetual argument over whether negative ads enhance or reduce voter turnout and participation in general—placing arguments that democracy is changing (and perhaps even flourishing) alongside those that point to diminishing levels of much-needed democratic norms.[11]

As changes unfold, the questions of political communication research have often focused on whether political information is living up to any number of its persuasion-oriented goals. Is the information produced and accessed ample for decisions and making judgments? How persuasive are messages across various media platforms? How much and what type of information do people retain? What content is most effective at converting opinions or causing action?[12] While some studies have focused on measuring the effectiveness of specific persuasive tactics, others have argued that Internet tools, in general, are not persuasive vessels for political information, arguing that "the increasing level of selective exposure based on partisan preference [which citizens can exercise online] thus presages a new era of minimal consequences, as least insofar as persuasive effects is concerned."[13] Rather than simply understanding digital campaign messages as failing to persuade, this chapter investigates the alternate goals new social media messaging practices point to. In social media content, not only do the texts focus on behind-the-scenes glimpses and digital retail politics, but they also move away from explicitly concerning themselves with persuasion, and toward a model that focuses on fostering emotional connection in service of mobilizing those who are already persuaded. This goal might be expected from the field office—those who solicit and organize volunteers to knock on doors, make phone calls, and lick envelopes—but for communications offices, it is less common. Occurring in more channels than campaigns' social media pages, a move toward playful and interpersonal content points to a larger phenomenon of realizing and leveraging practices that are largely ineffectual or inefficient ways to meet the most important of traditional campaign goals in order to develop feelings of connection that are important to mobilizing and engaging citizens at a deep level.[14]

Traditional Tactics, New Impulses

While social media have yielded hybrid campaign tactics in many areas, decisions regarding content in social media were especially haphazard in 2010. Ultimately though, they offer insight into the early stages of the stabilization of practices of content creation. Social media content illustrates what Andrew Chadwick has called the hybrid media system in which new and old tactics meet, with many posts highlighting messages and themes seen in other on- and offline spaces, while also introducing different types of content.[15] Traditional campaign texts such as press releases, candidate platforms, and web and TV advertisements can be found on "new" tools of official campaign websites and social media, while newer content like entire photo albums of events, messages or videos thanking supporters, or off-the-cuff notes that would not warrant a press release or email to supporters are also present. Within this hybrid landscape, social media were a place where emerging norms of interpersonal and amusing content—inefficient in terms of directly persuasive or mobilization goals—were taking root. Campaigns' combination of traditional content and new generic conventions illustrates the confusing march toward new practices—specifically toward information that focuses more on soft news and candidates' style than policy and a subsequent shift in emphasis from pure persuasion to mobilization.

MAINTAINING TRADITIONAL CONTENT

Despite the radical opening up of space for content and rise in interactive capabilities that have emerged through the affordances of digital tools, campaigns use digital tools to disseminate content that is often the same as its pre-Internet counterparts. Whereas printing technology brought an easy way to disseminate political messages, and political candidates once relied heavily on pamphlets to get their platforms and issues to citizens, this same type of content now makes up the bulk of campaign websites. Focusing on candidates' stances and issues they consider important, official websites stand as a clearinghouse for very traditional types of information about campaigns. They contain the very same content that can still be obtained by calling campaign headquarters; they highlight major issues just as pamphlets did (and still do); they further publicize existing content from news articles and endorsements. Electronic press releases are often housed on campaign websites and published to social media when released, yet they date back to analog days and are still used to push stories or versions of events to the press (see table 5.1 for a breakdown of content present within social media messages).

In Illinois in 2010, the creation of familiar content was likely due to multiple and reinforcing factors, including staffers with strong roots in traditional modes of communication, little training in digital media, and a lack of known best practices among all ranks of political analysts. These campaigns knew they had to use digital platforms and wanted to mirror the successes seen in 2008, but were largely understaffed and lacking the experience needed to use social media tools to their interactive potential. One communications director admits that their social media strategy looked remarkably similar to their overall messaging strategy of pushing content to citizens without engaging in many of the interactive affordances or media-specific content of the platforms, saying: "We would largely stick with messages that we wanted to get out."[16] Almost uniformly, with each new television ad campaign's rollout, the videos would be posted to campaign websites, social media pages, and pitched to local bloggers in order to increase viewing and ultimately increase breakthrough. One communications director explains how social media can provide the same free coverage as earned media, noting the importance of the medium in circulating traditional texts: "So you know on TV, you can have a story on the 7 or the 10 o'clock news that you don't pay for but it's worth thousands of dollars right, but then you can have an ad that follows it that costs $10,000 and you have to pay for it. Same thing on Facebook. You can post things on your account for free."[17] Another speaks of the online space in general terms as reaffirming traditional goals, saying, "I think it's just a way to put out more information," emphasizing the sheer amount, not the changes to the type of information.[18] This is especially true of video content, wherein traditional content is posted to social media platforms a great deal. Creating web videos that are little (or not at all) different from those that run on television and push a campaign's message can accomplish multiple goals. In addition to publicizing a message across digital channels, they can also garner earned media coverage in traditional media channels. "[Our digital director], early on, made a really creative web video that launched, and it got really popular," explains a communications director, detailing how the campaign pushed messages about an opponent's controversial voting record through social media. She continues, saying, "It was strictly a web video, but we got it on MSNBC, we got on hundreds of websites."[19] Beyond publicizing such videos through social media and hosting entire YouTube channels, campaigns are finding additional ways to drive viewers to this content. In recent well-funded elections, campaigns have bought advertising space on YouTube that runs their television (or even web-based) ads before other highly rated or related videos, or have purchased "featured video" status that places the ad next to other "recommended" videos.[20] As young people go online for television content in increasing numbers, these spaces become more and more important as a digital space for reaching audiences with the very same content campaigns have always relied upon.

Still, traditional content often blurs into newer messages, whether campaigns intend to evolve their practices or not. Scrawled on the wall of a communications office, a campaign's social messaging calendar exhibited this seemingly unintended evolution. When planning the social media calendar, the communications director would start with the regular messaging calendar. When the campaign was messaging about social security, social media would be messaging about social security.[21] A digital media director described her process of creating a digital messaging calendar as bringing together the calendars of the Communications, Field, and Finance offices to ensure the necessary issues and goals were reinforced. Traditional events such as policy releases, speeches, and fundraisers were all listed on the calendar, but their tone would change for social media publication. What had been listed as "Choice Endorsement" went up on Facebook as a photo album of a lunch with women that occurred after the endorsement; "Small Business" became pictures of men shaking hands. In these cases, despite campaigns' seeming attempts to maintain traditional issues-based calendars, messaging plans changed without much discussion or went forward without deliberate change in how events were to be framed in a social media environment. In fact, simple questions asking staffers and consultants to describe their content elicited descriptions covering both traditional and newer content: "I like using Facebook to highlight where we were going and what we've done, photos, posting news stories and press releases and whatnot."[22] In many ways, these practices contradict—staffers hold on to the tried and true while reaching into uncharted territory and new norms. More advanced digital strategists, however, often moved from traditional to new practices in a much more deliberate and planned fashion, culling important events, messaging strategies, and assessing campaigns needs over the coming weeks and months to draft comprehensive digital calendars that would incorporate all other departments of the campaign in a coherent way. The convergence present in these tactics is likely to be a significant element of digital strategy's evolution.

INTRODUCING AN INTERPERSONAL GENRE

Despite these similarities and political campaigns' notoriously slow pace of adopting new approaches to campaign tactics, both the material affordances of these new social media tools and their evolution at the hands of user-driven norms have led to at least some divergent, more interpersonal content in campaign messaging. Insofar as they have been collectively dubbed "social" media, interpersonal relationships have become the norm of these tools, and as they are adopted by campaigns, their social elements and aesthetic norms are conditions to which those producing campaign messages in such spaces must respond. Explaining the ways these tools have evolved to almost necessarily involve types of use that are interactive and interpersonal, one communication director describes them by saying, "The reason social media is called social media is because it's *social*, right?"[23] Comparing social media's drive to mirror or enable connections that are similar to interpersonal and face-to-face interactions, one consultant argues that "this room is created to get everyone in a room to talk to each other, to share the energy. Now we have online forums do the same." He goes on to show how those interpersonal impulses are the bread and butter of social media, saying, "My mom got on Facebook to see pictures of my sister's babies . . . I think a lot of communities try to be built around stuff where the user doesn't care. People don't really care about your press release."[24]

By enabling interpersonal texts such as pictures to be easily shared, the material affordances of platforms like Facebook or Twitter foster the social, interpersonal element that has grown to define these tools. Not only do these platforms create spaces where visual content exists at a much larger scale, but some features of social media encourage such content to dominate, while leaving purely text-based information by the wayside. For example it was well known by campaigns that Facebook's algorithm for public "news feeds"—the main way people see any content posted to Facebook—was more likely to show off a post that contained pictures, as opposed to just links or text. As a result, the platform not only enabled, but incentivized visual, photo-based content from campaigns. Even Twitter, a platform developed for simple text-based use, supported the proliferation of images via add-ons like TwitPic in 2010, and eventually defaulted to directly embedding photos in Twitter streams by 2013. Since the 2010 election, visually oriented social media platforms have only gotten more popular, with the rise of Instagram, Pinterest, and Tumblr. While some of these tools existed during the 2010 midterm elections, they were largely overlooked until 2012 when campaigns created profiles on the individual platforms, and often cross-pollinated their content, posting Instagram photos on Facebook and filling Tumblr pages with stylized campaign images. From 2010 to 2012, a move toward deeper attention to aesthetic sensibility can be seen, with even local candidates using photo editing apps and filters to improve and add text to the images they post.[25] In just four years, the very same campaigns that began these trends in 2010 have dramatically added to the aesthetic sensibility of their content. These messages still contain candid footage and unchoreographed shots from campaign headquarters and public events, but they also make use of editing software to request citizens take action or to highlight a message.

Discussing the plethora of digital media tools campaigns have at their disposal and the specific advantages social media offer, one consultant and digital media director describes the norms of social media by saying, "I fully agree that all [official campaign] statements should be put out there. But that's not why you come to Facebook. You go to Facebook, you want to see a glimpse inside a candidate as a person."[26] Twitter was originally designed with the idea of asking its users to directly express an answer to the question "What are you doing?" (the company officially changed its tagline to "What's happening?" in 2009),[27] and Facebook's addition of enabling "status updates" in 2006 requested a similar response from users. Materially, the abilities to easily post pictures and recirculate messages lend themselves to the interpersonal features of one-to-one communication and being physically present. "If you have a Twitter account you're tweeting and no one's following it, why bother? Or, if you have a Facebook page that's just—that's not interactive, or that's just posting stuff that you can find in other places, you're probably not going to get much of an impact."[28] While it is not entirely surprising that a form called *social* media would have this engaging and interpersonal element, the type of interpersonal content is new. Rather than websites with humanizing pictures of candidate's families (the same type of pictures that have long been present in direct mail as well), digital retail content and behind-the-scenes messages hold their interpersonal content as the message itself—entire Facebook albums or single pictures—rather than a supplementary image accompanying a larger message. Within the campaign's ongoing need to push information out, two related, emergent types of content—digital retail politics and behind-the-scenes images—emphasize goals very different goals from the political information citizens have long received.

Digital retail politics consist of the online reproduction of the campaign standby of face-to-face retail politics marked by campaign stops in diners, kissing babies or signing autographs on a rope line, and smaller meetings with members of a community in living rooms across a district, state, or country. Consultants sing the praises of personal contact with voters, and researchers have proven its benefits; especially on the local scale.[29] In their online equivalent, references to such events, the details of foods served and locations visited, and pictures of the activities give readers a sense of being part of campaign events. Behind-the-scenes content, on the other hand, provides readers with the feeling that they are part (or at least have some insight into) the activities of campaign staffers and volunteers, whether they are on the campaign trail or in headquarters. Comments, descriptions, and photo evidence of offices overrun with campaign signs, volunteers licking envelopes or phone-banking, and overworked staffers provide citizens with an insider perspective on "how the sausage is made." The glimpse behind the curtain such content provides has long been open to the public, though it has largely been the purview of journalists. Books chronicling the trials and tribulations of campaigns—from Hunter S. Thompson's *Fear and Loathing on the Campaign Trail '72* and Crouse's *The Boys on the Bus* to Halperin and Heilemann's *Game Change*—have long garnered interest from the public.[30] Even the demystifying done by photojournalism chronicling life inside the Kennedy administration continues to be of interest to contemporary publics.[31] The convention of behind-the-scenes news accounts remains popular with contemporary candidates as well, as the *New York Times* ran state-by-state photo series of the 2012 Republican primary, and journalists tweeted about the minutiae of traveling with the campaign press corps constantly during the subsequent presidential election.[32] As campaigns begin to adopt this practice themselves, they retain the popular appeal of insider accounts while wresting control of their message away from journalists. Whereas journalists may blow the lid off of campaign turmoil, campaigns' strategic use of similar content can be used to reinforce the persuasive messages they choose. Campaigns have also tried to multiply the power of retail politics by taking pictures of rope lines and pancake breakfasts to the digital sphere. In traditional campaign experiences, these two activities are very different—meeting a candidate on the rope line or at a coffeehouse is very different from glimpsing inside the campaign bus that's late to an event. However, when they are publicized and highlighted within digital media, the genres sometimes blend: a tweet about driving to the local fair both announces the fact of a retail politics event and provides some behind-the-scenes element of knowing exactly what the campaign is doing at that moment in time, away from the crowds and press coverage. Both of these types of content give audiences a view of what it's like to be alongside the campaign and an image of what it's like to share a moment with the candidate, her staffers, and even other supporters, whether in a crowd or on the bus.

In general, content that focuses on providing behind-the-scenes and digital retail content occurs in nearly all campaigns.[33] While traditional content such as links to mainstream news media coverage and links to other campaign messages (ads, press releases, invitations to events, etc.), as discussed, remained a significant element of social media content, content providing a behind-the-scenes view or emphasizing digital retail politics made a significant contribution to social media content. With just over two-thirds of the competitive Illinois races in the sample producing behind-the-scenes or digital retail content for at least 10% of Facebook posts and one-half of those campaigns producing this type of content for at least 30% of their posts, these messages are clearly of prominence within the social media space.

Of those overall numbers, a sizable amount of this content is made up of posts that specifically focus on creating content that displays retail politics within an online forum. Typical instances of such posts consist of notifications that the candidate is currently at a local event, pictures from an offline event within the community, and giving thanks to citizens with whom the candidate recently interacted. One communications director discussed her desire to tell supporters about retail events immediately, and efforts at "trying to use Facebook as more of a 'where and when.' 'Here's what we did today, here's where he was, here's a photo of him with a group.' So it's more of a day-to-day update and less policy."[34] Telling people the candidates were engaging in local activities was one helpful approach, and showing these activities was also a tactic considered productive. "People love pictures," began one digital media director. "So I was always trying to get a picture out—I would much rather post a picture than a statement. And people want to see the candidate interacting with other normal people, and they want to see him locally where they are."[35] Some campaigns even focused on highlighting supporters in these digital retail politics scenarios, flooding Facebook and Twitter with pictures of enthusiastic constituents at barbeques and "man on the street" videos highlighting their support for the candidate. By providing pictures, the face-to-face relationships so important to offline retail politicking can be highlighted. Behind-the-scenes content, while similar to digital retail messages, provides citizens with insight into the inner workings of the campaign, rather than just updates about the candidate. Typified by backstage updates from campaign buses and dimly lit rooms in campaign headquarters, behind-the-scenes content also provides an interaction with campaigns that is much closer to face-to-face interaction than traditional messages get (see figures 5.1 and 5.2).

Explaining how her campaign gravitated toward these types of messages, one digital director scoffed,

> You don't want constantly to be putting up "Here's our white paper on Social Security." It's not really what those media, I think, are best for. . . . People like the inside look or the behind-the-scenes aspects of politics. They want to know what's going on. What's the

Table 5.1 **Types of Content Present in Campaigns' Facebook Pages**

Candidate	Total posts	Cross-media campaign messages	News	Events	Behind the scenes / retail	Other
Brady (R, governor)	170	23	24	40	53	17
Quinn (D, governor)	125	36	23	27	19	17
Cohen (I, governor)	33	2	6	8	17	0
Whitney (I, governor)	120	26	34	35	12	5
Giannoulias (D, senator)	157	41	26	25	6	44
Kirk (R, senator)	223	84	76	30	12	17
Dold (R, congressperson)	110	12	12	7	62	15
Halvorson (D, congressperson)	82	32	16	5	6	19
Kinzinger (R, congressperson)	71	28	13	13	6	7
Pollak (R, congressperson)	270	112	51	40	35	27
Schakowsky (D, congressperson)	50	16	17	2	5	10
Schilling (R, congressperson)	79	10	18	8	13	22
Seals (D, congressperson)	73	18	16	12	7	16
Walsh (D, congressperson)	89	25	15	10	18	21

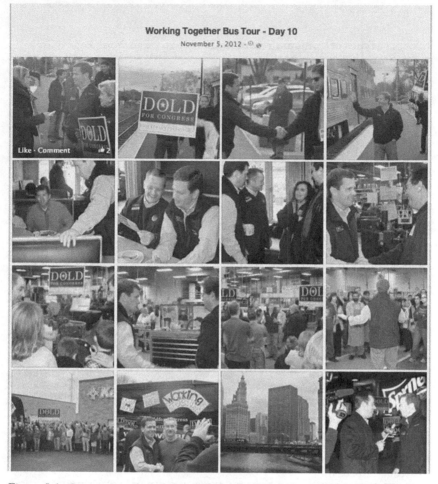

Figure 5.1 Congressional candidate Robert Dold's Facebook page, filled with photos of digital retail politics and behind-the-scenes coverage.

campaign doing? Where are people going? Why are they doing this? What's the candidate doing?[36]

Another asserts: "The behind-the-scenes stuff is good. . . . You start sharing photos and talking about events and fun stuff rather than issues and some of the more heavy things, which have their place obviously. But social media tends to be a little lighter in the messaging."[37] The combination of ease and perceived interest from citizens made these types of content a preference of consultants and staffers alike. "Yeah, one of my favorite things to do would

Figure 5.2 The William Foster for Congress campaign posts behind-the-scenes images from the campaign office alongside a common trope of retail politics: meeting voters in a local diner.

be ... if we had a very good phone bank going, I would take a picture of it with my phone and throw a Twitpic up and put it up on Facebook."[38] This inside perspective—"a glimpse inside a candidate's person; inside the life of the campaign"—was often referenced as a productive strategy.[39] It was often described as more than just a glimpse, though; as one consultant specializing in blogging observed, "It was all in service of getting people to understand that we were giving them stuff that was going to give real access."[40] This trend continued through the 2012 campaign as well, when a picture of the president and the First Lady hugging became the most retweeted message ever, was widely shared across Facebook, and was considered an extremely successful message (see figure 5.3).

A similar trend in content can be traced to the rise of campaign blogs as well. Dubbed the "journalistic signature of the 2004 campaign," blogs were used by journalists to cover campaign news and were adopted by campaigns. But more recently, scholars have found that it is candidates and campaigns who are "perhaps the most visible new bloggers," as they "use blogs to humanize themselves and appear accessible to interaction with voters."[41] Blogs not only allow campaigns to circumnavigate traditional media and provide content that is entirely on-message, but provide more avenues of connection between citizens and candidates, and foster connection and access.[42] Insofar as this means blogs promote networking, perhaps they are

Timeline Photos
Back to Album · Barack Obama's Photos · Barack Obama's Page   Previous · Next

Like   Comment

Barack Obama
Four more years.
Like · Comment · Share · November 6, 2012

👍 4,438,742 people like this.

🔁 572,886 shares

💬 View previous comments   43 of 216,587

Album: Timeline Photos
Shared with: 🌐 Public

Open Photo Viewer
Download
Embed Post
Report Photo

Figure 5.3 A photo of the president and First Lady became the "most liked" and "most retweeted" image on Facebook and Twitter, respectively, in 2012.

not too unlike what we consider social media. These trends and the descriptions of them show new types of content entering into the arena of political information.

Combining elements of behind-the-scenes and digital retail politics genres was key to providing this close feeling of access. Posts that blur the edges of these two lines are ones that might detail or preview a candidate's schedule for the day, which gives insight into the specific offline retail events as well as a behind-the-scenes look at what a day on the campaign trail looks like, or it may provide citizens with a message directly from the candidate during the everyday hubbub of a campaign. In some cases, not only did campaigns publish updates from the car or campaign bus en route to events or photos of candidates engaging in the common campaign activities of meet-and-greets and sharing a meal with constituents, but they also used social media to highlight and circulate off-the-cuff, unpolished messages to citizens, as would occur at an offline event. "We were trying to give people the sense that they're having a Skype conversation almost with [a well-known campaign manager]. But they *were really* having a meeting with the campaign manager," notes one digital media and blogging specialist who found the use of quick videos to supporters extremely fruitful.[43] Another digital media director describes his realization of similar opportunities that came immediately following a candidate's primary night victory, when he recognized that the campaign had a chance to virtually shake the hands of online supporters, just as you would volunteers who would spend time behind the scenes at campaign headquarters. "We were at the hotel where the victory party was going to be held, and we decided that we would film a special thank you to our Facebook fans right before the polls closed. And just in the hotel room we do two takes of a 30-second thank you, specifically for the Facebook fans."[44] Explaining the multiple times they did this over the course of the campaign, he speaks to the way campaigns use social media to increase citizens' feelings of "being there." "We put those online, so that people could see. . . . People could—say they were in Carbondale or they were in even somewhere like, somewhere not Chicago or Springfield—they could see what was going on with the candidate that I'm thinking about supporting." Further, "If you can't physically see the candidate, if you don't physically meet the candidate at a parade, at a fair, this is the way for you to get that personal connection."[45] This move toward interpersonal and behind-the-scenes content shows that with the rising use of social media, traditional forms of communication are not necessarily being supplanted by new ones. Instead, the goals of and feelings pursued in undertaking retail politics are being taken up in new spaces and growing.

Social Media and "Homestyle"

Sharing characteristics of personalizing candidates, displaying relationships between candidates and citizens, and providing citizens with a feeling of "being there" during numerous campaign events, this body of content emphasizes the closeness between candidates and everyday people. The rhetorical choices—in terms of both language and aesthetics—within behind-the-scenes and digital retail content display similarities to the "homestyle" Fenno describes as integral to congressional members' success.[46] Arguing that members of Congress adopt certain practices, affectations, tones, and even speech patterns when they return to their home districts in order to gain and maintain trust, Fenno articulates the nuanced presentation of self that is necessary for election to local office. Choices such as engaging with crowds and speaking to many individuals are vital components of homestyle, as are stylistic choices of rolled-up sleeves and unbuttoned collars. Campaigns must emphasize retail politics because "in the members own language, constituents want to judge you 'as a person.' . . . 'If people like you and trust you as an individual,' members often say, 'they will vote for you.' "[47] The genre of digital interpersonal content is therefore an embodiment of homestyle, wherein "every congress[person] also conveys a sense of *identification* with his constituents. Contextually and verbally, he gives them the impression that 'I am one of you'; 'I am like you'; I think the way you do and I care about the same things you do."[48] The concept of homestyle contains an emphasis on sharing physical space, or being in the immediate physical presence of citizens, which digitally mediated messages complicate. Even without distance-leveling tools, this style of interaction itself figuratively reduces the distance between politicians and citizens by forgoing the coiffed and strong presidential style for the rolled-up sleeves and unbuttoned collars of life away from Washington. This digital update allows homestyle to transcend geography. Citizens can see and experience candidates in a backyard or small café without either party being in their community. Moreover, citizens can do more than merely see these images; they can interact with them through comments, sharing, and favoriting to actually engage in the interpersonal elements of homestyle while nowhere near home.

Rooted in these relatively traditional campaign actions of meeting citizens face to face, these social media messages do mark a new genre of content found within campaign texts. Bringing the lived experience to a more static realm, but doing far more than pasting a picture of a candidate surrounded by constituents to a poster, digital retail politics and behind-the-scenes content mark new conventions in campaign communication. Moreover, as Karlyn Kohrs Campbell and Kathleen Hall Jamieson have argued that genre categories mark "substantive responses to perceived situational demands," these changes mark the fact that the contexts of campaign communication must be changing in important ways if such a shift is to occur.[49] Perhaps a not entirely shocking change in genre, many circumstances of campaign and communication technologies more generally seem to preempt such a change in generic conventions. First of all, a practice already rewarded within the world of local politics—that of homestyle—emphasizes the social relationships and interaction that also ground the way people use new social media technologies. Moreover, as campaigns have seen the popularity of content that brings citizens into the fold of campaigns—whether it was journalists' behind-the-scenes coverage or crowds at retail events—they would be remiss if they did not want to harness and control that type of content for themselves. As digital media in general provide a wealth of space in which to host and publicize content of that nature without having to pay to broadcast or print material, it is a logical home to this genre. As social media in particular provide a place where policy-oriented content is understood as not going over as well with audiences, the new genre's presence is even more valuable.

Still, these posts differ from homestyle in one fundamental way; despite their similar content, the purposes for creating and deploying the two genres are meaningfully different. Traditional homestyle is discussed as a persuasive tool that is not only helpful, but necessary to persuading voters to support a candidate. Its digital corollary, behind-the-scenes and digital retail content, is not for explicitly persuasive purposes. The following section explores the range of purposes, from vague shots in the dark to very specific goals, as they are articulated by consultants and staffers. Although its aims are far from solidified as tried-and-true practice, one thing about this content is sure: it has purposes that are markedly different from the assumed purpose of persuasion.

Connecting Citizens and Harnessing Closeness

If the well-oiled machinery of campaigns is producing this interpersonal content to such a degree, we might expect them to have considered how they directly contribute to any of the persuasive or mobilizing goals. Despite social media's place within the overall messaging calendar, however, their specific purposes were not as well thought out; even after the fast-moving pace of campaign season, where we can expect goals and purposes to go unarticulated in the drive to produce content quickly, consultants and staffers were unlikely to ascribe specific goals to the social messages they created. When goals were clear, they were not overtly persuasive or mobilization-oriented, and instead focused on a new, overarching goal of fostering connection with citizens. While connection was viewed as potentially helpful for more tangible goals such as GOTV efforts or persuasion, connection itself was sought out as beneficial. As a result, the informing done via social media messaging added a new goal of fostering connection to the existing ones of persuading and mobilizing.

Most campaigns, although they assign no specific, measurable goals to fostering feelings of connection in citizens, are aware that they do not push a specific goal with these messages and see the content as a way to communicate some of the more intangible elements of a campaign. "It may not be a specific message," admits one consultant, "but maybe an overall vision of the campaign's mission or the candidate.[50] Similarly, another communications director describes a similar feeling as the result of this type of content, saying, "A lot of candidates want to show that they're humans [chuckle]. They have a family, they went to a certain college, and things like that." Admitting that this isn't a traditional goal of campaigns, he goes on to say, "Yeah, I don't know if it gets [citizens] more involved—it gets them more sympathetic to the candidate, I think. It makes them feel more connected to him."[51] Some frame this connection in terms of what we might usually think of as ownership or loyalty to a campaign:

> I think it's kind of in the way that people will read sports columns on something ESPN.com because they want to feel like it felt like an inside track for what the Cubs are doing, and they want to feel closer to the team. I feel like people who are genuinely interested in politics will do the same thing with campaigns. I think that's why the MyBarackObama thing [MyBarackObama.com] is so clever, because it really, it makes . . . this large organization that otherwise wouldn't really seem close to the individual, it makes it their own.[52]

Referring to the multifaceted effects of behind-the-scenes content from a field office, consultants enjoy the mileage they could get from simple behind-the-scenes posts: "It was a way . . . to show the other campaign, 'Hey, like, we are *working*. I don't know what you guys are doing, but it's eight o'clock at night we're still making phone calls.' And part of it, too, was a way to really show our volunteers that we recognize their efforts. . . . So in that sense, it's part of thanking people. But it's also really trying to close the gap between your average voter and the campaign."[53] This feeling of connection is especially evident when juxtaposed to the lack of closeness felt through traditional messaging practices. One communications director, having worked for various campaigns for the past decade, describes the difference: "There's a much more personal connection to the office than to a mail piece once a year."[54] These claims are echoed by others who say, "You've sort of engaged supporters" or "We were giving them stuff that was going to give real access into the campaign, where it's going to open up the campaign, make it feel more personal, more transparent, more accessible."[55] Even in cases where people haven't figured out their specific reasons for these tactics, they are sure that citizens enjoy the content: "I think that there is something inside of all of us that wants to kind of understand how things work, and why things work the way they do. The funny thing is the joke in politics is no one wants to watch the sausage being made, you know, referring to creating legislation. And I think that that's exactly wrong. I think everybody wants to watch the sausage being made."[56]

While the importance of a deep connection can be helpful to many (and perhaps all) campaign goals, explicit requests were very seldom made during the campaign, and were not often attributed to the messages after the fact. These intangible goals of inducing feelings of connection, bonding, and closeness between candidates and citizens are the results most commonly hoped for by campaigns. Although consultants and staffers might not have specific or articulated purposes for the campaigns, that does not necessarily mean there is no method to this madness. Even when staffers and consultants find it difficult to pinpoint these purposes, the feelings created are viewed as of definite strategic value to campaigns: "When you go through your photo album and you're actually able to see, 'Oh I know that person,' it changes the dynamics, because you feel a connection. Photos do that. We do that more and more with social media. So we get to know people on a closer level."[57]

Vague purposes and hopes that potential feelings of closeness can lead to increased turnout is not enough for some campaigns, though—especially for the more specialized consulting population, which has thought through the benefits of cultivating strong relationships with citizens more reflectively. In order to *harness* these feelings of closeness or connection between citizens and candidates or campaigns, such consultants argue they must be put to a variety of mobilizing purposes, from GOTV to fundraising to increasing the rates of recirculation of campaign messages. Within these strategies, consultants and staffers overwhelmingly see the feelings of closeness enabled by social media as instrumental for encouraging action, rather than persuading voters, as most campaigns messages are designed to do. A communications director expresses frustration with what seems to be a history of dealing with campaigns that lack such clear goals:

> If everything is not producing either money, volunteers, good press, or votes, then there's no point in doing it. Just because it's a nice thing to do, or we can refer back to it on Facebook and it'll make a few volunteers happy, that isn't a compelling enough reason to do something. There has to be a return on the investment. That seems transactional, *but the whole nature of the campaign is you're trying to get something done. There's one goal in mind.*[58]

Reaffirming that even very traditional campaign goals require purposeful action, one netroots organizer argues, "So in campaigns again, you've still got to get loads of bodies, votes, and money. That is the theory of change. But change is more of a deliberate effort to do things that will make a difference and not just doing them for the sake of doing them or because they're cool."[59] Explaining further, she asserts the importance of the theory of change for very simple reasons—people need to know what's being asked of them: "You can't expect people to read your mind in terms of knowing what you want from them. And if you just tell them what you want from them, then they'll do it, but they have to have some guidance, and they particularly have to have guidance online." Among those who were attuned to the specific purposes of their behind-the-scenes content, persuasion was not invoked. Even in cases mentioning voting, the emphasis was not on winning citizens' support, but on mobilizing them to make it to the polls come Election Day.

> Obviously the senior staff wants numbers and they want numbers in terms of money, in terms of phone calls, in terms of bodies, in terms of votes. And that's quantifiable right? We understand those things. But my perspective—and it's probably colored by the culture of the new media that I come from—is that the real strength about it is this day-to-day bonding that goes on between the person and the candidate when they see, everyday, a picture a glimpse into their life, when they see them at a parade, or at a state fair or at a candy store in their area. And I think that that is going to make it. So come, November 2, are you excited about the candidate? Are you actually going to get out of your house, and get in your car and

go vote? And I think that the building up of the relationship that takes place through the new media channels particularly . . . in this camp particularly Facebook, and seeing them in your daily stream or Twitter, if a person's on Twitter—I think that is a nonquantifiable way that brings people to the polls.[60]

Other specific uses show up as well. Garnering donations—a digital director for a campaign relayed how they put a picture of the campaign office online that, when visitors scrolled their mouse over the picture, would highlight office supplies and ask for small donations—and getting people to show up at offline events are top among them.[61]

No matter the specificity or vagueness of the purposes assigned to this behind-the-scenes / digital retail politics genre of content, its notable feature is that it has goals that are overwhelmingly not that of persuasion. When reflecting upon the purposes of behind-the-scenes or digital retail content, very few consultants or staffers mention using such tactics to convert potential voters from the other side of the aisle or even undecideds. Emphasizing action items over conversion, one communications director's perspective is that "it's more about engagement . . . to keep your supporters interested, and engaged, and encourage them to be advocates."[62] This is not from an idealistic perspective, she argues, but from the very pragmatic perspective that in traditional media, the numbers needed to break through to an audience—to ensure a certain amount of persuadable people receive your message and that a certain percentage are likely to be influenced in some manner—are known quantities. Polling data, message testing, and ratings testing have been used to study the transmission and reception of messages through radio, television, and print ads for decades. Digital media, on the other hand, are an unknown quantity: "I would like to see more metrics on what the actual impact of all this is. How many people are we really reaching? And how many of those people that we're reaching are converting?" Thus, attempting to incite action among those who are "proactively engaged" with the campaign in the social media environment is a better tactic.[63] There were even explicit articulations of this content as distinctly created not to persuade. "We weren't really concerned with converting people who weren't already into [the candidate]," explains one consultant who specializes in digital messaging and blogging. "We were trying to get voters to become more active, more committed supporters, and then become evangelists. . . . We were trying to mostly build a movement by converting top supporters into hardcore supporters. Not even soft [support], but just have the supporters that can really act."[64] A communications director's story of a specific attempt to place persuasive messaging strategy into a retail politics message, and how that plan fell short, explains the need to emphasize action over persuasion. Wanting to put videos of people at events or volunteering up online, but always too pressed for time to do so, the campaign reverted to an old standby: "We did one kind of flip-cam-like mini-ad thing that was more focused on an issue, but I think if I could kind of integrate that more ... ," explained the director, still frustrated and trailing off before saying that what he really wanted was something that was less like a traditional ad or on-message statement, one that would "close the gap between your average voter and the campaign."[65] While some consultants are quick to assert that, in general, "social media is more people who are engaged already online," much content outside of the genres of behind-the-scenes and digital retail politics is directed at traditional goals of conversion, while these genres are specifically oriented toward this mobilization goal.[66]

The goals underwriting this genre of content, while reflecting certain elements of the situation of contemporary campaigning and the information age more generally, also ignore or elide influence from other important contexts. As these messages are being created for and within social media, they are also taking place within a larger discourse of information and communication technologies that should be used for encouraging participatory action rather than one-way dissemination. Especially prevalent in discussions of newer tools, and overwhelmingly common in discussions of social media, this drive to use social media content to foster participation could be influencing the goals campaigns have for these media channels in general. Moreover, as campaigns get more expensive, and the ground game becomes more dependent on large pools of volunteers, the needs for higher forms of participation become stronger, and therefore more likely the subject of messaging in any form.[67] Despite these reasonable explanations for a general move toward mobilizing citizens and away from informing them, equally plausible reasons to retain an emphasis on informing exist. As the amount of journalistic coverage dwindles, campaigns need methods to circulate informing messages throughout the public. Informing is actually becoming a greater priority for campaigns themselves, yet new genres do not reflect this need. Moreover, the communications office of a campaign—the individuals actually producing the social media content the vast majority of the time—are still primarily tasked with the responsibility of crafting and circulating messages that persuade people. While communications staffers might hope their message is strong enough to mobilize citizens to make it to their polling place, GOTV efforts are truly the area of the field team. As a result, an expectation of maintaining that emphasis on persuasion over that of mobilization would be expected of texts coming out of the communications office. Although moves away from issues potentially hinder citizens' ability to stay informed, digital content constructs a version of engagement in which mobilizing is a much more important action than gaining information.

Whither Information? Ramifications of Emerging Genres' Emphasis on Mobilization

The way political information circulates—and the content of this information—is certainly changing. While social media as a whole do feature significant content devoted to publicizing a candidate's position, such as press releases or external news coverage, and the overarching campaign goal of electoral victory is never far out of the mind of any staffer, there is a significant emerging genre of content that moves away from the goal of persuading undecided or wavering voters. In addition to traditional messaging tactics, campaigns have brought new genres of interpersonal content to their toolkit through social media: that of behind-the-scenes and digital retail politics. To some degree, this might seem like common sense—social media are channels through which citizens can opt in and are therefore likely receptive to a candidate if not outright supporters to begin with. Still, however, any move away from conversion is a surprise. After all, fundraising is less important if you lose on election night. But if specific media tools or genres of mediated content prioritize mobilization and commitment over conversion, inquiry into the efficacy and success of these tools must change. The implications of these new genres of content are multifaceted, showing potential for a move both toward more action-centered, mobilizing messages as well as a glut of inconsequential, superficially important content.

In many ways, the genre of content being added to the information landscape is problematic. Focusing on thank-you messages, updates from campaign busses and county fairs, and hundreds of images of candidates shaking hands strategically avoids talk of policy and of most content that could be used to engage in debates over issues or critical analysis of campaigns. In an era of dramatically and stubbornly low levels of political knowledge among citizens and decreased in-depth or analytical information, this absence becomes even more problematic. Moreover, as campaigns articulate their own self-produced social media content in an attempt to make up for decreases in news coverage, the substantive differences between these emerging conventions of social media information and those they are "replacing" must be looked at, and that comparison throws the dearth of substantive content into relief. Now, positive elements of a rise in similar content such as "soft" news and infotainment have been asserted: some have shown positive relationships between infotainment and levels of participation for some populations, which can also lead to further, more in-depth information-seeking behavior in the future and/or greater knowledge.[68] Still, most argue that the overall effects are damaging for both participation and levels of public knowledge of issues.[69] Moreover, contrasting the rise of online retail politics within social media spaces with the rise of highly informative fact-check-oriented content in campaign websites and related blogs (detailed in chapter 3) indicates the development of very separate informational spheres. While overlap does in fact occur because of campaign practices of also using social media to publicize traditional web content, the two spaces emerge as qualitatively different in content. Despite the presence of links to more informational content, the rise of online retail politics and behind-the-scenes content is problematic insofar as it makes it easier for citizens to self-select into less informative content. One silver lining remains, however. Failure to meet informative benchmarks is certainly the case, but that does not tell the whole story. The assumption that social media's purpose is to provide the information needed to render political judgment on a campaign or candidate may not be entirely relevant, as these messages seem to exhibit goals that are decidedly different from conversion or the development of a broadly informed political class, yet can still serve important democratic functions of deepening connection between citizens and politicians and setting the stage for mobilization.

Following in-depth measurement of the persuasive capabilities of digital tools such as campaign websites, the digital environment has often been deemed unproductive for efforts at persuasion. As persuasion has, largely without question, been considered the primary goal of all public campaign texts, what logically follows is a condemnation of these tools as ineffectual and unproductive. Yet by reassessing the possibilities of campaign goals—and, in fact, observing that these texts' producers do often have very different desires for them—the efficacy of these texts need not be immediately dismissed. Indeed, it is reasonable to believe that campaigns observed the same inadequacies related to persuasion that Bimber and Davis observed and analyzed, thereby changing their goals (and thereby changing the campaign content).[70] Moreover, this could even be productive. By accounting for the likely fact that citizens consuming social media content are already largely persuaded in terms of whom they support, the next step into deeper political engagement is mobilization of some sort. As discussed in the previous chapter, getting people on what consultants call the "ladder of engagement," pushing them up to higher rungs of that ladder, goes beyond attaining basic civic goals of becoming informed, and closer toward much-heralded participatory action.

While it may be easy to unequivocally condemn a move away from substantive, issue-based content the public has repeatedly demonstrated it lacks, a move to messages for mobilization may also contain positive attributes. Rather than presenting normative accounts of citizenship as fundamentally connected to being informed, this content provides a model of enacted citizenship that is more in tune with widespread and everyday participatory politics. If this norm is to have any hope of becoming prevalent and being taken up by citizens, campaigns must begin to put these emerging genres to purposeful use in the name of encouraging participatory action. The fact that many consultants are advocating for more purposeful uses of behind-the-scenes and digital retail content adds to the potential that its power will be harnessed for mobilization rather than simply contributing to greater information drought, and results in a less bleak picture of the current state of political information.

6

Confounding Control

In mid-August, over two weeks before the most intense and desperate period the election was to begin, the campaign had its first run-in with a member of the virtual opposition. Writing on the campaign's Facebook wall in all capital letters, posting links to extremely partisan sites and spouting them as "truth," this commenter sent a shock of disbelief through the communications staff. "What are we supposed to do with this?" read the quizzical looks on their faces. As everyone stared at the post on their respective computer screens, nervous, confused chuckles came from all corners of the room. There was no immediate discussion about whether to respond to or remove his two posts, and within 15 minutes, supporters of the campaign were responding by requesting credible sources and telling him to lay off the Caps Lock key. Staffers tracked the burgeoning Facebook debate compulsively, but no discussion of erasing his message ever took place. Looking deeper, staffers realized that this man was posting rants on the opponent's wall as well, objecting to the relatively moderate stance put forth by both candidates. The relief that accompanies a misery-loves-company attitude permeated the small room of the communications shop, and made it easier to shrug off the posts. Looking over my shoulder at eight back-and-forth comments, the communications director seemed pleased: "This is why we can just leave it up there—supporters will immediately respond." Ultimately, this man and his posts would become a recurring source of intrigue, frustration, and comic relief throughout the campaign. None of his comments were deleted.

On October 25, exactly one week out from the election, a woman posted on the campaign's Facebook wall. Her comment, a response to a recent news article highlighted by the campaign, expressed her desire to vote for the party, but said she was not particularly interested in the issue at hand. Instead, she wanted to know about jobs and the economy. Noticing the post, one communications staffer emailed the group, saying it seemed worth a response. The communications director agreed: "short—less said, best said," she tacked on, not desiring to post the candidate's whole economic platform on Facebook. A short note on the importance of these topics went up, and the woman quickly responded. "Go look at the lady's response," yelled a communications staffer from his room across the hall from their director. A refresh of the page, and five seconds later came the reaction: "Seriously?!" The response read suspiciously like the talking points being used by the opposing candidate, and the mood in the office turned from mild frustration to anger. "Say we'd love to explain our full policy, and tell her to call the office or look at our website, maybe link to that one fact-check. Then be done with it." The campaign posted this and began to watch without any intent of responding or getting bogged down talking to what was quickly viewed as a member of the opposition attempting to bait the campaign. A supporter posted in the campaign's defense, and the original woman responded, as did another echoing her viewpoint. The two detractors started a conversation among themselves within the same comment space, now decidedly not on the campaign's side. The staff had deleted content before, but they were concerned that if they deleted this exchange, other detractors would come back with a stronger negative response. While staffers weighed the pros and cons of erasing the content, the communications director saw how the conversation had unfolded and offered an immediate and unequivocal judgment. "Oh no, they're done now," she announced. Both were banned from the Facebook page, but the first comment that questioned the campaign's priorities while leaving room for debate (and the positive responses) remained.

In many ways, the 2010 midterm elections marked a change in campaigns' ability to control messages. Across the nation, communications offices still attempted to tamp down on messages that were misaligned with their own, and publicized those they preferred, but their ability to do so—or at least to do so overtly—was diminishing. While digital technologies are certainly used to control which potential voters get what messages, digital media are also confounding the traditional stranglehold campaigns have had on the information that circulates about a candidate. By encouraging practices of commenting and community-building discussions within their platforms, campaigns have also invested in norms of participation that include talking back to campaigns. As campaigns' tactics change, their decisions about how to handle online opposition are often made on the fly and without hard-and-fast rules to follow. Inflammatory comments may escape censorship in some cases, while they may never see the light of day in others. Commentary that is reasonably phrased, but viewed as baiting, rather than debating, might be deleted by some despite the opening for debate. Others may cut off such content before it is even published, thus prohibiting any public discussion at all. Some may try to steer clear of specific topics entirely to avoid this type of interaction. Despite a variety of approaches, what can be seen from the events of 2010 is a distinct move away from traditional and overt exertion of control. This chapter investigates how, driven by changes in media platforms and the internal organization of campaign staff, campaigns are moving toward actions that discreetly prohibit conflicting opinions from being publicized and covertly preempt disagreements. In doing so, this chapter examines how the very definitions of campaign "control" are shifting, and analyzes how these changes—designed and accidental, welcomed by and forced upon campaigns—point toward a specific set of practices regarding control moving forward. Moreover, it discusses how these changes to forms of control impact citizens' ability to engage in deliberation and debate.

Control and Publicity

In the contemporary media environment of immediate email updates, constant sharing of digital texts, and cross-media integration, campaigns seem to have lost the opinion that texts are entirely, or even significantly, controllable once they are in the world. While campaigns may have once gotten away with presenting slightly different views to various populations, or going to extremely partisan rallies without hopes of upsetting moderate voters, digital technologies have changed those assumptions. Currently, campaigns see the potential for radical publicity within any message they post to a website, send to an email list, or say at small public events. Explaining the difficulties in controlling a campaign's message in an era of digital media, one communications consultant simply warns, "Nothing is private. When you send an email to a list, it's out there. .... It can be printed on the front page of the *New York Times*."[1] Another specializing in digital strategy acknowledges the loss of power, saying: "The fact is that on the Internet, any pretense of being able to control that is a lie."[2] These conditions are a double-edged sword for campaigns, allowing them to reach an incredible amount of people, and running the risk of the wrong message getting to these same individuals.

There is no shortage of campaigns that have experienced this publicity firsthand, and now stand as cautionary tales. In the 2008 presidential race, Barack Obama was reminded of the difficulties controlling a message after telling a small crowd of supporters in California that voters in the Midwest cling to guns and religion, and ending up in a firestorm of accusations of elitism. Mitt Romney's 2012 "47%" comments are often argued to be the event that lost him the presidency. This does not pertain only to presidential candidates, either. In 2010, Republican Robert Dold, eventual winner of Illinois's heavily contested 10th Congressional District, found himself in hot water when an obscure Tea Party magazine claimed he "requested not to be rated by the magazine in an effort to appear more moderate" and news organizations reported on the implications that he was hiding something.[3] In one campaign a communications director recounted the days she spent lamenting her inclusion of "one stupid sentence" of a press release that garnered negative publicity from local blogs, partisan bloggers who were usually advocates for the candidate, and eventually national press. This single sentence became a two-day news story that she herself had to walk back.[4] In light of the ease with which this can happen to any campaign, maintaining a tight grip on information is often seen as a necessity. A common practice within the communications office was the temporary embargoing of the campaign's own content. "Let me decide if we want to press that event or not" was a common reaction to a suggestion to publish a story on social media platforms.[5] No longer does "pressing" an event necessarily mean actively driving content toward the press. In a digital environment, simply releasing information into the world via social media can often have the same effects.

The ease with which information travels—so long as it's the right kind of information—benefits campaigns as well, and leads to a grudging optimism. Campaigns can release and circulate information to highly targeted populations, for fractions of the cost of television or direct mail advertising. A candidate's positions and stances are widely available and easily locatable on the official campaign websites, and many have argued that it is easier than

ever for newcomers to get the information they want.[6] In addition to pushing information directly to potential voters, digital media equip campaigns
with new methods of reaching reporters. By and large, campaigns can see
some payoff in this turn of events, despite their fears. "Everything that you
say off-hand can be tweeted or Facebooked," begins one communication
director who recognizes both the appeal and the risk of this turn, "and you
can look at that as a bad thing or you can look at that as a very powerful
opportunity."[7]

Of course, some of this optimism can be seen as enabling myths that strategically situate consultants' work within contemporary discourses that lav-
ish praise on systems and interactions that are seen as open and enabling
of public deliberation.[8] After all, free and open space for deliberation is a
normative criterion for what constitutes democracy itself. Additionally, the
act of engaging in rational critical deliberation is a centerpiece for how we
understand political participation or what counts as "strong democracy."[9]
Political professionals' claims of strong democracy are more than lip service, too. Changes in how campaigns claim to value deliberative discussion
are occurring, along with actual changes to the levels of control campaigns
are willing to cede. In some cases, these changes appear to be purposeful,
though controversial. In others, they appear to be the result of unintended
consequences, such as limited resources or the adoption of certain digital
tools, the evolving affordances of which could not have been known. As
campaigns cautiously move into this world of radical publicity, the rules
concerning how to interact with citizens are far from cut and dried. While
staffers and consultants universally point to standard legal language posted
on social media sites that announces their right to police egregiously inappropriate content, deciding what counts as egregious falls to the communications office, and the term is interpreted in any number of ways. While the
spaces controlled by campaigns are usually viewed as anathema to deliberative politics, the 2010 midterm elections marked a moment in time during
which the tension between control and deliberation seemed to be especially
confounding, and began a move away from many traditional, strong forms
of control campaigns relied on in the past. The wrestling with whether and
how to control conversations that occurred in 2010 and years since simultaneously leaves openings for deliberation and political talk, while also fac-
ing the prohibitions placed on open communication. It is this process of
navigating what content to police that illuminates the changing nature of
control within campaigns. The question then becomes, how are campaigns'

attempts to control messages changing, and what are the normative implications of those changes?

In these the processes of campaign communication, there are myriad ways that campaigns relinquish control and open up dialogue, from enabling comments on blog posts, to allowing people to post on their Facebook pages, to asking specific and deliberate questions that spur discussion across digital media. Moreover, as campaigns use popular social media tools to reach out to citizens, their attempts to control discussion are often at the mercy of these tools' designers. Still, to argue that campaigns are simply careening down a path toward the absence of control is to oversimplify things. Instead, this chapter emphasizes how the effects of personnel choices and organizational hierarchies within campaigns, combined with the adoption of specific digital technologies, have placed campaigns within certain sets of constraints and affordances regarding control. Investigating campaigns' use of social media in 2010—especially Facebook—this chapter sheds light on campaign staffers and consultants' strategies of control and the role of flexible tools that allowed for a range of options for controlling messages that changed over time. Additionally, even within a flexible system, this chapter focuses on the impact of the evolution of campaigns' organizational structure—from a communications-dominated world to one where digital strategists play a powerful role—on the goals of campaign control. Ultimately, campaigns used social media tools in ways that made a significant move away from traditional, *overt control*, which involves the direct censorship of comments. Rather than relinquishing control entirely, they moved toward new methods of control that have varying levels of openness. These forms of control were adopted by a combination of changes to normative ideals of transparency in online spaces as well as unforeseen advances in the affordances of common, publicly produced communication technologies campaigns. Thus, even when campaigns are reluctant to give up control, they are forced to either change the forms of control they engage in or acquiesce. Most commonly, upon realizing that overt control is not as productive in a digital environment, campaigns moved on to *discreet control*, which involves disabling some interactive features of digital media and enabling back-end controls that allow for control without having to publicly erase content or completely prohibit interaction with citizens. Campaigns that were and continue to be more dedicated to openness engage in *indirect control*, which involves allowing for the actions associated with deliberation—spaces to voice opinions, disagree, and engage in reciprocal communication—while also exerting great power in setting an agenda that is of strategic benefit to the campaign regardless of topics' importance to the public. These forms of control exist on a continuum, and though campaign practices sometimes skirt the line between forms of control, the three categories are important insofar as they offer insight into differences in potential ramifications contained by attempts at control.

Overt Control

To say that there are shifting norms of control in the campaign environment is not to claim the absence of control. Overt forms of control such as the direct censorship of content were, on the contrary, on display in 2010. In fact, its many forms—the policing and deletion of comments on Facebook pages, campaign blogs, or websites; completely ignoring the feedback of citizens; and the like—are still available to campaigns. The women whose story opened this chapter were, after all, still banned from a candidates' social media page, and others like them experienced the same fate. Despite the ease of exerting overt control over content, the approaches to, excuses for, and conditions of its use are changing.

Even as campaigns exert overt forms of control, they show their lack of comfort with the idea as they continuously jump through rhetorical hoops to justify their practices. Most commonly, communications directors, consultants, and staffers draw a distinction between content that is "only" negative and therefore allowable, versus that which is counterproductive or "over the line," which campaigns are not only allowed to, but obliged to, delete. Explaining this, one communications director asserts, "Anything that was lewd or inappropriate, that we would remove. But we really did allow opposing viewpoints."[10] Another communications director, acknowledging that his campaign did, on occasion, delete citizen-produced comments, defines the act of censorship not as removing any content, but as removing a specific type of content. "We didn't really censor anything. Unless it literally was vulgar and whatever—there's no place for that. But we weren't really concerned about negative comments."[11] For him and other staffers, the act of censorship only existed in cases where content was acceptable, but was still taken down.

Of course, in practice, the line between "unacceptable" and "merely negative" is never clearly defined, and leaves campaigns with much leeway in their decisions regarding what to allow. One communications director ratio-nalizes the erasure of some negative content, so long as some amount of the oppositional side is represented: "We have the right to cut them out if they're unnecessarily harsh, but we let a couple through just to show the balance."[12] Some make distinctions between censorship policies deemed acceptable of campaigns and elected officials. One communication director who's worked on both sides of this line describes it this way:

> When you're elected and people are saying things you don't like, you kind of—you have to listen to them because you represent them and you give them a forum as long as you feel is necessary before they get inappropriate. . . . But when you're a candidate, you're not really beholden to anyone. . . . If it's just going to be like "You stink and so does your campaign," then I have no problem with a cam-paign just ripping that down, because it's our campaign, and there are real consequences.[13]

Going beyond drawing out the differences between appropriate and inap-propriate content, this approach also draws a distinction between content that argues or opposes an issue, and content that merely inflames, without the possibility for debate. For instance, describing one genre of insult that is widely seen as perfectly within range to delete, a communications consul-tant explains, "You get all caps, 'OBAMA IS A MUSLIM,' . . . we have to watch out for that sort of thing and take it off the page. I mean, it's unacceptable."[14] Others, however, may decide to leave something up if they feel it helps their case by reflecting poorly on their opposition. Arguments over what counts as questionable content rely on how much negative content already exists, who creates it, whether it was posted in government or campaign site, and so on.[15] Campaigns make these decisions strategically, rather than with clear moral stances in mind, but the strategic equations are changing, and these decisions are now up for grabs. In the event that opened this chapter—the two women who took to a candidate's Facebook page to argue against the candidate's stance on an issue—many of the staffers held different opinions on whether or not they should leave the comments up. Some voiced strategic concerns about a possible backlash, but others noted that the two women were actu-ally just providing counterarguments, not acting particularly aggressive or obscene. The communications director, who had a background in traditional press-oriented background, made the call to take the comments down quickly.

When questions about how much control should be wielded do arise, organizational divides usually occur along professional fault lines; those with traditional communications or press backgrounds on one side, and those who have come up as digital specialists on the other. In 2010, campaigns' hiring of digital directors shook up the usual organizational flow of campaigns. Whether campaigns hired digital directors—either with equal power as communications directors, or under their supervision—or just an individual to handle digital communications, the change in organizational structure of communications came with a change in how staffers understood the role of communication within a campaign. While the rule does not hold for each and every person with a press background or everyone coming from the digital side, the former are more likely to openly speak about the need to exert overt control over outside content, while the latter are much more likely to express their desire to let all content exist.

Communications directors, in particular spoke matter-of-factly about the need to exert control, discussing the campaigns' "right" to take down content, even as they argue they do not do so often. "My general rule said this is an open forum; however, it is still ours," begins the same communications director who voiced her willingness to "rip" unproductive comments down. "This is not owned by the people, this is our Facebook forum. We are providing it as a courtesy. We don't have to provide it."[16] Another echoes this practice with less deliberation: "You want an accurate reflection of the dialogue that's going on, but in communications you always want to make yourself look as good as possible. . . . People say you're not authentic, that you're putting up a facade. Well, the truth is that all campaigns are a facade."[17] As one consultant asserts: "That's the one thing that campaigns are sort of obsessed with: 'We have to control the message, we have to control the message.' "[18]

Idealistic (or perhaps naive) as it may sound, most digital hires expressed a different view. Those who came from a programming or digital analytics background saw technology as a tool that should be used for open communication, even as they understood the need for the campaign to get its message out. Even as they used these same tools to microtarget citizens and provide them with highly specialized information, they expressed discomfort with using them to take down citizens' contributions or hide information. "I come from sort of the generational culture, the tech culture, whatever," begins one such digital director, "that believes in more openness and more transparency. Put everything that you have out there and let people hash it out. Whereas the comms shop comes from the opposite culture: 'Don't say anything unless you have to.' "[19] One digital consultant discusses the fact that what she calls "old school" campaigns simply have to come to grips with the realities of diminishing control, saying: "They have to learn that the stuff is more decentralized and you can't control it." Emphasizing that campaigns must accept this even if it makes their lives more difficult, she goes on: "You can sort of facilitate [the message], but you're just not going to have 100% control anymore."[20] Navigating the first cycle in which digital directors were, in some cases, given a seat at the table that was equal to that of communications directors put these diverging perspectives on display. One communications director described the underlying issues that caused frustration in the campaign, arguing that the digital department often had differing views on what counted as on-message and did not want to delete outside content. His digital director, however, expressed her frustration at the resistance she encountered trying to mobilize the base through a variety of digital platforms. Not only were the red-meat attacks he thought the base would respond to off-limits, but he was also told that many online grassroots venues were too partisan to push news to or try to gain coverage from.[21] With consultants like these two having an equal seat at the table, it was not always clear when "communications strategy" trumped "digital strategy," or vice versa, and arguments erupted over what to publish and where to do so, as well as what to censor.

Perhaps a sign that practices of control will change as new media directors are brought to equal standing, digital specialists often voice their displeasure with communications departments' haste to delete comments. "I don't get it. It makes you look bad. And people *will* notice. Not just reporters . . . but the other side. They can take a screen grab and you end up on some [opposition] blog about how you're not transparent, you hide things." Adds another, "Frankly, I think organizations that don't realize that are going to be left behind." [22] And, despite some campaigns' refusal to allow divergent perspectives on their social media pages (see figure 6.1 for an example of content that was quickly deleted), it seems as if communications directors are slowly coming around. Not only does oppositional content live on the social media pages and websites of most campaigns, but more experienced consultants agree that "some campaigns, they're outdated in their refusal to allow anything through."[23]

As campaigns begin to step away from methods of overt control, to assume they do so purely out of dedication to democratic ideals is foolhardy. As digital media have exposed these forms of control, they are increasingly

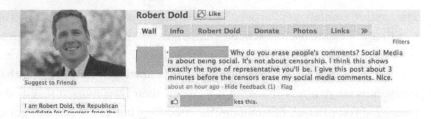

Figure 6.1 A citizen takes the Dold for Congress campaign to task for wielding overt control. Because of the ease with which such actions could be monitored and publicized by opponents, overt control became less helpful to campaigns in 2010.

distasteful to the public, and therefore reap the negative consequences that were previously absent (or at least less likely) from prior attempts at control. The potential downsides are many and were at the forefront of campaigns' minds during the election. Campaigns not only emphasized the fact that the act of deleting comments makes them seem untrustworthy and inauthentic, they also cited specific ways that doing so could blow up in a campaign's face. Some focused on the potential for negative publicity, saying things like: "People would begin to hate that if you [censored lots of content]. You don't want to do that. People will talk about that."[24] Another stressed the fact that in a digital environment, where both citizens and the opposing campaign can stake out your website or Facebook page and wait for a misstep, people will definitely find out if you engage in this behavior, and will publicize it.[25] And this concern is warranted—the amount of time campaigns spend on opponents' web pages and analyzing their communication is astonishing, and emails concerning the content of opponents' sites is routine, to the point of receiving multiple updates on the opposition's content daily.[26] Moreover, if and when publicized, these practices could take a campaign much farther off message than some silly comment, as happened to some campaigns. Even just changing one's position on an issue becomes a moment that can be documented with before and after screen grabs to illustrate someone's potential flip-flopping or pandering to voters. Additionally, one communication director described the backlash from citizens that deletions caused. "They came back stronger, we learned not to do that quickly."[27] Describing running into these problems as a trial-and-error approach to moderating, a communications director notes, "We found that if you try to filter, it causes more problems. It creates more problems than if you just let it all out there. . . . It was a learning process for me."[28] In cases where an active virtual opposition can result in being overrun by attacks on a campaign's own turf, the downsides to relinquishing control have also become even more painfully apparent. Tidal waves of opponents hit the Facebook walls of Jan Schakowsky (D, 9th District), Melissa Bean (D, 8th District), Phil Hare (D, 17th District), and Debbie Halvorson (D, 11th District). To delete content or block citizens often riled up these activists more, who would then highlight and criticize the censorship that was occurring and succeed doubly. In one such instance, a citizen posted, "I wrote something earlier today that disappeared. What I basically said was, when are we going to start getting [the candidate's] mailings." This was met with the disgruntled response from another citizen: "Typical, this campaign does not really communicate well. They are so watered-down with their message to win more votes."[29] As these strong measures of control gain greater risks, campaigns turn to less observable forms of control.

Discreet Control

As the risks of censoring content rise and acts of strong control have become more noticeable and are easily made public, other, more covert forms of control are still quite popular. Discreet control makes use of technologies' material capabilities on the back end, in spaces prior to what is seen by the public, in order to police citizen-produced content and control the information people encounter in secret. This means that discreet control can take place on two fronts: prohibiting people from engaging in certain interactions and controlling what is immediately available to them. In doing so, it also exerts control over the possibility of the public seeing censorship firsthand, and is thus a widely used alternative to strong control mechanisms. Although it avoids many of the pitfalls of strong control, it allows for a similarly intense level of policing content and is no more "authentic" than its more observable counterpart.

Although they are often shielded from the general public, discreet forms of control related to targeted messaging and advertising practices have been the subject of recent attention from political communication researchers. While targeting, or sending different messages to specific populations, has long been a norm of campaigns within media, as simple as speeches or direct mail, digital media enable this practice to an even greater degree. Because digital media allow for more accurate information to be gathered about citizens, and more specific channels through which to deliver content, targeting—and microtargeting—is seen as a problematic form of controlling content at two levels. On one hand, campaigns are able, through the help of both private and nonprofit organizations, to gather vast amounts of information about citizens. In doing so, they are able to better understand who will be persuaded or mobilized by what types of appeals, what issues, and segment their messages appropriately, amounting to what has been dubbed political redlining, or removing swaths of content from citizens' view. Additionally, with the rise of online advertising across a variety of platforms, and the ability to design websites so different content appears for different users, these messages can be sent specifically to desired populations. These practices of microtargeting are problematic insofar as they shape and confine the types and content of information people access.[30] A middle-aged housewife in Louisiana will likely be met by different content than a man in his early thirties who lives in a major metropolitan area when they both search out the website of major political parties or highly publicized races.[31] More importantly, this control becomes more powerful—and more problematic—because it can be exercised without informing its audiences of such differences. Both people in this example are likely to be none the wiser to these differences. In exercising this form of discreet control, campaigns hinder the circulation of common texts among large swaths of the public, and impede the development of a public that is informed on a diverse array of policies and issues. As Cass Sunstein and Nicholas Negroponte have argued, not only can people access a personalized version of the news they call the *Daily Me*, but people are force-fed this specialized and echoic content.[32] Just as these practices have definitely been seen in the previous election cycles, they are par for the course currently as well. Arguing against critics of this move, one communications director who "of course" tried to optimize content so that it would reach targeted populations notes, "And you know people go, 'Oh, that's so Big Brother.'" It's like, yeah, but people provide this information. It's not like we're snooping into their file cabinet.[33]

Although it is a less-studied phenomenon, campaigns also use discreet control to prevent content from entering the public. Similar to the strong control exercised when deleting posted comments from public view, campaigns have taken to controlling this content behind the scenes in order to escape the potential publicity that can come from censoring content in public. Unlike overt control mechanisms, they do not completely disallow interaction and input from citizens, but use the affordances of widely available tools to ensure they can filter, hide, or highlight content. In one particularly widespread use of this form of control, comments on blogs or message boards must be approved before they are published, thereby allowing campaigns not only to erase message-derailing information, but to prevent it from ever seeing the light of public discussion. By prohibiting content from reaching the public, campaigns undertake a form of discreet control that bears many similarities to strong control, while avoiding publicizing their exertion of power. While this practice is widespread among campaigns—and perhaps part of the reason that many campaign blog posts and websites are lacking in comments—it is also a practice of many advocacy organizations, which explicitly solicit content of people, and then selects specific examples to publicize. In a similar tactic in back-end control, campaigns can set social media privacy to allow for a number of levels of interactivity. Rather than allow anyone to post on a Facebook page, message board, or comment on a blog, campaigns can limit both the type of people who can post (i.e., no one, only registered users, specifically allowed political groups, "friends" or "fans," etc.) as well as the spaces where people can post (posting original content vs. only replying to posts produced by the campaign, or only on certain posts, etc.).[34] Any combination of these variables amounts to a different space on the continuum of control, and does so without resorting to deleting content.

In 2010, this form of control was not only popular (9 out of 16 of those in the greater Chicago area restricted the social media spaces in which people could post to some degree[35]), but was easily allowed by the campaign technologies most commonly employed. At the time, administrators of Facebook pages—the most common tool of the digital media staffers—could easily decide who, if anyone, could post responses to the campaign's posts or add content directly to a campaign's wall. Most often—and as is still the case—if citizens could post on a campaign's page at all, they were allowed to post responses or comments on content posted by the campaign, rather than post their own original content directly to the campaign page.[36] Moreover, while most candidates allowed people to post messages to their Facebook wall, the default setting on their pages was overwhelmingly set to show the public the voices of the campaign prior to those of citizens. At the time of the 2010 election, there was an option for pages to be set to first display posts only by the campaign, but readers could also click on a tab that made posts from everyone visible. While accessible, this content is only seen after taking one extra step, and may not be accessible by those who are of lesser skill level. Two campaigns that did allow people to post original content and highlighted this content by displaying it as their default setting were Republican congressional candidate Bobby Schilling and Independent gubernatorial candidate Scott Lee Cohen. This setting is in the campaign's control, and can be changed at any time. After the election, some campaigns opened up control—Mark Kirk (R, Senate), for instance, made his default set to public (and campaign) comments in the months following his victory. While far from censorship, this restriction does determine the prominence of citizen's comments on the page. Although people are free to write whatever they like, the convention of posting content that is responsive to that posted by the campaign is also amplified when this manner of control is exerted.

While campaigns exert their control over these features, there are still many things out of their control when using a third-party platform such as Facebook or Twitter. Illustrating the fact that changes in organizational practices are socio-technical in nature, change to the organizational structure of campaigns was not the only driver of changes in practices; changes in technology contributed as well. When the company introduces changes to the platform layout of affordances, these options may either be highlighted or made obsolete, possibly affecting influence over how and when campaigns choose to execute these various levels of control. Since the 2010 campaign began, changes to the very tools campaigns use have changed, forcing campaigns to accommodate new norms. Most notably, in 2011 Facebook prohibited a type of discreet control that allowed administrators of public pages close comments all together. Thus if campaigns are to use Facebook—basically a necessity in today's political landscape—they will necessarily offer a space where citizens can talk back. With the move away from overt control accepted by campaigns and opportunities for discreet control removed from the equation regardless of campaigns' willingness, the socio-technical evolution of the mechanisms of control has moved swiftly in the two cycles of 2010 and 2012.

Although campaigns' deployment of discreet control is less likely to be recognized and subsequently publicly condemned as inauthentic or hiding something, it performs many of the same functions as strong control. It allows the private deletion of citizen-produced content, and institutes invisible barriers to both the creation and consumption of information. As a result, when campaigns feel the traditional means of control they once had over campaign communications slipping away or becoming too risky to engage, their attempts to "just try to be pragmatic about the conversations happening online" often result in less public (but often quite direct) forms of control.[37]

Together, strong and discreet control make up the traditional approach to managing campaign messages, but these measures still leave room for a level of relinquished control that campaigns are either unprepared for or unwilling to tolerate. Additionally, with digital technologies enabling conversations and discussions among citizens, and a number of consultants and staffers seeming to legitimately desire this deliberative environment, these forms of control are prohibitive of the interactivity that both sides have come to expect from digital texts. Consequently, a final form of control has arisen as the latest method by which to engage members of the public while maintaining some degree of management over the content.

Indirect Control

Even in light of these opportunities and the continued need to control messages, campaigns are serious about encouraging deliberation and debate because of their strategic benefits of building communities, as discussed in the previous chapter. In order to allow for these actions without completely relinquishing their grip on messaging, campaigns are engaging in indirect control. This method of exercising power over messages attempts to shape public discourse through various agenda-setting tactics, rather than prohibiting content like strong and discreet control. Within a model of indirect control, campaigns often encourage discussion and debate and voice large concern about deleting anything but the most vitriolic language, but do so while making the topics of discussion relatively "safe," and cultivating a culture wherein supporters argue on their behalf to counter off-message content.

Changing the topic of conversation to "safe" topics can take many forms. Even before citizens' voices are part of the equation, campaigns go to great lengths to ensure that the content they produce matches the issues they want to highlight. In addition to the polling data that goes into crafting or refining an overall messaging strategy, the everyday content of campaigns is also determined by qualities of timeliness and relevance to local/national events, interestingness, and avoiding controversy within its virtual audience. Once the topic is decided, there are rounds of edits. Words are combed over with an attention to detail usually reserved for press releases, mass emails, and more buttoned-up media texts. The candidate's name is added to the text more times; contractions are made into two words. Multiple drafts go through the communications director until finally a social media message that is both on-message and designed to keep others on-message is published.[38] By giving such close attention to online messaging and opening up space for conversation and discussion in venues such as message boards, Facebook posts, blog comments, or responses via Twitter, campaigns are able to focus on content they want to be in public discussion, rather than risk going off message.

Methods of discreet control often enable technologies of deliberation and mechanisms for feedback that are responsive to campaign content, rather than allowing for completely original posts. As these discussions are responsive, campaigns can lead citizens to discuss and debate certain topics and stay away from others. Describing the campaign's consideration of what type of response its social media content would receive before posting it, one communications director notes: "We don't want to set ourselves up for situations where it would be easy for people to just bomb us."[39] First and foremost, this means avoiding discussion of polarizing topics or those that would incite the online ire of opponents. "We can foster debate about something that we want and we know that it'll probably go in the right direction. Other times, it's just kind of fostering a debate over more lighter subjects that are less contentious," explains one consultant, who shied away from hot-button issues, noting, "If we're going to foster a debate, it won't be about abortion."[40] While the issues that count as controversial vary according to district, attempts were made to avoid topics that would alienate the audiences within a specific district and within their specifically digital audience across all regions. As a result, issues that are generally polarizing are not the only risky topics for digital messaging. Sometimes, moderate positions can incite fringe groups on both sides of the aisle, including those who share a candidate's own party affiliation. Describing a moderate candidate's predicament, one consultant explained, "During the primary, we got almost nothing but vitriol on our Facebook page. It was almost all negative, all the time. And so to control that, we did not put every single statement on Facebook," noting that "you put those [moderate positions] in the mainstream press, but you don't put it online."[41] This is often due to the perception that the population of online activists is more extreme (either to the right or left) than the general voting public. High-profile movements such as MoveOn.org, with its roots in the anti–Iraq War movement, and the Tea Party's use of online technologies support this fear, although it is by no means the only place from which criticism stems. Whether moderate candidates would get more negative feedback from their own side or across the aisle depends on the specific case, and many communications directors for moderate candidates emphasized the need to rein in the base-directed online messages because of the potentially negative feedback from across the aisle. Fighting the urge to go too "red meat" with an online message, one communications director emphasized that despite the heavy presence of the party base online, digital content can't be more radical than the core campaign message: "There were a couple of times where I'd say, this is too much, we have to pull that back." So, while one campaign spoke about how it wouldn't list moderate events on an interactive map on the campaign website or check in on Foursquare, others noted how difficult it was to make decisions about whether to highlight their presence at highly partisan rallies or endorsements.[42] In either case, they exerted indirect control through their choices of when and how to engage the available tools.

In some races, the potential of being hit from both sides can feel paralyzing. In one very close and high-profile race, a campaign staffer devoted a week to creating an interactive map and cataloging the candidate's previous and upcoming appearances, only to have the map never go live, because of concerns over how moderate swing voters and strong members of the base would feel about the wide array of appearances being highlighted. After being told to assemble a list of the month's event's for a supporter e-newsletter, one staffer's assumption that they would use the entire list for the newsletter was met with incredulity, because he didn't understand that only a few on-message events would be publicized. Frequently, this fear of inciting negative feedback results in campaigns' reluctance to post content about issues in general. As one communications director confessed, "Any time we dabbled with actual policy on Facebook it was disaster."[43] While press releases and campaign websites are full of issue-based content, digital texts facilitate or have different norms. As discussed in chapter 5, a wealth of "behind the scenes" or retail politics coverage can serve this purpose; pictures of candidates kissing babies and shaking hands with the elderly are less controversial than policy speeches, and while it's just as easy to comment negatively on a picture, it is more difficult to comment negatively in a way that responds to the image and stays on topic.

While setting the agenda for feedback and discussion, many campaigns go so far as to ask citizens specific questions in order to facilitate a greater degree of interaction. "We do that with our email list a lot," reports one digital media staffer. "We definitely get a lot of feedback and we usually give the results. 'What do you think about,' for example, 'what's going on in Iraq?' Support or oppose, or whatever, and then we would actually calculate all the people's responses and put a graph up."[44] Most of the time, these questions concerned issues that the campaign expected to "win" on, and often policy points the campaign has polling data on that allow them to know citizens—either generally, or targeted populations—will agree with them.

> You get a response when you put a question mark on the end. People see it in their news feed or . . . on Facebook and it's almost like it's a question to you. . . . If you have an opinion on it, you're going to express it. And that's a good thing. And I learned this as we went along, but on Facebook, it's very helpful when you actually have a discussion going on. It puts you up higher [in people's news feeds].[45]

Even when using tactics of agenda setting and leading discussion to certain "safe" topic areas, citizens have many opportunities to derail a campaign's intended message. There is nothing stopping people from bringing up topics that are unrelated to those posted by the campaign, or from directly (and loudly) questioning or disagreeing with the policy being discussed. A specific tactic of issue-focused activists has, in fact, been to post their grievances or desires on every available space for comment, regardless of its fit for the conversation taking place in that venue. News articles or press releases focused on the economy can become the site of someone advocating for gay rights, a post about environmental policy can become a space to question a candidate's character. Moreover, in cases where people may only be allowed to respond to campaign content, rather than create their own original comment on a Facebook page, responding in this forum displays citizens' ability to avoid the elements of control levied against them.[46] As campaigns relinquish this control over messages, rather than simply prevent people from posting oppositional or message-damaging content, they have come to rely on supporters to come to the defense of candidates' positions or actions.

Deliberation and debate are much more electorally productive when campaigns know they have support on their side, and fostering a culture in which these supporters are active and vocal is a productive way to indirectly manage public discourses without resorting to direct control of content. Moreover, it fosters active engagement that has been shown to correlate to additional mobilization such as voting or donating money, while also holding out the possibility of persuading others. Some campaigns were quite proactive in their attempts to foster this behavior. A digital strategist who handles multiple campaigns' online content describes his proactive approach, saying, "We try to make it happen. We'll try to help the campaign organize some of their volunteers to be sort of online volunteers, so to speak."[47] This is especially helpful if many from the opposition side get heavily involved. "We'll immediately go into full recruit mode for getting more of our like-minded people to join the page to balance it out," says one consultant, noting how these volunteers also then become closer with the campaign: "Sometimes we'll call them ambassadors if we start to note we can trust them, so they can help disseminate the message and respond to negative criticism."[48] Even when campaigns did not have the time or resources to request this action of supporters, members of the campaign often tried to create an environment that welcomed this behavior. "We'll go to into the comment section and we'll answer people's questions that they have and we'll interact with them," said one political organizer, adding, "We say, 'If you're interested in this topic, you should check out this topic as well, or an organization that shares our position on that topic.' "[49] In being able to enter into a debate where citizens have already countered oppositional arguments, campaigns can avoid having to exclusively play defense in digital media forums. While this approach is productive, some campaigns have run into problems in this area because they are open to criticisms of engaging in pseudo-organic activism such as grasstops organizing or sockpuppeting.[50] News of one such instance broke in Chicago area election news when a communications director for a congressional race accidentally included a local reporter in an email asking supporters to please email letters to the editor and comment on various local blogs using specific, campaign-produced language.[51] Even those that did not premeditate their use of these networks of supporters have found them quite helpful in tamping down negative or harmful discussion. "You've got to assume your surrogates and your supporters are going to be out there advocating for you," says one communications director, and another saw social media pages themselves as most beneficial for supporters who were excited to engage in conversations and debates about the campaign and politics in general, saying, "It gave our good supporters resources."[52] Some were even surprised by how vocal and helpful to controlling the message citizens could be, as one communications director relayed the shock he felt when he began to see them come to the campaign's rescue, exclaiming, "They *really* back you up!"[53]

Citizens Who Talk Back

The fact that campaigns see their control as weakening should be no surprise—the actions they have always engaged in are becoming less socially acceptable, and the rules of engagement on the electoral battleground are being rewritten before their eyes. This rewriting, however, is done both by campaigns themselves via changes in their own professional organization, and by technologies over which they have no control. Whether campaigns consciously considered how the adoption of popular tools or the addition of new tiers of campaign leadership would impact their ability to wield control over public discourse or not, the unintended consequences of both social and technical change are clear. Still, digital campaigns are not the open and radically democratic spaces they are sometimes argued to be. Control's impact on campaigns and on citizenship is complex; within the presence of all three forms of control (strong, discreet, and indirect) attitudes toward each are changing. People's often contrary voices are increasingly published in a public forum that is potentially damaging to campaigns' bottom line of winning elections. Simultaneously, this allows campaigns to perform democratic ideals of transparency and deliberation. Even as they bemoan their loss of power, campaigns also show off and explicitly highlight their authenticity and dedication to the open debate and disagreement.

By viewing this shift purely as a reduction of control, campaigns and scholars alike ignore, whether intentionally or not, the very real ways in which control is being redefined. These redefinitions, in turn, contain very real ramifications for the way we see and engage in politics. Since they are a mixed bag of opening and closing avenues for participation, to mark these changes as solely productive or regressive oversimplifies their consequences. As citizens participate within spaces that are the site of indirect control, they are simultaneously provided more possibilities to engage as they please and provided a circumscribed set of spaces in which their participation is easily executed, and even encouraged. As citizens do, in fact, talk back, campaigns are forced to answer to new participants in the deliberative public. While campaigns have always had to answer to claims made by the opposition and by the press, they now are subject to citizens who are constantly given the opportunity to talk back. Sometimes a response is as simple as wielding the option for overt control and deleting content; other campaigns may rely on their own digital army to take on these new voices. In either case, citizens who talk back demand some sort of answer or response, even when it is not made publicly.

Through these spaces, citizens are met with potential increases in deliberation and voicing opinions via networked politics that exist simultaneously with a possible move away from the substantive, controversial issues that are in need of deliberation and debate. On one hand, there is a definite move toward allowing for and even fostering public deliberation and debate, and sites of engagement enabled by campaigns foster what Dryzek has labeled a "discursive design" or "a social institution around which the expectations of a number of actors converge."[54] These sites exhibit the necessary preconditions of deliberative practice, increasing and making available information, allowing the expression of arguments, and involving challengeable conclusions in the form of candidates' stances on issues of policy. By asking questions of citizens, and even training people to engage in voicing their opinions and countering political opposition, campaigns are providing a forum (and in some cases, instruction) to engage in these deliberatively democratic practices. As Seyla Benhabib relays a central tenet of theories of deliberative democracy, "The more collective decision-making processes approximate this model, the more [it] increases the presumption of their legacy."[55] Moreover, this fosters interactions that hold the potential to be more prolonged and less ephemeral than speaking in a public square. The relative stability of these dialogues and debates then leads to even greater potential for the informative benefit of deliberation, because deliberation itself is likely to make "individuals become more aware of such conflicts and feel compelled to undertake a more coherent ordering."[56] Even if these interactions do not always reach the standards of informed discussion or civil disagreement that are integral to some deliberative democrats, their presence is a further move toward encouraging a traditional measure of civic participation. Moreover, the act of communicating one's beliefs and opinions in public is more than a good in and of itself; it is seen as a way to encourage citizens to take future participatory action. Performing the actions of deliberation within a constrained environment can still be helpful to future political action. Thus, the networked politics discussed in chapter 4 are activated in this dynamic of deliberation and control. Campaigns often value online action as a means to the offline actions of volunteering or ultimately voting, and engaging people in conversation and deliberation connects people to the campaign and to politics in general. Thus, this move to foster deliberation and discussion online is simultaneously the means and end to an increase in political participation.

On the other hand, the issues that are the focus of deliberation and debate are of great importance too, and the forms of control campaigns currently exert are heavily focused on deciding content and setting the agenda in their favor. As a result, consultants pridefully proclaim a move toward "uncontroversial" topics that won't stir up strong opinions. Even when asking people's perspectives on a topic, and assuming some degree of disagreement, "debate" is fomented around topics campaigns feel they are on the right side of and have their constituents' support. This phenomenon, though it drives conversation away from pertinent issues much the way infotainment is alleged to do, acts more perniciously. Rather than being upfront about their lack of relevance to ongoing controversies, debates and discussions that campaigns encourage in social media are constructed to retain the form of deliberative democracy while glossing over the fact that their content is purposefully ineffective. Performing a false kind of openness conceals the control that is exerted, making it difficult for citizens to make claims on the need for open communication.

This approach, despite the fact that it literally raises questions, inhibits the goal of producing argument in favor of demonstrating a favorable position and affirming the positions of supporters. It is certainly not without the potential for upending, but it decisively attempts to produce a nondeliberative outcome within the form of deliberation. Citizens, if they are to engage in deliberation and debate outside the safe arenas proscribed by campaigns, must make purposeful attempts to raise questions other than those publicized by campaigns. Thus, while it is a mistake to ignore the very real deliberative and participatory possibilities offered by the turn toward indirect control, it is also of utmost importance to take sober account of lengths to which campaigns go to mitigate dissenting discourses—even when such discourse takes the form of a so-called ideal of contemporary democracy. In any case, rather than seeing this turn of events as an instance of campaign messaging, it should be understood as new norm of the contemporary campaign environment. Within the presence of all three forms of control (strong, discreet, and indirect), attitudes toward each are changing. The move toward greater use of indirect control reflects changes in how campaigns work and how participation can be enacted, and the fact that deliberative ideals and norms of control are not in direct opposition with one another.

7

Conclusion

Constructions of Citizenship Moving Forward

Somewhere right now, campaign communications offices are abuzz. They are drafting press releases that link to microsites and third-party fact-check groups, tacking on requests to pass campaign content along to friends in an email or social media message, monitoring discourses around their candidates while encouraging some forms of deliberation, asking citizens to participate in campaigns in new ways, and informing them about candidates' policy platforms and more humanizing characteristics. While the platforms they use to execute these tasks and the tactics deployed to do so may change, those strategies and messages will continue to tell us about our current position in democratic society, about what it means to be political.

In the short time from 2010 to now, changes to the technological landscape, the solidification of social norms across existing platforms, and the capabilities of campaign staffers brought onto campaigns all contributed to further changes to campaign strategies and subsequent constructions of citizenship. In most ways, the changes that began to emerge in 2010 and are enumerated in this volume have been reinforced. In 2012, national and local campaigns alike used microsites, social media was filled with interpersonal content and digital retail politics in 2014, and the ability to share content and users' propensity to do so has only grown since 2010. These changes show more than shifts in technical capabilities or new campaign tactics; they speak to new approaches to information and participation broadly. Additionally, in the years since 2010, additional emergent trends have developed. By comparing these disruptions and ongoing changes to traditional campaign practices, we can better understand how campaigns themselves are changing as well as how traditional understandings of campaign communication are evolving. Together, these emergent practices reveal contemporary understandings of citizenship that are more than merely utopian or dystopian, and a campaign landscape full of new practices and approaches.

From Emergent to Established

The emergent practices and subsequent norms of citizenship outlined here continued to take shape and solidify through the 2012 election. Their establishment was often simultaneously fostered and complicated by the constantly changing technical affordances of many of the tools and platforms used for digital messaging, a desire to mimic strategies that seem to work for others, and occasional interpersonal disagreements among staffers and consultants about how to best move forward. In many cases, while the platforms may change, the strategies that are at the heart of digital politicking have remained. These trends emerge across media platforms, even as they may be shifting slightly.

In the case of microsites, what were once novel have now become a transmedia genre. As they are in wide rotation on both sides of the aisle and have lost their novelty, they have become more similar to other political sites. However, while the sites themselves have gotten both larger and more generic, the form of the fact-check that so dominated these spaces has proliferated across campaign and news media. Certainly, their use within official campaign websites, "hit sites," and news coverage has continued, but their use has expanded as well. At the presidential level, the 2012 Obama campaign launched a "truth team" that anyone could join, so that "every time a baseless attack comes to light, we'll arm you with the truth so you can spread the word" (BarackObama.com/truth-team). In addition to the system of email notifications and updates within the BarackObama.com platform (the update to the 2008 campaign's social, action-oriented hub My.BarackObama.com), the truth team also involved a Facebook group and three other microsites: AttackWatch.com, KeepingGOPHonest.com, and KeepingHisWord.com. While the second clearly mimics the "hit sites" genre, the other two maintain positive content and involve a more holistic position that all kinds of information—not just attack information—need to be fact-checked. In addition to the steps of contextualizing and methodically proving information true or false that are described in chapter 3, the truth team adds additional modes by which to construct citizens as skeptical. Additionally, as members of the truth team, citizens are not merely expected to be skeptical of information they may receive, but are also expected to actively attempt to dispel other untruths.

Combining an emphasis on skeptical citizenship with a drive toward spreadable content, campaigns came to rely more heavily on infographics in 2012 and 2014. The infographics themselves serve as easily sharable documents, and citizens are explicitly asked to share this information and spread the truth. When truth team members look up, and seek to educate others about, controversial issues or incorrect rumors, they are provided not only with facts and figures from detailed sources, but are also provided with infographics, for a more easily translatable or understandable version of information at hand. Furthermore, by connecting citizens directly to a Facebook group devoted to the Truth Team, the sites facilitated sharing content, and citizens were encouraged to consider their role in a networked public that could connect the campaign to other social networks. Thus, the emerging norm of skeptical citizenship combines with that of active, networked citizens who share campaign messages and political information. The rise of infographics also continued to impact the aesthetic landscape of campaigns in 2010, 2012, and 2014. While the presidential campaigns of 2012 were certainly on the leading edge of this trend, senate and congressional races produced this content as well. While no more technically developed than any of the images shared in 2010—they are all simple PDFs, JPEGs, and so on.—infographics became more widely understood as a way to translate information and make difficult or complex ideas legible across all realms, and trainings for skills to produce these texts were in high demand.[1] While still overwhelmingly emphasizing visual elements, infographics provide a way to marry a public desire for visual content with a campaign's need for informative, issue-focused messaging.

If we consider the content of social media messages more generally, many of the phenomena described in chapter 5—an emphasis on interpersonal content and a marked shift away from issues—have remained prevalent in the years following 2010, and have been combined with an increased emphasis on professionally, aesthetically pleasing photographs and images for campaign communications. Whereas poorly executed photos, even blurry ones, made their way onto Facebook pages by the handful in 2010, 2012 was full of photos that were well lit, artistically composed, and varied in content and feel. Due in equal parts to improved cameras on mobile devices, the rapid adoption of photo editing mobile apps, and a subsequent expectation of aesthetically pleasing images, campaigns at the local level produced behind-the-scenes and digital retail content that was highly stylized, yet still fostered connection. Not just Facebook and Twitter, but more aesthetically driven platforms like Instagram, Pinterest, and Tumblr also figured into campaign strategy. As these social media tools have become further integrated and Internet culture that emphasizes images has pervaded much of society, a focus on image-driven content reigns in social media, and those pictures most often consist of behind-the-scenes content or digital retail politics.

More specifically, 2012 was dubbed by some the election cycle of memes. While 2008 had YouTube and 2010 had Facebook, 2012 was filled with the simple construction of still images (most often either pop culture references or a rather plain image of a candidate) plastered over with an amusing quote or misstep by a candidate. While memes are generally considered to be part of community-building and productive in fostering feelings of connection among creators and readers alike, their content is decidedly different from what has been described as interpersonal.[2] Fundamentally, these images are necessarily more issue-based or informative than digital retail politics, and often employ elements of parody. Despite their brevity, political memes overwhelmingly reference some issue or policy-related information, and necessitate that citizens know, understand, and synthesize that knowledge if memes are to be successful. Viewers will not be able to understand a reference to "binders full of women" if they do not know that Mitt Romney used that unfortunate language in an debate, and to understand the joke is to place it within a larger argument that either Romney or Republicans are bad on issues of gender equality. To laugh at an auto-tuned Obama "singing" "You didn't build that" is to understand that he was being criticized for implying well-off citizens were not self-made men and women. Now, this information may, as many have argued, be superficial and a poor stand-in for actual discussion of issues, but compared to other emerging trends in social media, it does reference issues, if not educate citizens about them. Using a slightly different rubric, Gerodimos and Justinussen's[3] recent analyses of posts at the presidential level show an overwhelming amount of emotional appeals within the posts, and while issue-related discussion exists, fact-based arguments are few and far between. Additionally, analysis of congressional Twitter and Facebook posts has shown that social media content via Twitter and Facebook has remained largely similar in its goals over time.[4] In the years following 2010, communications consultants and those specializing in digital or social media also continued to hammer home the message of using interpersonal content to foster or build community among citizens. Numerous panels of the 2011 and 2012 national consulting conference Netroots Nation were devoted to issues like community-building within campaigns—a goal that had not been given the same amount of import, and emphasizes the fact that connection is a goal unto itself.[5]

Finally, campaigns continue the trend of relinquishing control and encouraging citizens to pass along information, though it is becoming a more implicit and less clearly articulated strategy within the environment of campaigns' social media messages. With the development of the "share" button and the increased social norm of sharing or reposting content, campaigns rely less on overtly asking citizens to take such action. While these requests certainly still occur, the hope is implicit in nearly every message, as opposed to just those in which the request is explicitly made. These social norms are such that alongside the reduction in explicit requests to share information, the number of shares that posts receive was been much higher in 2012 and the years following.[6] Although the action itself—sharing a campaign message—is the same over time, the changing social norms around its execution may impact its meaning for citizenship. When an action becomes both easier and so common that it is not requested as often, it may take on a qualitatively different meaning. In some ways, this runs the risk of looking like clicktivism, rather than meaningful engagement. Rather than dismiss this practice, however, we must begin to ask if campaigns approach the concept of sharing differently or make use of citizens actions differently. As discussed in chapter 4, campaigns have reasons to encourage the recirculation of content beyond a base level need to amplify their message, and hope this action can begin citizens on the ladder of engagement, or an increasingly escalating scale of participatory action. Even if the action retains what Ethan Zuckerman has called "symbolic" elements of action, the question remains whether campaigns see this as an effective onboarding mechanism, or if they need more of citizens. For Zuckerman, these actions are in fact meaningful ways to produce citizenship, because voice begets voice and also has the power to set the agenda.[7] If sharing content becomes so rote an activity that it cannot meaningfully place citizens on the ladder of engagement, then the implications that such strategies hold for conceptions of citizenship may also shift.

Always Evolving: The Role of Social Platforms and the Data That Run Them

As the 2012 campaign reinforced and built upon the trends of 2010 in a significant way, it also was the site of its own emerging strategies. Most notably, it saw the rise of two trends: one that concerns the choices made when developing and circulating messages, and another that focused on the tools being used to circulate messages and get citizens to take action. First, there has been a significant rise in analytics-driven messaging strategy, or what has been called a "culture of testing" within campaigns. Second, campaigns across the board have adopted organizing platforms or action "hubs" that citizens can log into, keeping track of their own acts of participation and taking action directly from that space.

Long before the rise of digital strategy, campaigns have always tested the materials they produce. Employing a variety of methods, from focus groups to surveys to dial tests, campaigns routinely test what issues are salient to voters, poll public opinion on a variety of topics, and test the use of specific language or phrases, all before the "official" messages go out, in order to produce the most persuasive ones possible. But with the rise of digital messaging came the availability of analytic data that could capture what citizens did with messages—how often they opened emails, how long they spent on campaign websites, whether they shared content within social media platforms, and so on. With this data and increased technical capacity across the board came the ability to test most messages rapidly, and apply their findings to messages in an iterative way. Although major races like presidential campaigns have been empirically testing messages using controlled experiments since before 2010—the 2008 Obama campaign tested hundreds of versions of emails in real time in order to know which to send to whom and when—most campaigns only started to engage in such practices in the years following the 2010 campaign. While 2010 began to see the rise of A/B testing—when a campaign provides the public with one of two versions of a message for a very limited time, and then uses the message that tests better overall—the years following 2010 were full of calls to institute what many consultants called a "culture of analytics" or a "culture of testing." In doing so, major political consulting firms and groups well known for developing and institutionalizing cutting-edge strategy, such as the New Organizing Institute, the Analyst Institute, and Blue State Digital, called on campaigns of all sizes and levels to rigorously analyze the effects of their messages, share those effects, and begin to construct a more cohesive and nuanced understanding of best practices.[8] At national consulting conferences like Netroots Nation, panels focusing on explaining the benefits of a culture of analytics testing and detailing how to begin undertaking the necessary experiments were widespread from 2011 to 2013.[9] In addition to simply extolling the virtues of analytics-based testing, organizations increasingly held trainings in the skill, and it became a part of cutting-edge "curricula" and strategy manuals.[10]

Through this emphasis on digital analytics, campaigns are better equipped to produce persuasive and mobilizing messages alike, and the best practices that are learned from the tests enable campaigns to create and circulate messages with increased efficiency. While productive from a campaign point of view—this can save staff hours, in addition to providing compelling information—it may not bode as well for the image of citizenship it projects. Moreover, analytics-based decision-making necessarily means that the actions that have previously been and can easily be measured will be the primary modes of assessment, whether or not they are the most important forms of engagement. For instance, in assessing the success of email campaigns, consultants across the political spectrum were heavily reliant on open rates (the percentage of people who open an email sent to a list), despite the fact that the goal of most of these emails was not to inform people, but to get them to take action. Deeper forms of engagement—whether reflection occurs, how dedicated someone is to a candidate, and so on—are difficult to measure, and as a result, simplified variables are used as stand-ins, or other metrics are taken up completely. The primacy of efficiency within a campaign environment is by no means new, but recent developments like the emphasis on connection, rather than just mobilization or persuasion (as discussed in chapter 5), have gestured toward an expansion beyond efficiency. While important to campaigns, this emphasis on efficiency also comes at the cost of engaging with citizens in an interactive way, and citizens are often left with online and offline options that are transactional, rather than interactive. As a result, seemingly innovative "engagement" strategies are limited in their ability to lead to important indicators of citizenship, such as changes in citizens' practices, interest in civic issues, and feelings of connection or efficacy. This move toward the most efficient forms of information delivery or engagement has occurred within other realms of the political sphere, most notably in government, and the emphasis across arenas is troublesome if we consider deep or interactive engagement a primary goal.[11]

More than just changing the information they use to construct and circulate messages, campaigns are also adopting new digital platforms through which to both disseminate content and motivate citizens to take action. While publicly available and free platforms like Facebook, Twitter, Tumblr, and so on are still widely used by nearly every campaign, candidates are increasingly investing in off-the-shelf management systems or proprietary software that can provide a one-stop space for citizens to receive information, take action that will aid the campaign, and connect with others interested in similar issues or candidates. In 2008, the My.BarackObama.com (later known just as BarackObama.com) platform provided a hub for action and continued to engage citizens after the election. Because of comparatively lean times for campaigns during the midterms in 2010, this hub went unparalleled until the following presidential cycle. In the years that followed, however, activist organizations launched their own, and the capabilities were adopted at a rapidly increasing level. For example, FreedomWorks launched its FreedomConnector in 2011, and Democracy For America launched its YouPower in 2013 (see figures 7.1 and 7.2). Both of these sites focus on connecting online and offline action and enabling citizens to connect with one another in a social way as well.

While campaigns below the presidential level lack the resources necessary to develop full-fledged original social activism platforms, campaigns began to enlist the services of consulting firms to provide the same tools, or develop their official websites so that they had the look and feel of a platform, without needing to devote time to the complex development task of credentialing users with their own accounts. As a result, websites adopted the idea of a "hub" for action, without the features of enabling citizens to log in to their own account or trace and tally the actions they may have taken over time. Elizabeth Warren's campaign website, for example, contained an Action Center with nearly all of the same options for action provided by BarackObama.com, from receiving information or calling others, to joining groups within the campaign or attending events hosted by other citizens. Set off to the side of the website, and given the name of a "center," connoting its own separate space within the larger website, the Action Center draws on the rhetoric and aesthetic qualities of an original social activism platform while working within the resource constraints of a smaller race.

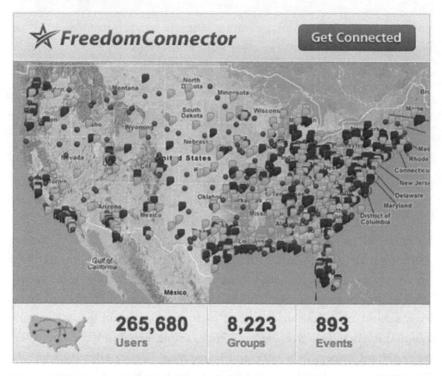

Figure 7.1 A screengrab of FreedomWorks' FreedomConnector, showing users the location of relevant political events and other users to connect with.

Figure 7.2 A screengrab of YouPower, a site that connects with Democracy For America's existing capabilities to locate and attend offline meetings, allowing users to start petition-like campaigns.

Figure 7.3 Screengrab of Warren's campaign website with the "Action Center" on the right.

While it provides a slightly different set of affordances than a complete platform, this workaround illustrates campaigns' dedication to providing a space where citizens can go to take any kind of campaign-related action. With the success of social activism platforms, and even the pseudo-platform from the Warren campaign (see figure 7.3), which won Reed Awards in 2013 for both Best Fundraising Program and Best Website, we can expect this style of creating a hub or central, identifiable space for taking action and gaining easily spreadable information to continue to expand.

These action-oriented hubs of social activism platforms emphasize a mode of citizenship that encourages political participation to be considered a social action, while also encouraging a citizen who takes a variety of types of action. While campaign offices still make ends meet by categorizing people based on what type of volunteer work they generally undertake—they often (and to great success) call a particular list of citizens they can count on to turn out at a rally or a talk and use an entirely different list for ones they can count on to phone-bank—social activism platforms ask a variety of actions of all users. The BarackObama.com platform does this most explicitly by tracking users' actions and showing the amount of each action they have (or have not yet) taken, but even the website-based hubs present all actions as options for citizens. In this way participatory citizenship is constructed as involving a breadth of forms of action.

Evolving Constructions of Citizenship

In both of these cases, the messages that campaigns create have more influence than can be measured by the number of supporters they garner or voters they turn out at the polls. As campaigns develop and circulate content, they are also producing visions of what it means to act as a participant in contemporary digital democracy. Whether it is in the service of a campaign website, a Facebook page, or in debate prep, the process of constructing messages and the messages themselves highlight the forces and institutions that constrain citizens' actions and illuminate those they are able and encouraged to take. As a result, these practices are a hybrid of new and old strategies, and none point to revolutionary democratizing forces. They do, however, point to new ways of understanding what it means to be a citizen, and new opportunities for productive political engagement. Throughout the previous chapters, messaging practices involving digital technologies reflect additions to traditional campaign goals and practices that subsequently imply shifts in what it means to be a citizen, whether it be how much deliberation or debate citizens are allowed to engage in, or what type of information they are exposed to. The relationship between the specific practices investigated in these chapters and the citizenship norms they engender occurs on multiple levels. On one hand, these changing practices are becoming typical in the sense that campaigns are requesting citizens undertake them in a recurring manner. On a deeper level, these practices become normative as they reflect more overarching models of how citizens act within our digitally mediated democratic culture. Thus, the practices of citizens publicly disagreeing with campaigns and related practices of campaigns allowing, anticipating, and sanctioning this behavior reflect a norm of citizens who have the right and the opportunity to talk back to campaigns. Similarly, specific practices of digital recirculation reflect a norm of active, actualized citizenship that can work within the constraints of campaign control.

Through these changing practices, it becomes clear that citizenship is not a failing enterprise; it is a changing one. While Robert Putnam and those following in his footsteps may argue that important social relationships and social capital are dissolving and forms of political participation are declining, and therefore citizenship is diminished in a digital era, this book argues that the possibilities that political relationships and modes of citizenship people can engage in are substantively different from those categorized under traditional rubrics of social capital, but should be recognized as potentially productive, nonetheless. The call to redefine what "counts" as political action is neither new, nor complete, but the findings presented here reflect legitimate reasons for optimism. Campaign texts invite practices that organize citizens in new ways and consist of new actions that are not covered by outdated measures that too often remain the primary ways of investigating the concept. Their changing digital practices are creating new spaces of possibility for political relationships and participatory action. The opportunities for participating and engaging political information that are enabled—and even fostered—by the digital messages campaigns produce should be understood as an effort to shed light on the places where possibilities for engaged citizenship are bubbling up. Passing along content to your network, engaging with microsites and fact-checks or with campaigns' social media photo albums, or entering in discussions and debates that are occurring within campaigns' social media pages all offer opportunities to engage in nuanced acts of citizenship, and should be recognized as such.

Countering this optimism, some critical scholars have argued that the prospects for digital democracy are bleak, and that, despite these opportunities, citizens have failed or been unable to take advantage of them. The most widely cited of these criticisms is Matthew Hindman's wide-ranging study of how citizens actually use allegedly democratic tools. From the hierarchies built into our overarching search engine platforms via algorithms, to the concentration of online news production and attention toward traditional news outlets rather than blogs, to political campaigns' reliance on distinctly transactional goals such as fundraising, Hindman argues that "vast swaths of the public are systematically unheard in civic debates."[12] The scope and detail of the analysis are impressive, and its findings certainly ought to act as a call for us to do better, but it does not, as it purports, prove digital democracy to be mere myth. It does not tell the whole story of what democracy can or even ought to be, and therefore is not the only rubric by which to measure the success or failure of digital democratic culture. While much of Hindman's work is premised upon the argument that we cannot make equivalences between the act of speaking and the fact of being heard, nor can we ignore the importance of campaigns' providing a space for citizens to speak and actively encouraging them to use such spaces to do so. Not only is the democratic output of such activity something to be measured in terms of the amount or reach of speech that results, but the interactive nature in which campaigns recognize and engage with citizens ought to be considered.

The rise of content creation by citizens—be it via blogs, social media, or commenting sections—should be seen as beneficial not only insofar as it adds new voices to the mix, but also because it provides other benefits of increasing or shifting the content of news or campaign communication. While campaigns' voices are still by far the loudest, that social media have given rise to content that is interpersonal, retail-oriented, and spreadable marks a change. Recirculating certain content exposes an individual's social network to her ideas, and serves an agenda-setting function within that space. Citizens' comments on social media or a blog post may not be widely read by other citizens or ever acknowledged by the campaign, but the fact that campaigns are inviting citizens to use their voice and opening themselves up to criticism is an expansion of democratic activity when compared to what came before. Fact-checks and microsites—even those created by regular citizens—are increasingly gaining news coverage. While the claims presented in this volume do not directly contradict or invalidate the specific empirical findings presented in such studies, they do nuance the dogmatic claims in service of which such findings have been used.

Even when campaigns do succeed in engaging citizens in clearly participatory acts, there is additional concern over the fact that digital democracy tends to be more usefully engaged by people who are already politically involved. In discussing our current "postbroadcast democracy," Markus Prior highlights this stratification of activism, showing how those who already participate are now finding more avenues to do so, and those who do not demonstrate interest in politics are left by the wayside.[13] While this studies show the status quo at the very outset of digital activism, more recent developments in engaging citizens in low-effort activism that involves speaking back to political institutions give reason to be optimistic. Yes, campaigns will continue to push those already on the ladder of engagement toward higher rungs, and citizens can cull a social network system so it has little to do with political content, but campaigns have also begun to take overt and purposeful efforts to include new citizens in their digital campaigning efforts. Chapter 4 shows how networked citizenship not only holds the potential to accidentally reach new audiences, but also is a space in which campaigns are actively seeking out new opinion leaders. As the bottom rung of that ladder of engagement has become easier to reach, the barriers to climbing the ladder lessen. Moreover, as chapter 5 details the rise of new interpersonal content, a change in the type of messages—away from the dry and strictly-on-message norms of public relations professionals and press secretaries—holds the potential to engage new citizens in the most basic of participatory acts, sharing content.

One of the criticisms of digital era democracy that is most difficult to shake is that, even within the aforementioned moments of success, citizens' actions and their ability to speak and be heard are all overwhelmingly controlled by campaigns. As a result, many have argued that political action—whether related to elections or governance—will therefore always be constrained.[14] While this is largely true (and somewhat inescapable), chapter 6's discussion of the disruption of traditional forms of campaign control shows that, although infrequent, there are moments of rupture in control and technical and organizational changes within campaigns have provided opportunities for citizens to sidestep those mechanics. People can, and do, talk back. Perhaps even more important than those fleeting moments is the overarching fact that campaigns have almost fully transitioned into a normative model of asking citizens to publicly provide their opinions and feedback. When citizens are asked to talk back and provided a space to do that (even if that space is, to varying degrees, controlled), expectations for talking back to political authorities grow, and expectations that feedback and criticism will not be deleted or overtly controlled develop.

Central to each of these arguments is that there is no way out of the limited participation they offer. Power laws mean that while citizens may speak, their opportunities for being heard are increasingly constrained, the control campaigns exert over what citizens can and cannot say or do on campaigns turf is unceasing, and online engagement only further increases the gap between those who participate and those who do not. This work nuances these arguments by showing that there are points of rupture in these dynamics, and that even as campaigns do exert these forms of control, there are ripple effects that ought to make our discussions of what counts as political participation more nuanced. Even in the midst of pessimistic accounts of the state of citizenship, these very real problems exist simultaneously alongside moments of autonomous and participatory action, and are even encouraged by digital campaign messages. While campaigns do manage the actions citizens are able to take, digital texts have also led to important points of rupture of campaigns' control over public discourses. While some traditional power structures may still reign in the digital space, newer relationships encouraged by campaign-requested acts of participation, such as circulating digital content, productively increase and diversify the public of messages. Although information within social media channels is potentially becoming less policy focused, it is also encouraging individuals to take a greater degree of action, and other spaces are inviting them to approach political information with a skeptical mindset that involves critically assessing and judging the validity of facts. All in all, this book should be understood as a project that brings to light the spaces in which new, active, and participatory forms of citizenship are enabled and encouraged through the messages campaigns create and circulate.

Even as they show possibilities for citizenship, these renderings of contemporary models of citizenship are by no means entirely utopian. They have potentially serious problems of minimizing the discussion of issues, being constrained, encouraging negative campaigning, and exerting forms of control. Perhaps most problematic of all, these messages are being constructed at the behest of the most powerful players in a political system that is filled with systematic inequalities. Politicians are more economically and socially powerful now than ever before. Despite a low public approval rating of their work, they hold the reins of decision-making power in this country, and the gaps between the vast majority of citizens, and the small minority of those with power—be it economic, social, or both—is still growing larger. Political campaigns are engorged with an unprecedented amount of money that will only reinforce existing power hierarchies; those who have power can, and likely will, buy more. In the face of such a problematic system, how can we relish the small new moments of citizenship that bubble up throughout the campaign environment? In addition to answering questions concerning whether these new and potentially productive forms of citizenship are possible, we must also answer the question of whether these forms of citizenship are plausible.

I believe they are. First of all, despite the discourses of apathy that constantly occupy news specials, citizens have exhibited a significant willingness to participate in recent years. The election of 2008 saw unprecedented amounts of people taking higher levels of political action such as donating to and volunteering in campaigns. Activists in this country have taken to the streets for both progressive and conservative causes such as Occupy Wall Street those of Tea Party organizations since that time, and have taken to the digital public sphere in bipartisan movements to halt the passing of Stop Online Piracy Act and the Protect IP Act (SOPA/PIPA) Internet regulation. Even amid talk of an apathetic and unenthusiastic Left, more volunteers rallied around President Obama's reelection campaign than in 2008. More specifically, signs point to the fact that practices such as fact-checks, requests to circulate digital content, requests for participation via interpersonal social media content, and mechanisms of indirect control are on the rise. Consultants often speak of these new practices as if even resistant campaign staffers would be forced to reconcile with them, and will be left behind if they insist on prior tactics. Moreover, similar practices are converging across media platforms—the fact-check form can be seen on campaign websites, press releases, within microsites, and on blogs, for instance. While the existence of more methods of participation does not necessarily mean more uptake, it will likely mean more exposure. Far from something to ignore as inconsequential, these forms of participation are important because exposure to participatory practices that are deemed legitimate and valued by those in control of the political system is how citizens come to understand what practices are involved in being political, even if they do not undertake them all.

The next steps of this research are clear: if these forms of citizenship are being put forth by the practices of producing campaign messages and the texts themselves, subsequent inquiry into whether and how citizens are engaging these norms is also necessary. If texts seem to be constructing citizens as skeptical subjects, the questions we must then ask are "Are citizens engaging with political information skeptically, and under what conditions?" "How often and over what issues are people publicly disagreeing with campaigns in digital public spaces?" Asking who's engaging in the forms of citizenship put forth here, and under what conditions, will give a fuller picture of how expectations or desires for citizens are currently being met, moving forward. In illuminating these routine practices and interactions, we can better understand what it means to be a political actor in a digital context.

Before that undertaking occurs, however, we can still draw meaningful insights from the messages campaigns are producing and their practices of production. Most significantly, these texts do not reflect common articulations of democracy fallen short. Rather than nostalgically lamenting our inability to duplicate the political actions and investments of a bygone era, these phenomena and the ways of being political that they promote show that hope is not lost. If, as I have argued, monitoring a wide array of political information or taking traditional political action is not the only or even the primary model of how citizens are asked to act politically, then measurements of these qualities showing shortcomings are not necessarily indicative of a rapid decline in citizenship. Instead, possibilities for action continuously bubble up alongside these declining measurements and deserve recognition. As political communication scholars take up this line of inquiry, citizens can be understood not merely as failing to act in particular ways, but as being provided many other additional opportunities for action. More than just providing alternatives, however, the phenomena illuminated and examined here, and the emerging ways of understanding engaged citizenship they reveal, make it painfully clear that traditional methods of measuring citizenship are falling short. Not only might they often fail to account for unnoticed or emerging modes of political action, but they are also inadequate because of citizenship's many oppositional forces and conflicting components. The drive to measure levels of citizenship, while perfectly able to give an account of people's action or attitudes, does not give an account of the available options, of potential changes to how society considers what it means to be political or to what those changes mean for democracy in general. As scholars increasingly call for assessments of citizenship for the digital age, a step away from measuring known forms of citizenship, and a step toward more inductive research that focuses on uncovering new visions of the concept, is needed. Similarly, while existing accounts of the state of citizenship often result in a judgment of success or failure, the reality is that the state of citizenship is much less cut and dried. As a nation, we may not return or reach the levels of action defined as "strong democracy" by Benjamin Barber or escape the professionalized politics described by Theda Skocpol, but the chapters presented here may very well point to the "ways to re-create the best of our civic past in new forms suited to a renewed democratic future" that Skocpol hopes are present within the scenario she outlines.[15]

Citizenship, like politics itself, is messy, and black-and-white proclamations of its failure or success gloss over its many shades of gray. Not only do the implications brought forth in the proceeding chapters illuminate some of these gray areas of new possibilities and pitfalls, they also reflect varied, competing, and sometimes conflicting perspectives. They show that far from being an either/or proposition, successes and problems within citizenship can often exist side by side and work at cross-purposes. The fact that the forms of control wielded by campaigns are changing is not merely a success story; it shows there are still pernicious and powerful constraints on citizens' capabilities for deliberation, yet there are more opportunities offered by campaigns than ever before. As a result, a new awareness of this mode of control will need to be developed if citizens are to take it on. Emerging genres of content within social media emphasize noninformative, mobilizing "information," while other popular practices such as the use of fact-checks and microsites not only inform, but also construct readers as necessarily skeptical and in need of being convinced. If we were to look at these events separately, they might seem to merely cancel one another out—democratic success on one side, failure on the other. But that designation is too simple. Rather than working against one another, these mechanisms work alongside one another. They do not occur in a vacuum, but influence and interact with other content. Citizens use a variety of media platforms to gain information, and most use these platforms simultaneously.[16] The phenomena described here are no different. Microsites' and fact-check websites' construction of citizens as skeptical interpreters of facts is unlikely to disappear with the click to another tab of a browser window. Perhaps people read behind-the-scenes content alongside "hard" information, and perhaps they are both mobilized and persuaded through content in different platforms. Although the content that citizens are asked to digitally circulate is often vague "support our campaign" messages or relegated to specific GOTV items, the fact is that campaigns encourage digital circulation in specifically the same medium that is home to emerging genres of interpersonal content, and the interaction between these types of information remains to be seen. Moreover, this increasing production of interpersonal content is also occurring in the same places where new, indirect forms of control seem to be making a major impact.

In the everyday grind of a campaign, life finds a way of gaining meaning through Election Day. The late nights crafting messages and deciding how to best reach audiences using a variety of tools are worth it because of the light at the end of the tunnel arriving on that first Tuesday in November. Seldom are the everyday practices of campaigns seen as the site of their substantive impact. In a moving instance of motivation, Illinois blogger Rich Miller described the experience of campaign hacks the best:

> The election is less than four weeks away, but you're certainly weary from the never-ending days and nights. You've no doubt been busting your hump for weeks or months on end. Living on coffee, cigarettes, cold pizza and warm beer. Your candidate may be behind, or maybe you're in a close race and fighting for what feels like your very life. . . . You may be losing your patience and your voice, but you can smell something familiar in the air: "The end." People are finally paying attention and you've been feeling that ol' adrenaline rush. You're gonna need it. It's the only thing that'll keep you going through the miserable days ahead.[17]

And when Miller goes on to describe the end result of these campaigns as "a zero-sum life. You win or you go home," he correctly identifies the importance placed on "E-Day." The day after an election, things feel finished. A losing campaign's staffers sleep in the next morning for the first time in months, returning to the office to literally clear the place out. Even a winning campaign, full of whooping congratulations and an eagerness to take on the path ahead, is left with a feeling of finality. Their celebrations are for the fact that they have the power to take up causes and produce change in the future. But that's not the whole story. While electoral victories and defeats are the most easily observed and directly influential result of campaigns, they also create forms of citizenship within their texts, and leave lasting change that way. The truth is that—in addition to the governing that winners of elections go on to—these campaign messages tell people how to be political. Their content and form argue that people should attend to and understand information in certain ways, place higher value on certain actions, and put forth accounts of the practices and constraining forces with which citizens are engaging. As campaigns use the wealth of tools—both traditional and digital—at their disposal, they build the democratic culture we live in today.

Appendix

Interview participants' contributions to this research were anonymous, so the following list contextualizes their input by providing the date of the interview and an overview of their political work in 2010 and beyond, while maintaining that anonymity.

January 19, 2011   Communications director for congressional race in 2010. Additional experience as communications director for federal-level candidates and officials, as well as advocacy/labor groups.

March 4, 2011   Digital consultant working for a firm handling multiple candidates nationwide in 2010, including two prominent mayoral races. Additional work with other municipal and federal candidates through same firm.

April 6, 2011   Communications director for federal-level race in 2010, in addition to working as a consultant with other federal- and municipal-level candidates through a media and communications consulting firm.

April 7, 2011   Communications director for federal-level race in 2010. Additional experience in media relations for for-profit organizations.

April 26, 2011   Communications director for gubernatorial campaign in 2010. Additional communication director and speech-writing experience for a large nonprofit.

April 27, 2011a   Communications director for gubernatorial campaign in 2010. Additional experience as communications director within elected officials' and state government offices.

April 27, 2011b	Communications director for Senate race in 2010. Additional experience as communications director at the presidential (regional director), federal, and municipal levels, as well as experience in nonprofit/labor.
April 30, 2011	Communications director for gubernatorial campaign in 2010. Additional experience as communications director for elected official.
May 5, 2011	Digital director for senate campaign in 2010. Additional experience as digital strategy activist, writer, and consultant.
May 7, 2011	Press secretary for Senate race in 2010. Additional experience as press secretary at state, regional, and national party levels.
May 19, 2011	Communications director for congressional election in 2010. Additional experience in for-profit communications.
May 20, 2011a	Digital communications consultant for national organization advocacy that focuses on training others in digital/communications strategy.
May 20, 2011b	Communications director for congressional campaign in 2010. Additional experience as communications director for elected official.
May 20, 2011c	Communications director for congressional campaign in 2010. Additional experience as communications director for multiple elected officials.
May 24, 2011	Cofounder of a grassroots digital advocacy organization, with experience in digital strategy for campaigns, nonprofit/labor advocacy.
June 1, 2011a	Digital director for senate campaign in 2010. Additional consulting experience with federal-level elections through a digital strategy firm and campaign experience at the presidential level.
June 1, 2011b	Campaign manager for a gubernatorial campaign in 2010. Additional experience as a communications and strategy consultant for a firm handling major federal and statewide candidates.
June 3, 2011a	Digital campaign coordinator for a national grass-roots organization in 2010. Additional experience as a communications consultant with nonprofit/advocacy groups.

June 3, 2011b	Digital director at a national grassroots organization in 2010. Additional experience as digital activist and writer, and as new media director for an advocacy organization.
June 7, 2011	Communications consultant for large communications/ strategy firm, consulting for campaigns at the gubernatorial and Senate level in 2010. Additional experience as a communications consultant at the congressional and statewide level as well.
June 9, 2011	Digital director for senate campaign in 2010. Additional experience as a digital director for nonprofit organization.
June 10, 2011	President and consultant at a digital consulting firm handling multiple Senate races in 2010. Additional experience as digital consultant for races at federal and presidential levels at own firm, as well as major digital strategy and technology development firms.
June 14, 2011	Principal at digital analytics, research, and strategy firm, consulting for clients at the federal level in 2010, as well as presidential- (and federal-) level and advocacy groups in 2008 and 2012.
June 16, 2011a	Digital communications consultant for national advocacy organization that focuses on training others in digital/communications strategy.
June 16, 2011b	Lead analyst for national organization advocacy that focuses on training others in digital/communications strategy and conducting analytics research in campaigns and advocacy organizations.
June 16, 2011c	Partner at digital communications consulting firm, specializing in advocacy and web development, with additional experience in digital advocacy at multiple digital strategy agencies.
June 17, 2011a	Digital strategy consultant at a mobile advocacy and strategy firm. Additional experience as a digital consultant working with federal, statewide, and international campaigns.
June 17, 2011b	Partner at a grassroots advocacy organization. Additional experience as an activist, communications strategist, and social media strategist.
June 17, 2011c	Partner at digital strategy firm specializing in national advocacy campaigns.

June 18, 2011a	Digital advocacy specialist and developer with experience in building tools to aid activists and advocacy groups.
June 18, 2011b	Digital entrepreneur focused on developing technologies and digital strategies for NGOs and local, state, and national governments. Specialist in user experience (UX).
June 18, 2011c	Cofounder of a grass-roots advocacy organization, with experience in organizing and communication strategy.
June 22, 2011a	In-house digital strategist at a major policy and advocacy group in 2010, with additional experience in communications and press relations.
June 22, 2011b	Communications consultant at a digital strategy firm handling a gubernatorial race in 2010. Additional experience in both non-profit and for-profit communications.
June 23, 2011	National director at a grass-roots digital advocacy organizations, focusing on analytics and strategy.
June 24, 2011	Digital communications consultant and author, focusing on election strategy.
June 27, 2011a	Digital strategist and journalist specializing in blogging strategy and constituent engagement. Additional experience as digital staffer at the presidential level and digital consultant at the federal level.
June 27, 2011b	Mobile strategy consultant specializing in local advocacy and mobilization strategies in national advocacy campaigns in 2010 and beyond.
July 5, 2011	Graphic designer and user interface specialist, focusing on web and mobile design, for a firm focused on advocacy and labor organizations.
July 14, 2011	Digital director for Senate-level race in 2010, with additional experience at the House, Senate, and presidential levels as a consultant for a major digital strategy firm. Specializes in direct contact/email and analytics-based messaging strategy.

Notes

Chapter 1

1. For a discussion of the slight changes in content and goals that have come about within a variety of media systems—from politics and advocacy to journalism—because of the changing digital landscape, see Andrew Chadwick, *The Hybrid Media System: Politics and Power* (New York: Oxford University Press, 2013). Chadwick's emphasis on emergence and small changes rather than radical revolution continues throughout this book as well.

2. While many books chronicled events and tactics of the 2008 Obama campaign (for examples, see Colin Delany, *Learning from Obama: A Comprehensive Guide to His Groundbreaking 2008 Online Presidential Campaign* [self-published, 2009]; Rahaf Harfoush, *Yes We Did! An Inside Look at How Social Media Built the Obama Brand* [New York: New Riders Press, 2009]; David Plouffe, *The Audacity to Win: The Inside Story and Lessons of Barack Obama's Historic Victory* [New York: Viking, 2009]), manuals concerning how to run digital campaigns more broadly only began cropping up after 2010. For one of the first well-regarded studies, see Colin Delany, *Online Politics 101: The Tools and Tactics of Digital Political Advocacy* (self-published, 2011).

3. Russell J. Dalton, "Citizenship Norms and the Expansion of Political Participation," *Political Studies* 56 (2008): 78.

4. David L. Swanson and Paolo Mancini, *Politics, Media, and Modern Democracy: An International Study of Innovations* (Westport, CT: Praeger, 1996); Cliff Zukin, Scott Keeter, Molly Andolina, Krista Jenkins, and Michael Delli Carpini, *A New Engagement? Political Participation, Civic Life, and the Changing American Citizen* (New York: Oxford University Press, 2006).

5. Swanson and Mancini, *Politics, Media*, 1.

6. Mark W. Brewin, *Celebrating Democracy: The Mass-Mediated Ritual of Election Day* (New York: Peter Lang International Academic Publishers, 2008).

7. Robert Bellah, Richard Madsen, William Sullivan, Ann Swidler, and Steven M. Tipton, *Habits of the Heart: Individualism and Commitment in American Life* (Berkeley: University of California Press, 1985). The question "How ought we to live?" in a democratic society has long concerned political scientists, political theorists, and sociologists alike, and is exemplified by Bellah et al., *Habits of the Heart*. While that text asked citizens about how they feel they ought to live, this book sets out to illuminate how political elites tell citizens they out to live in the digital era.

8. Sidney Blumenthal, *The Permanent Campaign: Inside the World of Elite Political Operatives* (New York: Simon and Schuster, 1982).

9. W. Lance Bennett, "Changing Citizenship in the Digital Age," in *Civic Life Online: Learning How Digital Media Can Engage Youth*, ed. W. Lance Bennett (Cambridge, MA: MIT Press, 2008).

10. Stephen Coleman, "Doing IT for Themselves: Management vs. Autonomy in Youth E-Citizenship," in Bennett, *Civic Life Online*.

11. Rasmus Kleis Nielsen, "Mundane Internet Tools, Mobilizing Practices, and the Coproduction of Citizenship in Political Campaigns," *New Media and Society* 13, no. 4 (2010): 4–5.

12. Campaign operations are divided into three pillars—communications, which creates messages that directly reach the public and is most clearly focused on persuasion; field, which aims its efforts at mobilizing supporters and is most concerned with getting out the vote (GOTV) on Election Day; and finance, the quiet fundraising engine that enables the other two to stay in operation. The three areas of field, finance, and communications have been, in some cases since 2008, joined by a fourth unique area, digital. The designation of digital effort as its own realm of the campaign, and dual existence as groups of staffers that answer to communications officers and as one group with its own seat at the table of senior staffers is discussed in chapter 6.

13. Rasmus Kleis Nielsen and Cristian Vaccari, "Do People 'Like' Politicians on Facebook? Not Really. Large-Scale Direct Candidate-to-Voter Online Communication as an Outlier Phenomenon," *International Journal of Communication* 7 (2013): 24.

14. Derek Benjamin Heater, *A Brief History of Citizenship* (New York: New York University Press, 2004); Bryan Turner, *Citizenship and Social Theory* (Thousand Oaks, CA: Sage, 1993); Michael Schudson, *The Good Citizen: A History of American Civic Life* (New York: Free Press, 1998); Robert Putnam, *Bowling Alone* (New York: Simon and Schuster, 2000). Turner's version of these histories explicitly argues that there have been multiple conflicting (and sometimes competing) definitions of citizenship throughout each of the eras, arguing that "a unitary theory of citizenship is inappropriate" (11).

15. James Bohman, "Expanding Dialogue: The Internet, the Public Sphere and Prospects for Transnational Democracy," *Sociological Review* 52 (2004): 131–55; Lincoln Dahlberg, "The Internet and Democratic Discourse: Exploring the Prospects of Online Deliberative Forums Extending the Public Sphere," *Information, Communication and Society* 4 (2001): 615–33.

16. Matthew Hindman, *The Myth of Digital Democracy* (Princeton, NJ: Princeton University Press, 2008); Michael Margolis and David Resnick, *Politics as Usual: The Cyberspace "Revolution"* (Thousand Oaks, CA: Sage, 2000); Jennifer Stromer-Galley, *Presidential Campaigning in the Internet Age* (New York: Oxford University Press, 2014).

17. Lincoln Dahlberg, "The Internet, Deliberative Democracy, and Power: Radicalizing the Public Sphere," *International Journal of Media and Cultural Politics* 3 (2007): 47–64; John Horrigan, R. Kelly Garrett, and Paul Resnick, *The Internet and Democratic Debate: Wired Americans Hear More Points of View about Candidates and Key Issues Than Other Citizens; They Are Not Using the Internet to Screen Out Ideas with Which They Disagree* (Pew Internet Research, 2004); Pippa Norris, *Digital Divide: Civic Engagement, Information Poverty, and the Internet Worldwide* (Cambridge: Cambridge University Press, 2001).

18. Cass Sunstein, *Republic 2.0* (Princeton, NJ: Princeton University Press, 2007); Bruce Bimber, "The Internet and Political Transformation: Populism, Community, and Accelerated Pluralism," *Polity* 31, no. 1 (1998): 133–60.

19. Eli Pariser, *Filter Bubble: How the New Personalized Web Is Changing What We Read and How We Think* (New York: Penguin, 2011).

20. Howard Rheingold, *The Virtual Community: Homesteading on the Electronic Frontier* (Reading, MA: Addison-Wesley, 1993); Clay Shirky, *Here Comes Everybody: The Power of Organizing without Organizations* (New York: Penguin, 2008).

21. Evgeny Morozov, *To Save Everything, Click Here* (New York: Public Affairs, 2013); Putnam, *Bowling Alone.*

22. Henrik Bang, "Among Everyday Makers and Expert Citizens," in *Remaking Governance: Peoples, Politics and the Public Sphere*, ed. Janet Newman (Bristol: Policy Press, 2005); Karen Mossberger, Caroline Tolbert, and Ramona McNeal, *Digital Citizenship: The Internet, Society, and Participation* (Cambridge, MA: MIT Press, 2007); Zukin et al., *A New Engagement?*

23. Schudson, *The Good Citizen.*

24. Theda Skocpol, *Diminished Democracy: From Membership to Management in American Civic Life* (Norman: University of Oklahoma Press, 2003). Despite the criticisms levied in *Diminished Democracy*, Skocpol's analysis is more nuanced than its title implies. In it, she argues that changes to relationships refigure how citizenship is currently enacted, that the civic reorganizations of our time are "changes that have made American both more and less democratic" (19), and that we can imagine new forms of participation within these relationships. David Karpf's *The Move On Effect* (Princeton, NJ: Princeton University Press, 2012) takes up questions of citizens' relationships to advocacy and issue organizations in the Internet age. While his analysis focuses on the impact to political organizations rather than citizens, implications for the type of political participation that is valued can be drawn out of his findings as well.

25. Philip Howard, *New Media and the Managed Citizen* (New York: Cambridge University Press, 2006).

26. Daniel Kreiss, "Developing the 'Good Citizen': Digital Artifacts, Peer Networks, and Formal Organization during the 2003–2004 Howard Dean Campaign," *Journal of Information Technology and Politics* 6, no. 3 (2009): 281–97.

27. Bennett, "Changing Citizenship," 14; Coleman, "Doing IT for Themselves"; W. Lance Bennett, Chris Wells, and Deen Freelon, "Communicating Civic Engagement:Contrasting Models of Citizenship in the Youth Web Sphere," *Journal of Communication* 61 (2011): 835–56.

28. Ethan Zuckerman, "New Media, New Civics?" *Policy and Internet* 6, no. 2 (June 1, 2014): 151–68.

29. Zizi Papacharissi, "The Citizen Is the Message: Alternative Modes of Civic Engagement," in *Journalism and Citizenship: New Agendas in Communication*, ed. Zizi Papacharissi (New York: Routledge, 2009).

30. This conception of citizenship norms is similar to Dalton's (2008): "a shared set of expectations about the citizen's role in politics ... they tell citizens what is expected of them, and what they expect of themselves" (78). The definition in this book, however, conveys the power of potential norms of citizenship—those just beginning to bubble to the surface—rather than just the ones directly articulated as desired or currently functioning.

31. Bang, "Among Everyday Makers"; Eric Gordon and Jessica Baldwin-Philippi, "Playful Civic Learning: Enabling Lateral Trust and Reflection in Game-Based Public Participation," *International Journal of Communication*, forthcoming; Bennett, "Changing Citizenship."

32. All of the stories and anecdotes in this book, unless otherwise cited, come from this campaign.

33. I use the term "affordances" to account for the fact that there are material components to the object of microsites that constrain (or enable) certain actions. In doing so,

I use the term in a way that is coherent with a science and technology studies perspective and indicates "functional and relational aspects which frame, while not determining, the possibilities for agentic action in relation to an objects." Ian Hutchby, "Technologies, Texts, and Affordances," *Sociology* 35, no. 2 (2001): 441–56.

34. Matthew Mahler, "Politics as a Vocation: Notes toward a Sensualist Understanding of Political Engagement," in *New Perspectives in Political Ethnography*, ed. Lauren Joseph, Matthew Mahler, and Javier Auyero (New York: Springer, 2007).

35. Sheila Jasonoff, ed., *States of Knowledge: The Co-production of Science and Social Order* (New York: Routledge, 2004); Anselm Strauss, "A Social World Perspective," in *Studies in Symbolic Interaction*, ed. Norman Denzin (Greenwich, CT: JAI Press, 1978).

Chapter 2

1. *Battle for the House* (Real Clear Politics, 2010), http://www.realclearpolitics.com/epolls/2010/house/2010_elections_house_map.html; *Most Expensive Races: Historical Elections* (OpenSecrets.org, 2010), https://www.opensecrets.org/bigpicture/topraces.php?cycle=2010&display=allcands.

2. Field notes, September 1, 2010. Until 2012, Facebook only allowed admins to target messages by geography, gender, and age, and target wall posts by geography and language.

3. This emphasis on technologies that connect voters with campaigns excludes a significant realm of technology use such as early email systems or intranets set up by campaigns to share information across geographical boundaries (Karen S. Johnson-Cartee and Gary Copeland, *Inside Political Campaigns: Theory and Practice* [Westport, CT: Praeger, 1997]), attempts to enhance polling data by using new technologies such as cell phones or online polls, or developing systems of e-voting. While these are interesting uses of technology, this book is concerned with ways that connect campaigns with audiences.

4. Personal communication, April 6, 2011.

5. Daniel Kreiss, *Taking Our Country Back: The Crafting of Networked Politics from Howard Dean to Barack Obama* (New York: Oxford University Press, 2012).

6. Georgia Logothetis, "The Wasteland," *Daily Kos*, January 7, 2011, http://www.dailykos.com/story/2011/01/07/934058/-The-Wasteland.

7. Journalists have detailed clashes between media consultant Jim Margolis and the cadre of young data scientists over whether to scrap a significant portion of the campaign's television buys (a notoriously expensive endeavor that embodies the throw-everything-at-the-wall approach) in favor of much smaller, more precise buys based on new analytics. Jim Rutenberg, "Data You Can Believe In: The Obama Campaign's Digital Masterminds Cash In," *New York Times Magazine*, June 20, 2013.

8. Pippa Norris, "A Virtuous Circle? The Impact of Political Communications in Post-industrial Democracies," in *Readings in Political Communication*, ed. Theodore F. Sheckels, Janette Kenner Muir, Terry Robertson, and Lisa Gring-Pemble (State College, PA: Strata Publishing, 2007), 137–61.

9. Rex Hardesty, "The Computer's Role in Getting Out the Vote," in *The New Style in Election Campaigns*, ed. Robert Agranoff (Boston: Holbrook, 1976).

10. Bruce Newman, *The Marketing of the President: Political Marketing as Campaign Strategy* (Thousand Oaks, CA: Sage, 1994).

11. Oscar Gandy, "Dividing Practices: Segmentation and Targeting in the Emerging Public Sphere," in *Mediated Politics: Communication in the Future of Democracy*, ed. W. Lance Bennett and Robert Entman (New York: Cambridge University Press, 2001); Norris, "A Virtuous Circle?"; Richard Semiatin, *Campaigns on the Cutting Edge* (Washington, DC: CQ Press, 2008).

12. Kreiss, *Taking Our Country Back*.

13. Access to party databases such as VoteBuilder/Demzilla and VoterVault is only granted once a candidate is the party nominee, and other wide-scale databases such as Catalyst, Aristotle, and those compiled by large political groups are used in primaries and by nonparty candidates.

14. Private platforms such as Facebook allow advertisers such as campaigns or advocacy groups access to their demographic and interest-based data, providing another potential layer by which to group or specify users. Many are critical of campaigns' (and consumer marketing groups) ability to access this information, despite the fact that it is provided to a third party (the platform) by users.

15. Costas Panagopoulos and Peter Wielhouwer, "The Ground War 2000–2004: Strategic Targeting in Grassroots Campaigns," *Presidential Studies Quarterly* 38 (2008): 347–62; Judith Trent and Robert Friedenberg, *Political Campaign Communication: Principles and Practices* (Lanham, MD: Rowman & Littlefield, 2008).

16. Michael Delli Carpini, "Gen.com: Youth, Civic Engagement, and the New Information Environment," *Political Communication* 17 (2000): 341–49.

17. Bimber, "Internet and Political Transformation"; Eric Lawrence, John Sides, and Henry Farrell, "Self-Segregation or Deliberation? Blog Readership, Participation, and Polarization in American Politics," *Perspectives on Politics* 8 (2010): 141–57; Sunstein, *Republic 2.0*.

18. Howard, *New Media*.

19. Savvy Internet users are often aware of the function served by cookies on their computer, and can take steps to inhibit such information from being accessed. Still, the vast majority are unaware of the scope of this data surveillance and use, and even more hidden monitoring is also taking place. Campaigns and organizations note where, when, and how people participate (or turn down requests to do so), and share can share this information within databases as well.

20. Kurt Lang and Gladys Engel Lang, *Television and Politics* (New Brunswick, NJ: Rutgers University Press, 2002); Joe McGinnis, *The Selling of the President* (New York: Penguin, 1988); Austin Ranney, *Channels of Power: The Impact of Television on American Politics* (New York: Basic Books, 1983).

21. Howard, *New Media*.

22. While the amount of people going online for information in 1994 was by no means massive, the idea that a message could be published without an intermediary was still used to create content similar to that on television and radio, despite their differing audiences.

23. Kirsten Foot and Steven Schneider, *Web Campaigning* (Cambridge, MA: MIT Press, 2006); David A. Dulio, Donald L. Goff, and James Thurber, "Untangled Web: Internet Use during the 1998 Election," *PS: Political Science & Politics* 32 (1999): 53–59.

24. Stromer-Galley, *Presidential Campaigning*.

25. Girish Gulati and Christine Williams, "Congressional Candidates Use of YouTube in 2008: Its Frequency and Rationale," *Journal of Information Technology & Politics* 7 (2010): 93–109; Girish Gulati and Christine Williams, "Diffusion of Innovations and Online Campaigns: Social Media Adoption in the 2010 U.S. Congressional Elections," available at SSRN 1925585, 2011.

26. Edelman, *Capitol Tweets: Yeas and Nays of the Congressional Twitterverse* (Washington, DC: Edelman Insights, March 21, 2012), http://www.slideshare.net/EdelmanInsights/capitol-tweets-yeas-and-nays-of-the-congressional-twitterverse; Matthew Eric Glassman, Jacob R. Straus, and Colleen J. Shogan, *Social Networking and Constituent Communications: Member Use of Twitter during a Two-Month Period in the 111th Congress* (Washington, DC: Congressional Research Service, 2010). Numbers and lists of Congress members on Twitter can also be accessed via

OpenCongress.org, a website dedicated to keeping tabs on the Twitter discussions of members of Congress and senators.

27. Chapman Rackaway, "Trickle-Down Technology? The Use of Computing and Network Technology in Legislative Campaigns," *Social Science Computer Review* 25, no. 4 (2007): 466–83.

28. Foot and Schneider, *Web Campaigning*; Stromer-Galley, *Presidential Campaigning*.

29. Antoinette Pole, *Blogging the Political: Politics and Participation in a Networked Society* (New York: Routledge, 2010).

30. See David Perlmutter, *Blogwars* (New York: Oxford, 2008) for an in-depth treatment of the norms and roles of blogs. Regarding niche or geographically specific blogs, partisan blogs often exist according to region: "Beltway" blogs (such as Congressional Quarterly's RollCall.com, TheHill.com), statewide blogs (such as ChicagoGOP. com, ProgressIllinois.com, or the nonpartisan TheCapitolFax.com), and local-level blogs (in one Illinois congressional district encompassing two counties, there exist three well-read local politics blogs: Ellenofthetenth.blogspot.com, TeamAmerica. blogspot.com, and 10thDems.org). Local blogs are especially prevalent in areas where races are routinely close, as is the case in the previous example.

31. Edwin Diamond, Martha McKay, and Robert Silverman, "Pop Goes Politics: New Media, Interactive Formats, and the 1992 Presidential Campaign," *American Behavioral Scientist* 37 (1993): 257–61; Aaron Smith, *The Internet's Role in Campaign 2008* (Pew Research Center, 2009); Darrell M. West, "Political Advertising and News Coverage in the 1992 California U.S. Senate Campaigns," *Journal of Politics* 56 (1994): 1053–75.

32. Aaron Smith, *The Internet and Campaign 2010* (Pew Internet & American Life Project, 2011).

33. Aaron Smith, *22% of Online Americans Used Social Networking or Twitter for Politics in 2010 Campaign* (Pew Internet & American Life Project, 2011).

34. Lee Rainie and Aaron Smith, *Politics Goes Mobile: 26% of Americans Used Their Cell Phones to Connect to the 2010 Elections* (Washington DC: Pew Internet & American Life Project, December 23, 2010).

35. Personal communication, January 18, 2011.

36. Michael McGerr, *The Decline of Popular Politics* (New York: Oxford University Press, 1986); Caroline Tolbert and Ramona McNeal, "Unraveling the Effects of the Internet on Political Participation?" *Political Research Quarterly* 56 (2003): 175–85.

37. Personal communication, June 27, 2011a.

38. Stephen Frantzich, *Computers in Congress: The Politics of Information* (Thousand Oaks, CA: Sage, 1982).

39. Personal communication, January 19, 2011.

40. Personal communication, May 19, 2011.

41. Personal communication, June 27, 2011a; personal communication, March 3, 2011.

42. Eventually covered as a major story by Sean Gregory in *Time* magazine, Corey Booker's use of Twitter during the winter following the 2010 election campaign garnered immediate and widespread attention in political circles and was a breakout moment for the then-mayor.

43. Jessica Baldwin-Philippi, "What's the Big Deal about Small Sites? How Political Microsites Reflect Shifting Norms of Participation," presented at "Social Media as Politics by Other Means," New Brunswick, NJ, 2011.

44. The first YouTube debate in 2007 featured the candidates for the Democratic presidential primary; Obama hosted town halls on Facebook and Twitter in the summer of 2011, and Republican presidential primary candidates hosted a Twitter debate in 2011.

45. Smith, *Internet and Campaign 2010*.

46. Nielsen, "Mundane Internet Tools."
47. Rainie and Smith, *Politics Goes Mobile.*
48. Smith, *Internet and Campaign 2010.*
49. Rainie and Smith, *Politics Goes Mobile.*
50. Morozov, *To Save Everything*; Stuart Shulman, "The Case against Mass E-Mails: Perverse Incentives and Low Quality Public Participation in U.S. Federal Rulemaking," *Policy & Internet* 1 (2009): 23–53. For a counterargument, see David Karpf, "Online Political Mobilization from the Advocacy Group's Perspective: Looking beyond Clictivism," *Policy & Internet* 2 (2010): 7–41.
51. Personal communication, May 20, 2011a.
52. Personal communication, July 14, 2011.
53. Personal communication, July 14, 2011.
54. Groups that are specifically dedicated to training campaign and advocacy workers in digital strategies, such as the New Organizing Institute, cover a variety of areas of focus, from messaging to data management, to fundraising and all-encompassing boot camps. Even large-scale advocacy organizations such as FreedomWorks have begun to offer trainings as part of their mobilization efforts.
55. Personal communication, June 16, 2011a.
56. Personal communication, June 22, 2011a.
57. Personal communication, June 1, 2011a.
58. Personal communication, June 10, 2011.
59. The Analyst Institute has conducted many behavioral experiments to test best practices in randomly controlled samples, and have demonstrated that text message campaigns reminding citizens to vote increase turnout by significantly more percentage points than phone calls. The Analyst Institute and New Organizing Institute, both liberal organizations, also consult and lead trainings on how to rigorously test messages, rather than rely on gut instinct. Still, even in cases where best practices have been empirically measured across a variety of contexts and populations, campaigns can be reluctant to accept universal norms. Campaign managers who trust their "gut" and argue that their town is different are depending on a notion that is not only romantic, but carries much sway at the decision-making table.

Chapter 3

1. The producers of these were the Republican National Committee, RightChange, and Buzzbomb, which is a still-developing offshoot of LiberalArt.
2. Field notes. This sentiment was specifically noted at the beginning of the brainstorming on September 22, 2010, September 26, 2010, and on October 14, 2010.
3. James Avery, "Videomalaise or Virtuous Circle? The Influence of the News Media on Political Trust," *International Journal of Press/Politics* 14 (2009): 410–33; Joseph N. Capella and Kathleen Hall Jamieson, "Spiral of Cynicism: The Press and the Public Good," *American Behavioral Scientist* 20 (1997): 1–16; Michael J. Robinson, "Public Affairs Television and the Growth of Political Malaise," *American Political Science Review* 70 (1975): 209–32.
4. Papacharissi, "Citizen Is the Message."
5. Joshua Cohen, "Deliberation and Democratic Legitimacy," in *The Good Polity*, ed. P. Pettit and A. Hamlin (Oxford: Blackwell, 1989); Robert Dahl, *On Democracy* (New Haven, CT: Yale University Press, 1998); Amy Gutmann and Dennis Thompson, *Why Deliberative Democracy?* (Princeton, NJ: Princeton University Press, 2004); Jürgen Habermas, *The Theory of Communicative Action, vol. 1: Reason and the Rationalization of Society*, trans. Thomas McCarthy (Boston: Beacon Press, 1984).

6. Walter Lippmann, *Public Opinion* (New York: Harcourt, Brace, 1922).

7. John Zaller, "A New Standard of News Quality: Burglar Alarms for the Monitorial Citizen," *Political Communication* 20 (2003): 109–30; Erik Amna and Joakim Ekman, "Standby Citizens: Diverse Faces of Political Passivity," *European Political Science Review*, Firstview article published online (2013): 1–21; Schudson, *The Good Citizen*.

8. Michael Delli Carpini and Scott Keeter, *What Americans Know about Politics and Why It Matters* (New Haven, CT: Yale University Press, 1996); Jane Junn, "Participation and Political Knowledge," in *Political Participation and American Democracy*, ed. William Crotty (New York: Greenwood Press, 1991); Henry Millner, *Civic Literacy: How Informed Citizens Make Decisions* (Hanover, NH: University Press of New England, 2002).

9. Lawrence K. Grossman, *The Electronic Republic: Reshaping Democracy in the Information Age* (New York: Viking, 1995), 25.

10. Jeffrey M. Ayres, "From the Streets to the Internet: The Cyber-diffusion of Contention," *Annals of the American Academy of Political and Social Science* 566 (1999): 132–43; R. Kelly Garrett, Erik Nisbet, and Emily Lynch, "Undermining the Corrective Effects of Media-Based Political Fact Checking: The Role of Contextual Cues and Naïve Theory," *Journal of* Communication 63, no 4 (2013): 617–37; Cass Sunstein, *On Rumors: How Falsehoods Spread, Why We Believe Them, What Can Be Done* (New York: Farrar, Straus and Giroux, 2009); Mark Andrejevic, *Infoglut: How Too Much Information Is Changing the Way We Think and Know* (New York: Routledge, 2013); Bruce Bimber, *Information and American Democracy: Technology in the Evolution of Political Power* (New York: Cambridge University Press, 2003).

11. For work in the area of information seeking and avoiding, see Scott Althaus, Anne Cizmar, and James Gimpel, "Media Supply, Audience Demand, and the Geography of News Consumption in the United States," *Political Communication* 26 (2009): 249–77; R. Kelly Garrett, "Politically Motivated Reinforcement Seeking: Reframing the Selective Exposure Debate," *Journal of Communication* 59 (2009): 676–99; Natalie Stroud, "Media Use and Political Predispositions: Revisiting the Concept of Selective Exposure," *Political Behavior* 30 (2007): 341–66; Stroud, "Polarization and Partisan Selective Exposure," *Journal of Communication* 60, no. 3 (2010): 556–76. For retention and salience, see Kelly Kaufhold, Sebastian Valenzuela, and Homero Gil de Zuñiga, "Citizen Journalism and Democracy: How User-Generated News Use Relates to Poltiical Knowledge and Participation," *Journalism and Mass Communication Quarterly* 87 (2010): 515–29; Kate Kenski and Natalie Stroud, "Connections between Internet Use and Political Efficacy, Knowledge, and Participation," *Journal of Broadcasting and Electronic Media* 50 (2006): 173–92. For work on the role of information in theories of citizenship, see W. Lance Bennett and Shanto Iyengar, "A New Era of Minimal Effects? The Changing Foundations of Political Communication," *Journal of Communication* 58, no. 4 (2008): 707–31; R. Lance Holbert, R. Kelly Garrett, and Laurel S. Gleason, "A New Era of Minimal Effects? A Response to Bennett and Iyengar," *Journal of Communication* 60 (2010): 15–34.

12. Schudson, *The Good Citizen*; Doris Graber, "The Rocky Road to New Paradigms: Modernizing New and Citizenship Standards," *Political Communication* 20 (2003): 145–48; Amna and Ekman, "Standby Citizens."

13. Studies concerning the news' capability to frame political information and set the agenda for the types of political information the public discusses ("what to think about and how to think about it") are largely the extent of inquiry into interpretations of political information beyond retained and not retained.

14. Jennifer Stromer-Galley's *Presidential Campaigning in the Internet Age* details consultant Rob Arena's recommendation of creating a separate "attack site" to be named either PeopleLast.com or RealClinton.com. Despite his efforts, the site was not made, and in 2000, the Gore campaign produced BushInsecurity.com. Quotations are from personal communication for the following dates: June 9, 2011, July 5, 2011, June 18, 2011a, respectively.
15. Garance Franke-Ruta, "RNC 'Fire Nancy Pelosi' Moneybomb Raises Nearly $1.5 Million," *Washington Post*, July 29, 2011.
16. Personal communication, June 10, 2011.
17. In 2012, the DNC produced MittVMitt.com, which focused on the fact that Mitt Romney had changed his position on numerous issues; the Romney campaign produced FortyFore.com, and the Obama campaign producing AttackWatch.com.
18. Personal communication, July 5, 2011.
19. Communications director, personal communication, January 19, 2011.
20. The sample of microsite texts consists of all of those produced in Illinois in 2010—nine microsites created by six campaigns, and two theorized sites. The blogs discussed are combination of three Illinois-based blogs: EllenOfTheTenth.blogspot.com, ChicagoGOP.com, and TheCapitolFax.com. The first is a liberal, primarily local blog featuring mostly original content that is largely commentary-based (focusing specifically on the congressional race in the in the 10th District, but also on the gubernatorial and senatorial races). The second is a statewide conservative blog featuring content produced by campaigns and political organizations, as well as original content. The third is a statewide news blog, written by journalist and *Sun-Times* columnist Rich Miller. It aggregates and analyzes both news and campaign texts, and often breaks news as well. Fact-checks come in two forms: those that are campaign-produced, and those that have some ties to journalistic writing, such as FactCheck.org and PolitiFact.org.
21. Quotes, respectively, come from new media consultant, personal communication, July 5, 2011; new media consultant, personal communication, June 27, 2011a; communications director, personal communication, January 19, 2011.
22. In eight days prior to the election, there were 14 "articles" that were direct reprints of press releases or messages directly from these campaigns: Dold (two); Pollak (three); Brady (two); Kirk (two); Kirk and Brady, jointly (three); statewide GOP campaign event (one); State Senator Dan Rutherford (one). These stories ran the gamut from being about major candidates for high office, such as Pat Quinn (Peter Bella, "'I Think Senator Brady Has a Lot of Apologizing to Do for His Record'—Pat Quinn," *ChicagoGOP*, 2010), mayoral candidates for whom elections would not happen for months (*ChicagoGOP*, 2011), and eccentric candidates for lower-level offices, such as Chicago rapper Rhymefest (Bella, "Rhymefest for Alderman!!!!!!!!!!!!!!!!!," *ChicagoGOP*, 2010). Stories focusing on the alleged liberal bias in the media are William Kelly's "Liberal Media Bias: What the Chicago Tribune Wouldn't (Couldn't) Print," *ChicagoGOP*, 2010.
23. Blog can be found at EllenOfTheTenth.blogspot.com. The blog's namesake, Ellen Beth Gill, and Carl Nyberg both author posts on the blog.
24. Field notes, September 27, 2010.
25. Field notes, September 27–September 31, 2010.
26. For a description of how these networks are leveraged on a national level, see Daniel Kreiss, "Acting in the Public Sphere: The 2008 Obama Campaign's Strategic Use of New Media to Shape Narratives of the Presidential Race," *Media, Movements, and Political Change* 33 (2012): 195–223.
27. The first is the slogan of PolitiFact.com, and the second is the slogan of FactCheck.org.

28. FactCheck.org, "Fiscal FactCheck: Does Washington Have a Spending Problem or an Income Problem? We Offer Some Key Facts," September 15, 2011.

29. Martha Hamilton, "Fact-Checking Boehner and Obama on Debt Duel," *PolitiFact*, 2011; Louis Jacobson, "Sorting Out the Truth about the Debt Ceiling," *PolitiFact*, July 14, 2011.

30. The FOIA request resulted in documents providing the data for an analysis of buildings and individuals who were beneficiaries of tax breaks from the Board of Review (and their lawyers), which Berrios sat on, presented alongside their contributions to his campaign. Donations and groups who provide campaigns assistance through independent expenditures (IEs), though they are readily searchable online, are a common strategy of this move to reveal. This was also highlighted on Claypool's website (www.forrestclaypool.com/cloutonamap.html, archived at the WayBack Machine) and picked up by local press, as well as *HuffPo Chicago*.

31. Perlmutter, *Blogwars*, 148.

32. As Axel Bruns, "News Blogs and Citizen Journalism: New Directions for E-Journalism," in *E-Journalism: New Media and News Media*, ed. Kiran Prasad (New Delhi: BR Publishing, 2009), argues, the digest function of blogs is particularly important in guiding people through information, as he dubs citizen journalists "guide dogs" or "gatewatchers" in opposition to the traditional "watch dog" and "gatekeeper" roles played by journalism.

33. Russ Stewart, "Democrats Try to Cope with 'Obama Obstacle,'" *ChicagoGOP*, October 27, 2010; Kelly, "Liberal Media Bias."

34. Carl Nyberg, "Prior to WWII the Republican Party Had Strong Nazi Sympathies," *Ellen of the Tenth*, 2010; Nyberg, "Bomb from Yemen Sent to Chicago Area Synagogue," *Ellen of the Tenth*, 2010.

35. In Illinois, the major political blogs covered the minutiae of campaigns and dedicated many posts to strange, but otherwise unnewsworthy events, such as a celebrity entry in a race for alderman (Bella, "Rhymefest for Alderman!!!!!!!!!!!!!!!!!!"), and highlighting rogue mobilizing efforts led by supporters of campaigns (Miller, "While Tea Partiers Surge in Illinois, Democrats Don't," *Capitol Fax*, October 28, 2010).

36. Bruns, "News Blogs."

37. Lauren McKenna and Antoinette Pole, "What Do Bloggers Do: An Average Day on an Average Political Blog," *Public Choice* 134 (2008): 97–108.

38. Although microsites are a tool that could benefit from online ads, even people specializing in microsites describe their modes of circulation as relying predominantly on supporters networks and SEO. Moreover, when campaign staffers did discuss their online ad buys (across multiple platforms), they were overwhelmingly used to direct traffic to campaigns' main websites. Some campaigns even regretted not using this specific tactic more, displaying a belief in its power. Moreover, those visiting political blogs and/or fact-check sites are likely to be invested in these descriptive and precise accounts of what happened. (This information all gained via personal communication: January 19, 2011; June 3, 2011a; June 3, 2011b; June 10, 2011; May 19, 2011; April 26, 2011, respectively.)

39. David Slayden and Rita Kirk Whillock, *Soundbite Culture: The Death of Discourse in a Wired World* (Thousand Oaks, CA: Sage, 1999).

40. Prime examples of FactCheck.org's coverage of these conventions can be found in "Debt Limit Debate Round-Up," July 29, 2011, and "Fiscal FactCheck: Does Washington Have a Spending Problem or an Income Problem? We Offer Some Key Facts," September 15, 2011.

41. Stewart, "Democrats Try to Cope."

42. Rich Miller, "'Democrats Accidentally Suppressing Their Own Voters,'" *Capitol Fax*, October 27, 2010.

43. Rich Miller, "***UPDATED x2*** Saturday Updates: Numbers, Cash, and Videos," *Capitol Fax*, October 30, 2010; Miller, "More New Lows," *Capitol Fax*, October 29, 2010; Russell Lissau, "Seals Camp Slams . . . ," *Daily Herald*, September 20, 2010; Bella, "'I Think Senator Brady Has a Lot of Apologizing to Do for His Record'—Pat Quinn," *ChicagoGOP*, October 26, 2010.

44. Bruns, "News Blogs," 13.

45. Foot and Schneider, *Web Campaigning*.

46. Bruce Bimber and Richard Davis, *Campaigning Online: The Internet in U.S. Elections* (New York: Oxford University Press, 2003).

47. Andrew Keen, *The Cult of the Amateur: How Today's Internet Is Killing Our Culture* (New York: Doubleday, 2007).

48. Just a decade after the *New York Times'* post-9/11 declaration of the "end of irony," it published a widely-read opinion piece by Christy Wampole that proclaimed irony as the "ethos of our generation" in a piece called "How to Live without Irony," published November 17, 2012. Despite a perhaps harsh treatment of the role of the skeptic, Richard Rorty's *Contingency, Irony, and Solidarity* (New York: Cambridge University Press, 1989) casts skepticism as a personal irony, categorizing the "cultural politician" who has managed to employ, but not be subsumed by, such dispositions as an ideal. Rex Huppke, "Facts, 360 B.C.–A.D. 2012: In Memoriam: After Years of Health Problems, Facts Has Finally Died," *Chicago Tribune*, April 19, 2012.

49. Dashboard for all Republican primary debates for the 2012 election here: http://elections.nytimes.com/2012/debates/2012-01-26-republican-debate

50. Personal communication, June 10, 2011.

51. Personal communication, July 5, 2011.

52. Microsites and campaign-created texts are often A/B tested by the campaigns themselves, but are seldom tested beyond that. The purpose for which fact-checks are most often used—correcting misinformation—has been studied by the field of political communication, and has resulted in establishing multiple variables that mediate the productive potential of fact-checks within fact-checks themselves (how long after an event they are produced, partisan cues, place of publication, and more) and within their audience (selective exposure, ideological bias, and so on (Garrett et al. "Undermining the Corrective Effects of Media-Based Political Fact Checking," 2011; Lucas Graves and Tom Glaisyer, "The Fact-Checking Universe in Spring 2012," *New America Foundation Media Policy Initiative Research Paper*, 2012; Brendan Nyhan and Jason Reifler, "Misinfornation and Fact-Checking: Research Findings from Social Science," *New America Foundation Media Policy Initiative Research Paper*, 2012).

53. Capella and Jamieson, "Spiral of Cynicism." While this book does not investigate citizens' engagement of microsites or other digital tools, Gary Hanson, Paul Haridakis, Audrey Wagstaff, Rekha Sharma, and J. D. Ponder's study of cynicism and social media platforms (MySpace, Facebook, and YouTube), "The 2008 Presidential Campaign: Political Cynicism in the Age of Facebook," *Mass Communication and Society* 13 (2010): 584–607, shows a correlation between increased use of social media and *decreased* cynicism. While the authors suggest the personal relationships involved in these platforms are the root of this result, the very fact that citizens' approaches to political information has been shown to be different across various media channels is encouraging for the concept of the skeptical citizen.

54. Paul Freedman, Michael Franz, and Kenneth Goldstein, "Campaign Advertising and Democratic Citizenship," *American Journal of Political Science* 48 (2004): 723–41.

Chapter 4

1. Yochai Benkler, *The Wealth of Networks: How Social Production Transforms Markets and Freedom* (New Haven, CT: Yale University Press, 2006); Manuel Castells, *The Rise of the Network Society* (West Sussex, UK: Blackwell, 2010).

2. G. Robert Boynton, "Going Viral—The Dynamics of Attention," in *Conference Proceedings: YouTube and the 2008 Election Cycle*, ed. Stuart Shulman and Michael Xenos, 11-38, 2009.

3. This chapter uses both of the terms "public" and "audience" to describe the organization of citizen readers not to further reify the binary between publics and audiences, but to differentiate between a view of a group of potential recipients of a message as clearly definable and/or targeted (audience[s]) and a group in which there is a broader potential for publicity as well as relatively shared normative expectations (public[s]). This is not to say that political content or action civilizes audiences and turns them into publics—indeed, as Sonia Livingstone has pointed out, audiences are often political/civic in nature, and traditional designations between audience and public may no longer hold. In the discussion of networked public(s), the intention is to speak to the blurring of these lines, and to describe what happens when those who would have previously been understood as audiences of messages are approached in newly mediated ways and asked to take action that catapults them beyond the traditional definitions of audience—even of participatory audiences. Sonia Livingstone, *Audiences and Publics: When Cultural Engagement Matters for the Public Sphere* (Bristol, UK: Intellect, 2005).

4. Kreiss, *Taking Our Country Back*.

5. Andrew Chadwick, *Internet Politics* (New York: Oxford University Press, 2006); Shirky, *Here Comes Everybody*.

6. Mizuko Ito, "Introduction," in *Networked Publics*, ed. Kazys Varnelis (Cambridge, MA: MIT Press, 2008); danah boyd, "Why Youth (Heart) Social Network Sites: The Role of Networked Publics in Teenage Social Life," in *Youth, Identity, and Digital Media*, ed. David Buckingham (Cambridge, MA: MIT Press, 2008).

7. Bennett, "Changing Citizenship"; Bennett, Wells, and Freelon, "Communicating Civic Engagement"; Coleman, "Doing IT for Themselves."

8. Matthew Hindman, *The Myth of Digital Democracy* (Princeton, NJ: Princeton University Press, 2008).

9. Personal communication, June 7, 2011.

10. Personal communication, January 19, 2011.

11. Personal communication, June 16, 2011a.

12. Personal communication, June 27, 2011b.

13. Personal communication, June 17, 2011a.

14. Personal communication, June 18, 2011a.

15. Personal communication, June 16, 2011c.

16. Personal communication, June 22, 2011a and January 19, 2011, respectively.

17. Content that causes an emotional reaction, as argued in Jonah Berger's *Contagious: Why Things Catch On* (New York: Simon and Schuster, 2013), is more likely to go viral, and although campaigns use this tactic to increase the reach of messages, it was not part of conversations about taking content viral.

18. Bill Brady (R) and Rich Whitney (I) were both challengers to incumbent Democrat Pat Quinn. Despite it being a close race, Quinn's campaign was slow to adopt social media strategies across the board. Although members of his staff later expressed some regret at this fact, their reliance on the traditional workings of the Chicago political machine—the city of Chicago turned out in impressive numbers to elect

Quinn, to the consternation of those in the suburbs and "collars" who overwhelmingly voted for Brady.

19. Rackaway, "Trickle-Down Technology?"
20. Personal communication, March 6, 2011.
21. Personal communication, March 7, 2011.
22. Personal communication, May 19, 2011.
23. One campaign in the Chicago area that was in an extremely tight race described being so concerned with gaining Facebook friends that it went beyond requests to existing supporters. Instead of limiting the campaign to this tactic, a member of the communications/digital team (in this campaign's case, the team was one and the same) went so far as to purchase Facebook friends. Realizing that this strategy held many problems, not least of all that it fails to reach actual voters and could make the candidate come off as a carpetbagger, the campaign discontinued this practice and spent many of its valuable hours ridding its Facebook page of faux friends.
24. Personal communication, May 20, 2011a.
25. Personal communication, March 7, 2011.
26. Personal communication, May 19, 2011.
27. Personal communication, June 1, 2011b.
28. Personal communication, January 19, 2011, and June 7, 2011, respectively.
29. Personal communication, May 20, 2011b.
30. Personal communication, June 1, 2011b.
31. Personal communication, June 18, 2011b.
32. Personal communication, June 17, 2011a.
33. Personal communication, March 4, 2011.
34. Personal communication, June 17, 2011b.
35. Personal communication, June 22, 2011.
36. Matthew Nisbet and John Kotcher, "A Two-Step Flow of Influence? Opinion-Leader Campaigns on Climate Change," *Science Communication* 30 (2009): 328–54.
37. Michael Warner, *Publics and Counterpublics* (New York: Zone Books, 2002), 87.
38. Ibid., 391.
39. Kreiss, *Taking Our Country Back*.
40. Benedict Anderson, *Imagined Communities* (New York: Verso, 1991).
41. The "knowability" of the public of a social network also extends to cases in which individuals may not be able to put "real" identities to those within the network, but understand them as having some form of stable identity (sharing with a community of redditors, for example, likely involves considering both a community of individuals who are "known" to some degree by their handle, as well as "known" as a group of individuals who can and may respond to your remarks.
42. Similar to the difference between "bridging" and "bonding" capital, this move marks substantive changes to existing bonds (which may not be permanent, but are definitely substantive), rather than the creation of new bonds.
43. Skocpol, *Diminished Democracy*; Zizi Papacharissi, *A Private Sphere: Democracy in a Digital Age* (Malden, MA: Polity, 2010).
44. Betsy Sinclair, *The Social Citizen: Peer Networks and Political Behavior* (Chicago: University of Chicago Press, 2012), highlights how social and political networks overlap and intertwine, even prior to social network systems.
45. Issues of message control and citizens cooptation of messages will be expanded up on in chapter 6.
46. Personal communication, May 20, 2011b.
47. Personal communication, May 19, 2011.

48. Personal communication, June 1, 2011b.
49. Personal communication, January 19, 2011.
50. Personal communication, June 7, 2011.
51. Personal communication, May 20, 2011c.
52. Personal communication, January 19, 2011.
53. David Karpf, "Measuring Influence in the Political Blogosphere: Who's Winning and How Can We Tell?" *Politics and Technology Review*, Institute for Politics Democracy and the Internet, George Washington University (2008), 33–41; Hindman, *Myth of Digital Democracy.*
54. Personal communication, March 27, 2011.
55. Personal communication, June 10, 2011.
56. Personal communication, March 27, 2011.
57. Personal communication, May 20, 2011a.
58. Personal communication, July 5, 2011.
59. Personal communication, May 20, 2011a.
60. Personal communication, July 5, 2011.
61. Personal communication, June 3, 2011a.
62. Field notes, October 12, 2010, and October 22, 2010, respectively.
63. Personal communication, June 3, 2011b.
64. Personal communication, June 1, 2011a.
65. Personal communication, July 5, 1120.
66. Jennifer Stromer-Galley, "On-Line Interaction and Why Campaigns Should Avoid It," *Journal of Communication* 50, no. 3 (2000): 111–32.
67. Personal communication, January 19, 2011.
68. Personal communication, March 4, 2011.
69. Howard, *New Media*; Kreiss, *Taking Our Country Back.*
70. Papacharissi, *A Private Sphere*; Skocpol, *Diminished Democracy.*

Chapter 5

1. Personal communication, April 6, 2011.
2. Personal communication, January 19, 2011.
3. After over 20 years as mayor of Chicago, Richard M Daley announced that he would step down on September 10, 2010, sending shockwaves through the local elections and stealing coverage from all levels of election in Illinois. As a primary runoff election would be held in Chicago in January, candidates began to campaign for mayor before the midterms had even occurred, spreading political journalists thin and crowding the airwaves as candidates jockeyed for coverage.
4. Personal communication, May 24, 2011.
5. Capella and Jamieson, "Spiral of Cynicism"; Shanto Iyengar, Helmut Norpoth, and Kyu Hahn, "Consumer Demand for Election News: The Horserace Sells," *Journal of Politics* 66 (2004): 157–75.
6. For analysis of the persuasive value of endorsements, see Kim Fridkin Kahn and Patrick Kenney, "The Slant of the News: How Editorial Endorsements Influence Campaign Coverage and Citizens' Views of Candidates," *American Political Science Review* 96 (2002): 381–94. Beyond that, however, direct persuasion is not the only benefit of editorial endorsements. In order to secure endorsements, candidates provide large amounts of information through both interviews and detailed surveys, which is usually made public and becomes part of information landscape.
7. Personal communication, April 6, 2011.
8. Personal communication, May 20, 2011a.

9. For infotainment, see Patricia Moy, Michael Xenos, and Verena K. Hess, "Communication and Citizenship: Mapping the Political Effects of Infotainment," *Mass Communication and Society* 8 (2005): 111–31; Markus Prior, "Any Good News in Soft News? The Impact of Soft News Preference on Political Knowledge," *Political Communication* 20 (2003): 149–71. For sound bite culture, see Daniel Hallin, "Sound Bite News: Television Coverage of Elections, 1968–1988," *Journal of Communication* 42 (2006): 5–24; Slayden and Whillock, *Soundbite Culture*. For the rise of parodic content, see Johnathan Gray, Jeffrey P. Jones, and Ethan Thompson, *Satire TV: Politics and Comedy in the Post-network Era* (New York: New York University Press, 2009); Amanda Lotz, *The Television Will Be Revolutionized* (New York: New York University Press, 2007); Geoffrey Baym, *From Cronkite to Colbert: The Evolution of Broadcast News* (Boulder, CO: Paradigm, 2010); Jeffrey P. Jones, *Entertaining Politics: Satiric Television and Political Engagement* (Lanham, MD: Rowman & Littlefield, 2010).

10. Ted Brader, "Striking a Responsive Chord: How Political Ads Motivate and Persuade Voters by Appealing to Emotions," *American Journal of Political Science* 49 (2005): 388–405.

11. Stephen Ansolabehere and Shanto Iyengar, *Going Negative: How Political Advertisements Shrink and Polarize the Electorate* (New York: Free Press, 1995); Richard R. Lau and Gerald M. Pomper, "Effects of Negative Campaigning on Turnout in U.S. Senate Elections, 1988–1998," *Journal of Politics* 63, no. 3 (August 1, 2001): 804–19.

12. For examples of these questions, see June Woong Rhee, "Strategy and Issue Frames in Election Campaign Coverage: A Social Cognitive Account of Framing Effect," *Journal of Communication* 47 (1997): 26–48; Michael D. Slater, "Reinforcing Spirals: The Mutual Influence of Media Selectivity and Media Effects and Their Impact on Individual Behavior and Social Identity," *Communication Theory* 17 (2007): 281–303; William P. Eveland, Andrew Hayes, Dhavan Shah, and Nojin Kwak, "Understanding the Relationship between Communication and Political Knowledge: A Model Comparison Using Pane Data," *Political Communication* 22 (2005): 423–66; Gregory A. Huber and Kevin Arceneaux, "Identifying the Persuasive Effects of Presidential Advertising," *American Journal of Political Science* 51 (2007): 957–77; Holbert, Garrett, and Gleason, "New Era of Minimal Effects?"

13. Bennett and Iyengar, "New Era of Minimal Effects?" 725.

14. Eric Gordon and Stephen Walter, "The Good User: Technology-Mediated Citizenship in the Modern American City," forthcoming, discusses meaningful inefficiencies in terms of practices related to public deliberation and consensus building. While this chapter discusses the ways goals of campaigns change rather than how inefficient participation can improve original goals, similarities between the two practices exist. Most notably, for both the electoral and deliberative settings, fun, playful, and *inefficient* content is about creating deeper forms of engagement that hinge upon social connections to others and to institutions.

15. Andrew Chadwick, *The Hybrid Media System: Politics and Power* (New York: Oxford University Press, 2013).

16. Personal communication, June 1, 2011b.

17. Personal communication, January 19, 2011.

18. Personal communication, April 6, 2011.

19. Personal communication, April 27, 2011a.

20. In campaigns, web-based and television ads are not designated only by the medium in which they appear, but by FEC regulations. If an ad is produced for television, the candidate herself must appear on screen and voice her approval of the ad. Web-based advertisements need only to provide the paid-for language of the campaign on the

screen. So, a television ad is often run on the campaign's website and platforms such as YouTube, as well as on television. Featured or recommended videos can be either web or television ads, and are content that the campaign pays to have put at the top of lists of related content.

21. Personal communication, July 14, 2011.

22. Personal communication, May 20, 2011b.

23. Personal communication, April 6, 2011.

24. Personal communication, June 16, 2011a.

25. In 2010, campaigns were more than willing to post poorly cropped or slightly blurry photographs. Following campaign events where staffers or volunteers were suddenly called on to take pictures with little more than a direction about where the camera's power button was (and, yes, campaigns largely used digital cameras, not smartphones for photos), I personally uploaded many of them, and combed through to find the least blurry of the bunch. By 2012, the images on local and national campaigns alike had improved dramatically and become the norm. Even blogs that are not explicitly interested in electoral politics, such as culture blog TheAwl.com, began to assess (and critique) the differences in aesthetics between the Romney and Obama campaigns in 2012. (Ana Marie Cox and Jason Linkins, "The Annotated Flickr Feeds of Barack Obama and Mitt Romney," *The Awl*, October 15, 2012.)

26. Personal communication, June 9, 2011.

27. An official blog post from Twitter discussing this change in Twitter's perceived purpose can be found at http://blog.twitter.com/2009/11/whats-happening.html.

28. Personal communication, April 6, 2011.

29. Lynn Vavreck, Constantine Spilotes, and Linda L. Fowler, "The Effects of Retail Politics in the New Hampshire Primary," *American Journal of Political Science* 46 (2003): 595–610; Trent and Friedenberg, *Political Campaign Communication.*

30. Hunter S. Thompson, *Fear and Loathing on the Campaign Trail '72* (New York: Warner Books, 1983); Timothy Crouse, *The Boys on the Bus* (New York: Ballantine Books, 1974); Marc Halperin and John Heilemann, *Game Change: Obama and the Clintons, McCain and Palin, and the Race of a Lifetime* (New York: Harper, 2010).

31. Tracey Barry and Peter Davidson, *The Kennedy Mystique: Creating Camelot*, National Geographic Channel, 2004.

32. The *New York Times* interactive feature "The 2012 Republican Primary in Pictures" was updated regularly following a state's primary and each state had a dedicated album (NewYorkTimes.com, *The 2012 Republican Primary in Pictures.*) The trend of tweeting behind the scenes of campaigns was problematic for campaigns, as detailed in Peter Hamby, *Did Twitter Kill the Boys on the Bus? Searching for a Better Way to Cover a Campaign* (Cambridge, MA: Shorenstein Center on Media, Politics, and Public Policy, 2013). He details the way that reporters being constantly tuned in to details about the heat of a bus, slow wireless connection, or sartorial choices of candidates negatively affected relationships between campaigns and press, which in turn hurt aspects of messaging strategy.

33. Content that is counted as "behind the scenes" or "digital retail politics" was defined as anything mentioning either an action that the public would not have been able to see in public (e.g., a tweet mentioning the schedule for the day, which is never public information, discussing being "on the road" or en route to campaign events, or pictures from campaign headquarters) or depicting or reviewing a retail politics event that has occurred (e.g., posting pictures from a parade or campaign event, updating social or digital media content to acknowledge being at an event, or sending out a message of thanks to those who attended).

34. Personal communication, April 7, 2011.

35. Personal communication, June 9, 2011.
36. Personal communication, April 6, 2011.
37. Personal communication, June 22, 2011b.
38. Personal communication, May 20, 2011c.
39. Personal communication, June 7, 2011.
40. Personal communication, June 27, 2011a.
41. George Packer, "The Revolution Will Not Be Blogged," *Mother Jones*, May–June 2004; Davis, *Typing Politics: The Role of Blogs in American Politics* (New York: Oxford University Press, 2009), 90.
42. Richard Kahn and Douglas Kellner, "New Media and Internet Activism: From the 'Battle of Seattle' to Blogging," *New Media and Society* 6 (2004): 87–95; Pole, *Blogging the Political*.
43. Personal communication, June 27, 2011b.
44. Personal communication, June 9, 2011.
45. Personal communication, June 9, 2011.
46. Richard F. Fenno Jr., *Home Style: House Members in Their Districts* (New York: Longman, 2003).
47. Ibid., 55–56.
48. Ibid., 58.
49. Karlyn Kohrs Campbell and Kathleen Hall Jamieson, "Form and Genre in Rhetorical Criticism: An Introduction," in *Form and Genre: Shaping Rhetorical Action*, ed. Karlyn Kohrs Campbell and Kathleen Hall Jamieson (Falls Church, VA: Speech Communication Association, 1978), 19.
50. Personal communication, April 6, 2011.
51. Personal communication, June 22, 2011b.
52. Personal communication, May 20, 2011c.
53. Personal communication, May 20, 2011c.
54. Personal communication, January 19, 2011.
55. Personal communication, May 20, 2011b, and June 27, 2011b, respectively.
56. Personal communication, July 5, 2011.
57. Personal communication, April 27, 2011a.
58. Personal communication, January 19, 2011, emphasis added.
59. Personal communication, May 20, 2011a.
60. Personal communication, June 9, 2011.
61. Personal communication, June 1, 2011a, and June 22, 2011b, respectively.
62. Personal communication, April 6, 2011.
63. Two consultants specifically used this phrase, though its sentiment of reaching people already somehow involved was echoed across numerous interviews. Personal communication, March 6, 2011, and June 9, 2011.
64. Personal communication, June 27, 2011a.
65. Personal communication, May 20, 2011c.
66. Personal communication, March 4, 2011.
67. Rasmus Kleis Nielsen, *Ground Wars: Personalized Communication in Political Campaigns* (Princeton, NJ: Princeton University Press, 2012).
68. Moy, Xenos, and Hess, "Communication and Citizenship"; Matthew Baum, "Sex, Lies, and War: How Soft News Brings Foreign Policy to the Inattentive Public," *American Political Science Review* 96 (2002): 91–110; Matthew Baum and Angela S. Jamison, "The Oprah Effect: How Soft News Helps Inattentive Citizens Vote Consistently," *Journal of Politics* 68 (2006): 946–59.
69. Prior, "Any Good News?"
70. Bimber and Davis, *Campaigning Online*.

Chapter 6

1. Personal communication, May 19, 2011.
2. Personal communication, July 5, 2011.
3. News media of all levels picked up this story, and it ran on local, state level, and national partisan blogs. Rich Miller, " 'They Bring It on Themselves,' " *Capitol Fax*, September 21, 2010; Abdon Pallasch, "Battle for the Center in North Shore Race to Replace Kirk," *Chicago Sun-Times*, September 29, 2010.
4. Field notes, September 22, 2010.
5. Field notes, September 13, 2010, October 13, 2010, October, 17, 2010, and October 23, 2010, respectively.
6. Personal communication, May 20, 2011b, and July 5, 2011, respectively.
7. Personal communication, May 20, 2011.
8. Recently, the popularity of the OpenGov movement has blended discourses that praise the openness of government and political systems with traditionally valued concepts of deliberative democracy. These normative values are certainly connected insofar as the information or data made available in the successes of the OpenGov movement contribute to the feasibility of discussing facts and debating issues publicly (see the Sunlight Foundation's work or the White House's ongoing Open Government Initiative for productive examples). Increasingly, they are being explicitly linked through organizations that advocate not only for open information but for digital spaces of deliberation that are not closed off to anyone and where comments cannot be censored, deleted, or even made more difficult to see through tweaks to the user interface Best Practices.
9. Benjamin Barber, *Strong Democracy: Participatory Politics for the New Age* (Berkeley: University of California Press, 1984); John S. Dryzek, *Discursive Democracy: Politics, Policy, and Political Science* (New York: Cambridge University Press, 1990); Habermas, *Reason and Rationalization.*
10. Personal communication, June 1, 2011b.
11. Personal communication, May 19, 2011.
12. Personal communication, April 27, 2011a.
13. Personal communication, January 19, 2011.
14. Personal communication, June 22, 2011.
15. In addition to the reasons for control enumerated here, another tactic is to displace the responsibility entirely. Some campaigns have said that "there are clinical consultants who, as part of the contract, monitor various types of blogs and stuff. So this was something like that. I didn't have direct oversight of it" (personal communication, April 26, 2011). In taking this position, campaign staffers show that they've considered the problematic elements of controlling messages and chosen to pass off responsibility precisely because of its importance.
16. Personal communication, January 19, 2011.
17. Personal communication, March 25, 2011.
18. Personal communication, July 5, 2011.
19. Personal communication, June 9, 2011.
20. Personal communication, May 20, 2011.
21. Both of these staffers worked on the same campaign and, much like Alexis Madrigal in "When the Nerds Go Marching In," *Atlantic*, November 16, 2012, describe the clash of cultures in the 2012 and 2008 Obama campaigns, engaged in fundamental disagreements over messaging strategies and even what the goals of certain messages should be.
22. Personal communication, May 5, 2011, and personal communication, May 20, 2011, respectively.

23. Personal communication, April 27, 2011a.
24. Personal communication, May 5, 2011.
25. Personal communication, May 19, 2011 and May 5, 2011, respectively.
26. Field notes, October 30, 2010. This process occurred long before that date as well. It was part of the daily grind of the campaign when I began in August, although it did severely ramp up throughout the month of October.
27. Personal communication, May 20, 2011c.
28. Personal communication, April 7, 2011.
29. Field notes, October 15, 2010. The second commenter had a history of taking a vocal stand against the campaign (and others') policies of deleting comments.
30. Howard, *New Media*; Daniel Kreiss, "Yes We Can (Profile You): A Brief Primer on Campaigns and Political Data," *Stanford Law Review Online* 64 (2012): 70–74.
31. At this point in time, this is largely only true for national parties and large-scale political organizations and *exceptionally* high-profile races. High-profile here means only presidential elections and potentially primary front-runners, as well as well-publicized, well-financed Senate races.
32. Pariser, *Filter Bubble*; Sunstein, *Republic 2.0*; Nicholas Negroponte, *Being Digital* (New York: Vintage Books, 1996).
33. Personal communication, January 19, 2011.
34. In some cases, allied groups or political organizations are enabled to post messages directly to a candidate's wall as well. This adds additional voices to those prioritized and highlighted within the deliberative space, but does so without risking controversy or generating off-message topics of discussion.
35. The campaigns that controlled their content to some degree were, in alphabetical order, Melissa Bean (D, Congress), Bill Brady (R, governor), Debbie Halvorson (D, Congress), Phil Hare (D, Congress), Adam Kinzinger (R, Congress) Mark Kirk (R, Senate, who allowed comments only toward the very end of his campaign), Pat Quinn (D, governor), Jan Schakowsky (D, Congress), Rich Whitney (I, governor). While there is a difference between the parties' tendency to engage this type of control in 2010, I believe that to be due to the level of vocal and active online opposition, rather than the specific party of opposition. In other words, were Democrats the loudest voices (or, possibly even the out-group in general), Republicans would be equally likely to levy control at a greater ratio.
36. During the 2010 election, campaigns could set their preferences so others could not even post a comment on public updates. This rule has since changed, and any time a public post is made, anyone can comment on it (likewise, any time a post is made to only followers or friends, any of those populations can comment).
37. Personal communication, June 1, 2011a.
38. The norms listed here are less important than the fact that they illustrate the immense amount of detail that goes into constructing the messages. For instance, one campaign's decision to use very proper language and forgo contractions is not how all campaigns operate within social media, and was the subject of some disagreement within the office (field notes, October 25, 2010).
39. Personal communication, June 1, 2011a.
40. Personal communication, April 6, 2011.
41. Personal communication, June 9, 2011.
42. Personal communication, April 27, 2011b, June 9, 2011, and April 7, 2011, respectively.
43. Personal communication, April 7, 2011.
44. Personal communication, June 9, 2011.
45. Personal communication, May 19, 2011.

46. Moreover, even in cases where comments are allowed, but are a click deeper into the page, responding to the campaign-produced messages places such comments in a more visible position than intended by the campaign.

47. Personal communication, March 4, 2011.

48. Personal communication, June 22, 2011a.

49. Personal communication, June 22, 2011b.

50. Grasstops activism is defined in opposition to grassroots politics, as shallow, nonorganic, and therefore illegitimate activism, while sockpuppeting means pretending to be someone else online. While the second phenomenon is executed less often (or perhaps just caught less often), campaigns have been accused of the behavior when staffers comment on blogs posing as outsiders to the campaigns, and when a campaign is suspected of directly feeding citizens lines to relay to these blogs or newspapers.

51. Russell Lissau, "10th Congressional Candidate Urging Supporters to Post Comments Online," *Daily Herald*, August 15, 2010; Zorn, "Adventures in Sock Puppetry," op-ed, *Chicago Tribune*, August 16, 2010.

52. Personal communication, April 6, 2011, and June 1, 2011a, respectively.

53. Personal communication, June 1, 2011b.

54. Dryzek, *Discursive Democracy*, 43.

55. Seyla Benhabib, "Toward a Deliberative Model of Democratic Legitimacy," in *Democracy and Difference: Contesting the Boundaries of the Political*, ed. Seyla Benhabib (Princeton, NJ: Princeton University Press, 1996), 63.

56. Benhabib, *Democracy and Difference*, 71.

Chapter 7

1. Training panels at national conferences began to emphasize the role of the visual in 2012 and 2013, with Netroots Nation panels devoted to topics like "Visual Storytelling" and "Using Data Visualisation to Understand What You've Done, Are Doing and Should Do." In 2012, panels focused on the role of images when providing advice on how to run "issue-based campaigns for college students" (2012).

2. Henry Jenkins, Sam Ford, and Joshua Green's 2013 *Spreadable Media: Creating Value and Meaning in a Networked Culture* (New York: New York University Press, 2013) details the power of messages like memes that circulate fluidly, as well as the drive to create those messages.

3. Roman Gerodimos and Jakob Justinussen, "Obama's 2012 Facebook Campaign: Political Communication in the Age of the Like Button," *Journal of Information Technology and Politics*, advance online publication, DOI: 10.1080/19331681.2014. 982266 (2014).

4. Jennifer Lawless, "Twitter and Facebook: New Ways for Members of Congress to Send the Same Old Messages?" in *iPolitics*, ed. Richard L. Fox and Jennifer M. Ramos (New York: Cambridge University Press, 2012).

5. Titles from Netroots Nation 2011 include "Sustaining Engagement in the Off Years: How Electeds use Community Organizing and Social Media to Engage Their Constituents" and "Building a Community for Your Campaign." Panels from Netroots Nation 2012 included "The Face of New Progressive Online Communities," a session about the role of personal content in social media platforms called "Winning the Interwebs through Epic Sharability" and many discussions about looking to community-oriented platforms like Tumblr.

6. Gerodimos and Justinussen, "Obama's 2012 Facebook Campaign."

7. Ethan Zuckerman, "New Media, New Civics?," *Policy and Internet* 6, no. 2 (2014): 151–68.

8. Field notes, June 17–19, 2011; June 7–10, 2012. Although the organizations that are leading this charge are those on the left, the manuals and case studies that these findings produce are used by practitioners on both sides of the aisle, and therefore impact those beyond the immediately present audience.

9. In 2013 alone, these presentations included titles like "What the F*** Do We Know? Applying Scientific Research to Elections," "Key Experiments and Discoveries in the World of Online Fundraising," and "The Online Lab." They were led by a combination of research scientists hired by political parties and campaigns, staffers who had worked for major national and close Senate races, and consultants from a variety of top-level firms. For more information on the development of the culture of analytics within electoral and advocacy campaigns, see Jessica Baldwin-Philippi, "The Cult(ure) of Analytics in 2014," in *Communication and the Midterm Elections: Media, Message, and Mobilization,* ed. John Allen Hendricks and Daniel Schill (New York: Palgrave, 2015).

10. The New Organizing Institute routinely holds trainings it calls "Roots Camps," which highlight the need and methods behind testing and controlled experiments with messages (see RootsCamp.NewOrganizing.com). Additionally, cutting-edge manuals like the wildly popular book by Sasha Issenberg, *The Victory Lab: The Secret Science of Winning Campaigns* (New York: Crown Books, 2012), those produced by epolitics. com (Colin Delany, "How to Use the Internet to Win in 2014: A Comprehensive Guide to Online Politics for Campaigns & Advocates," 2013), and memos from the likes of national publications like *Campaigns and Elections* (Charles Holland, "A Different Way to Test Your Message," 2012) contribute to building cohesive strategies around data and analytics.

11. Jessica Baldwin-Philippi and Eric Gordon, "Designing Citizen Relationship Management Systems to Cultivate Good Civic Habits," Radcliffe Center, Harvard University, Boston Area Research Initiative, 2013; Gordon and Walter, "The Good User."

12. Hindman, *Myth of Digital Democracy,* 12.

13. Markus Prior, *Post-broadcast Democracy: How Media Choice Increases Inequality in Political Involvement and Polarizes Elections* (Cambridge, MA: Cambridge University Press, 2007).

14. Stromer-Galley, *Presidential Campaigning;* James E. Katz, Michael Barris, and Anshul Jain, *The Social Media President: Barack Obama and the Politics of Digital Engagement* (New York: Palgrave Macmillan, 2013); Howard, *New Media.*

15. Barber, *Strong Democracy;* Skocpol, *Diminished Democracy,* 292.

16. Kristen Purcell, Lee Rainie, Amy Mitchell, Tom Rosenstiel, and Kenny Olmstead, *Understanding the Participatory News Consumer: How Internet and Cell Phone Users Have Turned News into a Social Experience* (Pew Research Center, 2010).

17. Rich Miller, "For the Hacks," *Capitol Fax,* October 6, 2010.

References

Althaus, Scott, Anne Cizmar, and James Gimpel. "Media Supply, Audience Demand, and the Geography of News Consumption in the United States." *Political Communication* 26 (2009): 249–77.

Amna, Erik, and Joakim Ekman. "Standby Citizens: Diverse Faces of Political Passivity." *European Political Science Review.* Firstview article published online (2013): 1–21.

Anderson, Benedict. *Imagined Communities.* New York: Verso, 1991.

Andrejevic, Mark. *Infoglut: How Too Much Information Is Changing the Way We Think and Know.* New York: Routledge, 2013.

Ansolabehere, Stephen, and Shanto Iyengar. *Going Negative: How Political Advertisements Shrink and Polarize the Electorate.* New York: Free Press, 1995.

Avery, James. "Videomalaise or Virtuous Circle? The Influence of the News Media on Political Trust." *International Journal of Press/Politics* 14 (2009): 410–33.

Ayres, Jeffrey M. "From the Streets to the Internet: The Cyber-diffusion of Contention." *Annals of the American Academy of Political and Social Science* 566 (1999): 132–43.

Baldwin-Philippi, Jessica. "The Cult(ure) of Analytics in 2014." In *Communication and the Midterm Elections: Media, Message, and Mobilization,* edited by John Allen Hendricks and Daniel Schill. New York: Palgrave, 2015.

———. "What's the Big Deal about Small Sites? How Political Microsites Reflect Shifting Norms of Participation." Presented at "Social Media as Politics by Other Means," New Brunswick, NJ, 2011.

Baldwin-Philippi, Jessica, and Eric Gordon. "Designing Citizen Relationship Management Systems to Cultivate Good Civic Habits." Radcliffe Center, Harvard University, Boston Area Research Initiative, 2013.

Bang, Henrik. "Among Everyday Makers and Expert Citizens." In *Remaking Governance: Peoples, Politics and the Public Sphere,* edited by Janet Newman, 159–79. Bristol: Policy Press, 2005.

Barber, Benjamin. *Strong Democracy: Participatory Politics for the New Age.* Berkeley: University of California Press, 1984.

Barry, Tracey, and Peter Davidson. *The Kennedy Mystique: Creating Camelot.* National Geographic Channel, 2004.

Battle for the House. Real Clear Politics, 2010. http://www.realclearpolitics.com/epolls/2010/house/2010_elections_house_map.html.

Baum, Matthew. "Sex, Lies, and War: How Soft News Brings Foreign Policy to the Inattentive Public." *American Political Science Review* 96 (2002): 91–110.

197

Baum, Matthew, and Angela S. Jamison. "The Oprah Effect: How Soft News Helps Inattentive Citizens Vote Consistently." *Journal of Politics* 68 (2006): 946–59.

Baym, Geoffrey. *From Cronkite to Colbert: The Evolution of Broadcast News*. Boulder, CO: Paradigm, 2010.

Bella, Peter. "'I Think Senator Brady Has a Lot of Apologizing to Do for His Record'—Pat Quinn." *ChicagoGOP*, (2010).

———. "Rhymefest for Alderman!!!!!!!!!!!!!!!!" *ChicagoGOP* (2010).

Bellah, Robert, Richard Madsen, William Sullivan, Ann Swidler, and Steven M. Tipton. *Habits of the Heart: Individualism and Commitment in American Life*. Berkeley: University of California Press, 1985.

Benhabib, Seyla. *Democracy and Difference: Contesting the Boundaries of the Political*. Princeton, NJ: Princeton University Press, 1996.

———. "Toward a Deliberative Model of Democratic Legitimacy." In *Democracy and Difference: Contesting the Boundaries of the Political*, edited by Seyla Benhabib, 67–94. Princeton, NJ: Princeton University Press, 1996.

Benkler, Yochai. *The Wealth of Networks: How Social Production Transforms Markets and Freedom*. New Haven, CT: Yale University Press, 2006.

Bennett, W. Lance, and Shanto Iyengar. "A New Era of Minimal Effects? The Changing Foundations of Political Communication." *Journal of Communication* 58, no. 4 (2008): 707–31.

Bennett, W. Lance. "Changing Citizenship in the Digital Age." In *Civic Life Online: Learning How Digital Media Can Engage Youth*, edited by W. Lance Bennett, 1–24. Cambridge, MA: MIT Press, 2008.

Bennett, W. Lance, Chris Wells, and Deen Freelon. "Communicating Civic Engagement: Contrasting Models of Citizenship in the Youth Web Sphere." *Journal of Communication* 61 (2011): 835–56.

Berger, Jonah. *Contagious: Why Things Catch On*. New York: Simon and Schuster, 2013.

Best Practices. Utah Transparency Project, 2012.

Bimber, Bruce. *Information and American Democracy: Technology in the Evolution of Political Power*. New York: Cambridge University Press, 2003.

———. "The Internet and Political Transformation: Populism, Community, and Accelerated Pluralism." *Polity* 31, no. 1 (1998): 133–60.

Bimber, Bruce, and Richard Davis. *Campaigning Online: The Internet in U.S. Elections*. New York: Oxford University Press, 2003.

Blumenthal, Sidney. *The Permanent Campaign: Inside the World of Elite Political Operatives*. New York: Simon and Schuster, 1982.

Bohman, James. "Expanding Dialogue: The Internet, the Public Sphere and Prospects for Transnational Democracy." *Sociological Review* 52 (2004): 131–55.

boyd, danah. "Why Youth (Heart) Social Network Sites: The Role of Networked Publics in Teenage Social Life." In *Youth, Identity, and Digital Media*, edited by David Buckingham, 119–42. Cambridge, MA: MIT Press, 2008.

Boynton, G. Robert. "Going Viral . . . the Dynamics of Attention." In *Conference Proceedings: YouTube and the 2008 Election Cycle*, edited by Stuart Shulman and Michael Xenos, 11–38. 2009.

Brader, Ted. "Striking a Responsive Chord: How Political Ads Motivate and Persuade Voters by Appealing to Emotions." *American Journal of Political Science* 49 (2005): 388–405.

Brewin, Mark W. *Celebrating Democracy: The Mass-Mediated Ritual of Election Day*. New York: Peter Lang International Academic Publishers, 2008.

Bruns, Axel. "News Blogs and Citizen Journalism: New Directions for E-Journalism." In *E-Journalism: New Media and News Media*, edited by Kiran Prasad. New Delhi: BR

Publishing, 2009. http://snurb.info/files/News%20Blogs%20and%20Citizen%20 Journalism.pdf.

Campbell, Karlyn Kohrs, and Kathleen Hall Jamieson. "Form and Genre in Rhetorical Criticism: An Introduction." In *Form and Genre: Shaping Rhetorical Action*, edited by Karlyn Kohrs Campbell and Kathleen Hall Jamieson, 9–32. Falls Church, VA: Speech Communication Association, 1978.

Capella, Joseph N., and Kathleen Hall Jamieson. "Spiral of Cynicism: The Press and the Public Good." *American Behavioral Scientist* 20 (1997): 1–16.

Castells, Manuel. *The Rise of the Network Society.* West Sussex, UK: Blackwell, 2010.

Chadwick, Andrew. *The Hybrid Media System: Politics and Power.* New York: Oxford University Press, 2013.

———. *Internet Politics.* New York: Oxford University Press, 2006.

Cohen, Joshua. "Deliberation and Democratic Legitimacy." In *The Good Polity*, edited by Phillip Pettit and Alan Hamlin, 17–34. Oxford: Blackwell, 1989.

Coleman, Stephen. "Doing IT for Themselves: Management vs. Autonomy in Youth E-Citizenship." In *Civil Life Online: Learning How Digital Media Can Engage Youth*, edited by W. Lance Bennett, 189–206. New York: Routledge, 2008.

Cox, Ana Marie, and Jason Linkins. "The Annotated Flickr Feeds of Barack Obama and Mitt Romney." *The Awl*, October 15, 2012.

Crouse, Timothy. *The Boys on the Bus.* New York: Ballantine Books, 1974.

Dahl, Robert. *On Democracy.* New Haven, CT: Yale University Press, 1998.

Dahlberg, Lincoln. "The Internet and Democratic Discourse: Exploring the Prospects of Online Deliberative Forums Extending the Public Sphere." *Information, Communication and Society* 4 (2001): 615–33.

———. "The Internet, Deliberative Democracy, and Power: Radicalizing the Public Sphere." *International Journal of Media and Cultural Politics* 3 (2007): 47–64.

Dalton, Russell J. "Citizenship Norms and the Expansion of Political Participation." *Political Studies* 56 (2008): 76–98.

Davis, Richard. *Typing Politics: The Role of Blogs in American Politics.* New York: Oxford University Press, 2009.

Delany, Colin. "How to Use the Internet to Win in 2014: A Comprehensive Guide to Online Politics for Campaigns & Advocates." Epolitics.com, 2013.

———. *Learning from Obama: A Comprehensive Guide to His Groundbreaking 2008 Online Presidential Campaign.* Self-published, 2009.

———. *Online Politics 101: The Tools and Tactics of Digital Political Advocacy.* Self-published, 2011.

Delli Carpini, Michael. "Gen.com: Youth, Civic Engagement, and the New Information Environment." *Political Communication* 17 (2000): 341–49.

Delli Carpini, Michael, and Scott Keeter. *What Americans Know about Politics and Why It Matters.* New Haven, CT: Yale University Press, 1996.

Diamond, Edwin, Martha McKay, and Robert Silverman. "Pop Goes Politics: New Media, Interactive Formats, and the 1992 Presidential Campaign." *American Behavioral Scientist* 37 (1993): 257–61.

Dryzek, John S. *Discursive Democracy: Politics, Policy, and Political Science.* New York: Cambridge University Press, 1990.

Dulio, David A., Donald L. Goff, and James Thurber. "Untangled Web: Internet Use during the 1998 Election." *PS: Political Science and Politics* 32 (1999): 53–59.

Edelman. *Capitol Tweets: Yeas and Nays of the Congressional Twitterverse.* Washington, DC: Edelman Insights, March 21, 2012. http://www.slideshare.net/EdelmanInsights/ capitol-tweets-yeas-and-nays-of-the-congressional-twitterverse.

Eveland, William P., Andrew Hayes, Dhavan Shah, and Nojin Kwak. "Understanding the Relationship between Communication and Political Knowledge: A Model Comparison Using Panel Data." *Political Communication* 22 (2005): 423–66.

FactCheck.org. "Debt Limit Debate Round-Up." 2011. http://www.factcheck.org/2011/07/debt-limit-debate-round-up/.

———. "Fiscal FactCheck: Does Washington Have a Spending Problem or an Income Problem? We Offer Some Key Facts." September 15, 2011. http://www.factcheck.org/2011/07/fiscal-factcheck/.

Fenno, Richard F., Jr. *Home Style: House Members in Their Districts.* New York: Longman, 2003.

Foot, Kirsten, and Steven Schneider. *Web Campaigning.* Cambridge, MA: MIT Press, 2006.

Franke-Ruta, Garance. "RNC 'Fire Nancy Pelosi' Moneybomb Raises Nearly $1.5 Million." *Washington Post,* July 29, 2011. http://www.factcheck.org/2011/07/debt-limit-debate-round-up/.

Frantzich, Stephen. *Computers in Congress: The Politics of Information.* Thousand Oaks, CA: Sage, 1982.

Freedman, Paul, Michael Franz, and Kenneth Goldstein. "Campaign Advertising and Democratic Citizenship." *American Journal of Political Science* 48 (2004): 723–41.

Gandy, Oscar. "Dividing Practices: Segmentation and Targeting in the Emerging Public Sphere." In *Mediated Politics: Communication in the Future of Democracy,* edited by W. Lance Bennett and Robert Entman, 141–59. New York: Cambridge University Press, 2001.

Garrett, R. Kelly. "Politically Motivated Reinforcement Seeking: Reframing the Selective Exposure Debate." *Journal of Communication* 59 (2009): 676–99.

Garrett, R. Kelly, Erik C. Nisbet, and Emily K. Lynch. "Undermining the Corrective Effects of Media-Based Political Fact Checking? The Role of Contextual Cues and Naïve Theory." *Journal of Communication* 63 (2011): 617–37.

Gerodimos, Roman, and Jakob Justinussen. "Obama's 2012 Facebook Campaign: Political Communication in the Age of the Like Button." *Journal of Information Technology and Politics,* advance online publication. DOI: 10.1080/19331681.2014.982266 (2014).

Glassman, Matthew Eric, Jacob R. Straus, and Colleen J. Shogan. *Social Networking and Constituent Communications: Member Use of Twitter during a Two-Month Period in the 111th Congress.* Washington, DC: Congressional Research Service, 2010.

Gordon, Eric, and Jessica Baldwin-Philippi. "Playful Civic Learning: Enabling Lateral Trust and Reflection in Game-Based Public Participation." *International Journal of Communication,* forthcoming.

Gordon, Eric, and Stephen Walter. "The Good User: Technology-Mediated Citizenship in the Modern American City." Forthcoming.

Graber, Doris. "The Rocky Road to New Paradigms: Modernizing New and Citizenship Standards." *Political Communication* 20 (2003): 145–48.

Gray, Jonathan, Jeffrey P. Jones, and Ethan Thompson. *Satire TV: Politics and Comedy in the Post-network Era.* New York: New York University Press, 2009.

Graves, Lucas, and Tom Glaisyer. "The Fact-Checking Universe in Spring 2012." *New America Foundation Media Policy Initiative Research Paper,* 2012.

Grossman, Lawrence K. *The Electronic Republic: Reshaping Democracy in the Information Age.* New York: Viking, 1995.

Gulati, Girish, and Christine Williams. "Congressional Candidates Use of YouTube in 2008: Its Frequency and Rationale." *Journal of Information Technology and Politics* 7 (2010): 93–109.

Gutmann, Amy, and Dennis Thompson. *Why Deliberative Democracy?* Princeton, NJ: Princeton University Press, 2004.

Habermas, Jürgen. *The Theory of Communicative Action.* Vol. 1: *Reason and the Rationalization of Society.* Translated by Thomas McCarthy. Boston: Beacon Press, 1984.

Hallin, Daniel. "Sound Bite News: Television Coverage of Elections, 1968–1988." *Journal of Communication* 42 (2006): 5–24.

Halperin, Marc, and John Heilemann. *Game Change: Obama and the Clintons, McCain and Palin, and the Race of a Lifetime.* New York: Harper, 2010.

Hamby, Peter. *Did Twitter Kill the Boys on the Bus? Searching for a Better Way to Cover a Campaign.* Cambridge, MA: Shorenstein Center on Media, Politics, and Public Policy, 2013.

Hamilton, Martha. "Fact-Checking Boehner and Obama on Debt Duel." *PolitiFact*, 2011. http://www.politifact.com/truth-o-meter/article/2011/jul/26/fact-checking-boehner-and-o bama-debt-duel/.

Hanson, Gary, Paul Haridakis, Audrey Wagstaff, Rekha Sharma, and J. D. Ponder. "The 2008 Presidential Campaign: Political Cynicism in the Age of Facebook." *Mass Communication and Society* 13 (2010): 584–607.

Hardesty, Rex. "The Computer's Role in Getting Out the Vote." In *The New Style in Election Campaigns*, edited by R Agranoff. Boston: Holbrook, 1976.

Harfoush, Rahaf. *Yes We Did! An Inside Look at How Social Media Built the Obama Brand.* New York: New Riders Press, 2009.

Heater, Derek Benjamin. *A Brief History of Citizenship.* New York: New York University Press, 2004.

Hindman, Matthew. *The Myth of Digital Democracy.* Princeton, NJ: Princeton University Press, 2008.

Holbert, R. Lance, R. Kelly Garrett, and Laurel S. Gleason. "A New Era of Minimal Effects? A Response to Bennett and Iyengar." *Journal of Communication* 60 (2010): 15–34.

Holland, Charles. "A Different Way to Test Your Message." *Campaigns and Elections* 32 (January 1, 2012): 37. http://technews.tmcnet.com/news/2012/03/07/6171623.htm.

Horrigan, John, R. Kelly Garrett, and Paul Resnick. *The Internet and Democratic Debate: Wired Americans Hear More Points of View about Candidates and Key Issues Than Other Citizens; They Are Not Using the Internet to Screen Out Ideas with Which They Disagree.* Washington, DC: Pew Internet Research, 2004.

Howard, Philip. *New Media and the Managed Citizen.* New York: Cambridge University Press, 2006.

Huber, Gregory A., and Kevin Arceneaux. "Identifying the Persuasive Effects of Presidential Advertising." *American Journal of Political Science* 51 (2007): 957–77.

Huppke, Rex. "Facts, 360 B.C.–A.D. 2012: In Memoriam: After Years of Health Problems, Facts Has Finally Died." *Chicago Tribune*, April 19, 2012. http://articles.chicagotribune.com/2012-04-19/news/ct-talk-huppke-obit-fa cts-20120419_1_facts-philosopher-opinion.

Hutchby, Ian. "Technologies, Texts, and Affordances." *Sociology* 35, no. 2 (2001): 441–56.

Issenberg, Sasha. *The Victory Lab: The Secret Science of Winning Campaigns.* New York: Crown Books, 2012.

Ito, Mizuko. "Introduction." In *Networked Publics*, edited by Kazys Varnelis, 1–14. Cambridge, MA: MIT Press, 2008.

Iyengar, Shanto, Helmut Norpoth, and Kyu Hahn. "Consumer Demand for Election News: The Horserace Sells." *Journal of Politics* 66 (2004): 157–75.

Jacobson, Louis. "Sorting Out the Truth about the Debt Ceiling." *PolitiFact*, July 14, 2011. http://www.politifact.com/truth-o-meter/article/2011/jul/14/sorting-out-truth-ab out-debt-ceiling/.

Jasonoff, Sheila, ed. *States of Knowledge: The Co-production of Science and Social Order.* New York: Routledge, 2004.

Jenkins, Henry, Sam Ford, and Joshua Green. *Spreadable Media: Creating Value and Meaning in a Networked Culture.* New York: New York University Press, 2013.

Johnson-Cartee, Karen S., and Gary Copeland. *Inside Political Campaigns: Theory and Practice.* Westport, CT: Praeger, 1997.

Jones, Jeffrey P. *Entertaining Politics: Satiric Television and Political Engagement.* Lanham, MD: Rowman & Littlefield, 2010.

Junn, Jane. "Participation and Political Knowledge." In *Political Participation and American Democracy,* edited by William Crotty, 193–212. New York: Greenwood Press, 1991.

Kahn, Kim Fridkin, and Patrick Kenney. "The Slant of the News: How Editorial Endorsements Influence Campaign Coverage and Citizens' Views of Candidates." *American Political Science Review* 96 (2002): 381–94.

Kahn, Richard, and Douglas Kellner. "New Media and Internet Activism: From the 'Battle of Seattle' to Blogging." *New Media and Society* 6 (2004): 87–95.

Karpf, David. "Measuring Influence in the Political Blogosphere: Who's Winning and How Can We Tell?" *Politics and Technology Review* (Institute for Politics Democracy and the Internet). https://davekarpf.files.wordpress.com/2009/03/politech-article.pdf.

———. *The MoveOn Effect.* Princeton, NJ: Princeton University Press, 2012.

———. "Online Political Mobilization from the Advocacy Group's Perspective: Looking beyond Clictivism." *Policy and Internet* 2 (2010): 7–41.

Katz, James E., Michael Barris, and Anshul Jain. *The Social Media President: Barack Obama and the Politics of Digital Engagement.* New York: Palgrave Macmillan, 2013.

Kaufhold, Kelly, Sebastian Valenzuela, and Homero Gil de Zúñiga. "Citizen Journalism and Democracy: How User-Generated News Use Relates to Political Knowledge and Participation." *Journalism and Mass Communication Quarterly* 87 (2010): 515–29.

Keen, Andrew. *The Cult of the Amateur: How Today's Internet Is Killing Our Culture.* New York: Doubleday, 2007.

Kelly, William. "Liberal Media Bias: What the Chicago Tribune Wouldn't (Couldn't) Print." *ChicagoGOP,* October 26 2010. http://www.chicagogop.com/home/liberal-media-bias-what-the-chicago-tribune-wouldnt-couldnt-print.html.

Kenski, Kate, and Natalie Stroud. "Connections between Internet Use and Political Efficacy, Knowledge, and Participation." *Journal of Broadcasting and Electronic Media* 50 (2006): 173–92.

Kreiss, Daniel. "Acting in the Public Sphere: The 2008 Obama Campaign's Strategic Use of New Media to Shape Narratives of the Presidential Race." *Media, Movements, and Political Change* 33 (2012): 195–223.

———. "Developing the 'Good Citizen': Digital Artifacts, Peer Networks, and Formal Organization during the 2003–2004 Howard Dean Campaign." *Journal of Information Technology and Politics* 6, no. 3 (2009): 281–97.

———. *Taking Our Country Back: The Crafting of Networked Politics from Howard Dean to Barack Obama.* New York: Oxford University Press, 2012.

———. "Yes We Can (Profile You): A Brief Primer on Campaigns and Political Data." *Stanford Law Review Online* 64 (2012): 70–74.

Lang, Kurt, and Gladys Engel Lang. *Television and Politics.* New Brunswick, NJ: Rutgers University Press, 2002.

Lau, Richard R., and Gerald M. Pomper. "Effects of Negative Campaigning on Turnout in U.S. Senate Elections, 1988–1998." *Journal of Politics* 63, no. 3 (August 1, 2001): 804–19. doi:10.2307/2691714.

Lawless, Jennifer. "Twitter and Facebook: New Ways for Members of Congress to Send the Same Old Messages?" In *iPolitics,* edited by Richard A. Fox and Jennifer M. Ramos, 206–32. New York: Cambridge University Press, 2012.

Lawrence, Eric, John Sides, and Henry Farrell. "Self-Segregation or Deliberation? Blog Readership, Participation, and Polarization in American Politics." *Perspectives on Politics* 8 (2010): 141–57.

Lippmann, Walter. *Public Opinion.* New York: Harcourt, Brace, 1922.

Lissau, Russell. "Seals Camp Slams . . .," *Daily Herald*, September 20, 2010. http://prev.dailyherald.com/story/?id=409440.

———. "10th Congressional Candidate Urging Supporters to Post Comments Online." *Daily Herald*, August 15, 2010. http://prev.dailyherald.com/story/?id=401002

Livingstone, Sonia. *Audiences and Publics: When Cultural Engagement Matters for the Public Sphere*. Bristol, UK: intellect, 2005.

Logothetis, Georgia. "The Wasteland." *Daily Kos*, January 7, 2011. http://www.dailykos.com/story/2011/01/07/934058/-The-Wasteland.

Lotz, Amanda. *The Television Will Be Revolutionized*. New York: New York University Press, 2007.

Madrigal, Alex. "When the Nerds Go Marching in." *The Atlantic*, November 16, 2012.

Mahler, Matthew. "Politics as a Vocation: Notes toward a Sensualist Understanding of Political Engagement." In *New Perspectives in Political Ethnography*, edited by Lauren Joseph, Matthew Mahler, and Javier Auyero, 224–46. New York: Springer, 2007.

Margolis, Michael, and David Resnick. *Politics as Usual: The Cyberspace "Revolution"*. Thousand Oaks, CA: Sage, 2000.

McGerr, Michael. *The Decline of Popular Politics*. New York: Oxford University Press, 1986.

McGinnis, Joe. *The Selling of the President*. New York: Penguin, 1988.

McKenna, Lauren, and Antoinette Pole. "What Do Bloggers Do: An Average Day on an Average Political Blog." *Public Choice* 134 (2008): 97–108.

Miller, Rich. "'Democrats Accidentally Suppressing Their Own Voters.'" *Capitol Fax*, October 27, 2010. http://capitolfax.com/2010/10/27/democrats-accidentally-suppressing-their-own-voters/

———. "For the Hacks." *Capitol Fax*, October 6, 2010. http://capitolfax.com/2010/10/06/for-the-hacks/.

———. "More New Lows." *Capitol Fax*, October 29, 2010. http://capitolfax.com/2010/10/29/more-new-lows/.

———. "Bringing It On Themselves." *Capitol Fax*, September 21, 2010. http://capitolfax.com/2010/09/21/bringing-it-on-themselves/

———. "Saturday Updates: Numbers, Cash, and Videos." *Capitol Fax*, October 30, 2010. http://capitolfax.com/2010/10/30/saturday-updates-numbers-cash-and-videos/.

———. "While Tea Partiers Surge in Illinois, Democrats Don't." *Capitol Fax*, October 28, 2010. http://capitolfax.com/2010/10/28/while-tea-partiers-surge-in-illinois-democrats-dont/.

Millner, Henry. *Civic Literacy: How Informed Citizens Make Decisions*. Hanover, NH: University Press of New England, 2002.

Morozov, Evgeny. *To Save Everything, Click Here: The Folly of Technological Solutionism*. New York: PublicAffairs, 2013.

Mossberger, Karen, Caroline Tolbert, and Ramona McNeal. *Digital Citizenship: The Internet, Society, and Participation*. Cambridge, MA: MIT Press, 2007.

Most Expensive Races: Historical Elections. OpenSecrets.org, 2010. https://www.opensecrets.org/bigpicture/topraces.php?cycle=2010&display=allcands.

Moy, Patricia, Michael Xenos, and Verena K. Hess. "Communication and Citizenship: Mapping the Political Effects of Infotainment." *Mass Communication and Society* 8 (2005): 111–31.

Negroponte, Nicholas. *Being Digital*. New York: Vintage Books, 1996.

Newman, Bruce. *The Marketing of the President: Political Marketing as Campaign Strategy*. Thousand Oaks, CA: Sage, 1994.

New York Times. *The 2012 Republican Primary in Pictures*. 2012. http://www.nytimes.com/interactive/2012/01/24/us/politics/2012-republican-primaries-in-pictures.html?ref=politics.

Nielsen, Rasmus Kleis. *Ground Wars: Personalized Communication in Political Campaigns*. Princeton, NJ: Princeton University Press, 2012.

Nielsen, Rasmus Kleis. "Mundane Internet Tools, Mobilizing Practices, and the Copro-duction of Citizenship in Political Campaigns." *New Media and Society* 13 (2010): 1–17.

Nielsen, Rasmus Kleis, and Cristian Vaccari. "Do People 'Like' Politicians on Facebook? Not Really. Large-Scale Direct Candidate-to-Voter Online Communication as an Outlier Phenomenon." *International Journal of Communication* 7 (October 30, 2013): 24.

Nisbet, Matthew, and John Kotcher. "A Two-Step Flow of Influence? Opinion-Leader Campaigns on Climate Change." *Science Communication* 30 (2009): 328–54.

Norris, Pippa. *Digital Divide: Civic Engagement, Information Poverty, and the Internet Worldwide.* Cambridge: Cambridge University Press, 2001.

———. "A Virtuous Circle? The Impact of Political Communications in Post-industrial Democracies." In *Readings in Political Communication,* 137–61. State College, PA: Strata Publishing, 2007.

Nyberg, Carl. "Bomb from Yemen Sent to Chicago Area Synagogue." *Ellen of the Tenth,* October 30, 2010.

———. "Prior to WWII the Republican Party Had Strong Nazi Sympathies." *Ellen of the Tenth,* October 10, 2010. http://ellenofthetenth.blogspot.com/2010/10/prior-to-wwii-republican-party-had.html.

Nyhan, Brendan, and Jason Reifler. "Misinfornation and Fact-Checking: Research Findings from Social Science." *New America Foundation Media Policy Initiative Research Paper,* 2012.

Packer, George. "The Revolution Will Not Be Blogged." *Mother Jones,* May–June 2004. http://motherjones.com/politics/2004/05/revolution-will-not-be-blogged.

Pallasch, Abdon. "Battle for the Center in North Shore Race to Replace Kirk." *Chicago Sun-Times,* September 29, 2010.

Panagopoulos, Costas, and Peter Wielhouwer. "The Ground War 2000–2004: Strategic Targeting in Grassroots Campaigns." *Presidential Studies Quarterly* 38 (2008): 347–62.

Papacharissi, Zizi. "The Citizen Is the Message: Alternative Modes of Civic Engagement." In *Journalism and Citizenship: New Agendas in Communication,* edited by Zizi Papacharissi, 29–43. New York: Routledge, 2009.

———. *A Private Sphere: Democracy in a Digital Age.* Malden, MA: Polity, 2010.

Pariser, Eli. *Filter Bubble: How the New Personalized Web Is Changing What We Read and How We Think.* New York: Penguin, 2011.

Perlmutter, David. *Blogwars.* New York: Oxford, 2008.

Plouffe, David. *The Audacity to Win: The Inside Story and Lessons of Barack Obama's Historic Victory.* New York: Viking, 2009.

Pole, Antoinette. *Blogging the Political: Politics and Participation in a Networked Society.* New York: Routledge, 2010.

Prior, Markus. "Any Good News in Soft News? The Impact of Soft News Preference on Political Knowledge." *Political Communication* 20 (2003): 149–71.

———. *Post-broadcast Democracy: How Media Choice Increases Inequality in Political Involvement and Polarizes Elections.* Cambridge, MA: Cambridge University Press, 2007.

Purcell, Kristen, Lee Rainie, Amy Mitchell, Tom Rosenstiel, and Kenny Olmstead. *Understanding the Participatory News Consumer: How Internet and Cell Phone Users Have Turned News into a Social Experience.* Washington, DC: Pew Research Center, 2010.

Putnam, Robert. *Bowling Alone.* New York: Simon and Schuster, 2000.

Rackaway, Chapman. "Trickle-Down Technology? The Use of Computing and Network Technology in Legislative Campaigns." *Social Science Computer Review* 25, no. 4 (2007): 466–83.

Rainie, Lee, and Aaron Smith. *Politics Goes Mobile: 26% of Americans Used Their Cell Phones to Connect to the 2010 Elections.* Washington, DC: Pew Internet and American Life Project, December 23, 2010.

Ranney, Austin. *Channels of Power: The Impact of Television on American Politics*. New York: Basic Books, 1983.

Rhee, June Woong. "Strategy and Issue Frames in Election Campaign Coverage: A Social Cognitive Account of Framing Effect." *Journal of Communication* 47 (1997): 26–48.

Rheingold, Howard. *The Virtual Community: Homesteading on the Electronic Frontier*. Reading, MA: Addison-Wesley, 1993.

Robinson, Michael J. "Public Affairs Television and the Growth of Political Malaise." *American Political Science Review* 70 (1975): 209–32.

Rorty, Richard. *Contingency, Irony, and Solidarity*. New York: Cambridge University Press, 1989.

Rutenberg, Jim. "Data You Can Believe In: The Obama Campaign's Digital Masterminds Cash In." *New York Times Magazine*, June 20, 2013.

Schudson, Michael. *The Good Citizen: A History of American Civic Life*. New York: Free Press, 1998.

Semiatin, Richard. *Campaigns on the Cutting Edge*. Washington, DC: CQ Press, 2008.

Shirky, Clay. *Here Comes Everybody: The Power of Organizing without Organizations*. New York: Penguin, 2008.

Shulman, Stuart. "The Case against Mass E-Mails: Perverse Incentives and Low Quality Public Participation in U.S. Federal Rulemaking." *Policy and Internet* 1 (2009): 23–53.

Sinclair, Betsy. *The Social Citizen: Peer Networks and Political Behavior*. Chicago: University of Chicago Press, 2012.

Skocpol, Theda. *Diminished Democracy: From Membership to Management in American Civic Life*. Norman: University of Oklahoma Press, 2003.

Slater, Michael D. "Reinforcing Spirals: The Mutual Influence of Media Selectivity and Media Effects and Their Impact on Individual Behavior and Social Identity." *Communication Theory* 17 (2007): 281–303.

Slayden, David, and Rita Kirk Whillock. *Soundbite Culture: The Death of Discourse in a Wired World*. Thousand Oaks, CA: Sage, 1999.

Smith, Aaron. *The Internet and Campaign 2010*. Washington, DC: Pew Internet and American Life Project, 2011.

———. *The Internet's Role in Campaign 2008*. Washington, DC: Pew Research Center, 2009.

———. *22% of Online Americans Used Social Networking or Twitter for Politics in 2010 Campaign*. Washington, DC: Pew Internet and American Life Project, 2011.

Stewart, Russ. "Democrats Try to Cope with 'Obama Obstacle.'" *ChicagoGOP*, October 27, 2010.

Strauss, Anselm. "A Social World Perspective." In *Studies in Symbolic Interaction: An Annual Compilation of Research*, edited by Norman Denzin, 119–28. Greenwich, CT: JAI Press, 1978.

Stromer-Galley, Jennifer. "On-Line Interaction and Why Campaigns Should Avoid It." *Journal of Communication* 50, no. 3 (2000): 111–32.

———. *Presidential Campaigning in the Internet Age*. New York: Oxford University Press, 2014.

Stroud, Natalie. "Media Use and Political Predispositions: Revisiting the Concept of Selective Exposure." *Political Behavior* 30 (2007): 341–66.

———. "Polarization and Partisan Selective Exposure." *Journal of Communication* 60, no. 3 (2010): 556–76.

Sunstein, Cass. *On Rumors: How Falsehoods Spread, Why We Believe Them, What Can Be Done*. New York: Farrar, Straus and Giroux, 2009.

———. *Republic 2.0*. Princeton, NJ: Princeton University Press, 2007.

Swanson, David L., and Paolo Mancini. *Politics, Media, and Modern Democracy: An International Study of Innovations*. Westport, CT: Praeger, 1996.

Thompson, Hunter S. *Fear and Loathing on the Campaign Trail '72*. New York: Warner Books, 1983.

Tolbert, Caroline, and Ramona McNeal. "Unraveling the Effects of the Internet on Political Participation?" *Political Research Quarterly* 56 (2003): 175–85.

Trent, Judith, and Robert Friedenberg. *Political Campaign Communication: Principles and Practices*. Lanham, MD: Rowman & Littlefield, 2008.

Turner, Bryan. *Citizenship and Social Theory*. Thousand Oaks, CA: Sage, 1993.

Vavreck, Lynn, Constantine Spilotes, and Linda L. Fowler. "The Effects of Retail Politics in the New Hampshire Primary." *American Journal of Political Science* 46 (2003): 595–610.

Wampole, Christie. "How to Live without Irony." *New York Times*, November 17, 2012.

Warner, Michael. *Publics and Counterpublics*. New York: Zone Books, 2002.

West, Darrell M. "Political Advertising and News Coverage in the 1992 California U.S. Senate Campaigns." *Journal of Politics* 56 (1994): 1053–75.

Zaller, John. "A New Standard of News Quality: Burglar Alarms for the Monitorial Citizen." *Political Communication* 20 (2003): 109–30.

Zorn, Eric. "Adventures in Sock Puppetry." Op-ed. *Chicago Tribune*. August 16, 2010. http://blogs.chicagotribune.com/news_columnists_ezorn/2010/08/adventures-in-sock-puppetry.html.

Zuckerman, Ethan. "New Media, New Civics?" *Policy and Internet* 6, no. 2 (June 1, 2014): 151–68. doi:10.1002/1944-2866.POI360.

Zukin, Cliff, Scott Keeter, Molly Andolina, Krista Jenkins, and Michael Delli Carpini. *A New Engagement? Political Participation, Civic Life, and the Changing American Citizen*. New York: Oxford University Press, 2006.

Index

"f" indicates material in figures. "n" indicates material in endnotes. "t" indicates
material in tables.